SCIENTOLOGY
THE BIG LIE

HOW I MADE AN EVIL CULT LOOK GOOD

SCIENTOLOGY THE BIG LIE

HOW I MADE AN EVIL CULT LOOK GOOD

By

MITCH BRISKER

M.D. BRISKER INC.

SCIENTOLOGY
THE BIG LIE

First Edition: November 2023

Published in the United States of America by
M.D. Brisker Inc.

Book cover and interior design by Mermaid Cafe.

ISBN: 979-8-9894086-0-3
Library of Congress Control Number: 2023921319

The text of this book was set in Adobe Garamond.

For information, permissions, and appearances, please visit:
scientologythebiglie.com
facebook.com/mitchbrisker
instagram.com/mitchbrisker
@mitchbrisker

Table of Contents

AUTHOR'S NOTE

I DEFINE ADDICTION AS anything a person does compulsively that they cannot stop doing, and that is ruining their life. I don't know how that definition squares with existing academic definitions of addiction, nor do I particularly care. It works for me.

The first time I set foot in a Church of Scientology I was a twenty-three year old, heroin-addicted, film school drop-out. Six weeks later I was drug-free and on my way back to college and a career in filmmaking. While that might sound like I'm claiming to be a Scientology success story, I am not; whatever forces got me tangled up with drugs in the first place did not abate. What Scientology provided was a mechanism to disrupt the cycle of addiction, allowing me to become free of its grip. In spite of Scientology's promise of spiritual awareness, I was left utterly unprepared to deal with whatever led me to begin using drugs in the first place.

My main objective in writing this book is to tell the story of my involvement with Scientology as a Scientologist and as a hired professional making films for the Church. Out of respect for their privacy, my family is largely omitted. As I've grown to understand the effect Scientology had on my two sons, I hope what I've written will help them to better understand what I was going through while being mostly absent from their day-to-day lives.

Much has been written about Scientology and its founder L. Ron Hubbard. There have been meticulously researched scholarly biographies concerning Hubbard's life as well as personal memoirs from former members who left and spoke out. All of these biographies ultimately arrive at the same conclusion—L. Ron Hubbard was a con man, a master manipulator, and quite possibly severely mentally ill.

Most of the material in this book consists of my own personal experiences from having spent nearly 50 years in Scientology and almost three decades working at the highest levels of the organization, most specifically working closely with David Miscavige, the man who emerged as the ultimate leader of Scientology after Hubbard's death.

Some of the material in this book is based on publicly available and verifiable information. Some of it is based on my own personal opinions and observations from memory, with the disclaimer that memory can be a fragile thing. This book is more of a collection of reflections than a memoir.

Individuals' names have been included only where identifying them served the story and did not pose an unwarranted threat to their privacy or security.

In approaching this book, the first question I had to grapple with was where to begin the story—how far back do I retrace my steps? Like a smash cut in the opening of an action film, I tried to begin at the moment all hell broke loose shortly before I first walked into Celebrity Centre back in 1973. Under that scenario, what was missing were the myriad steps I'd taken up till then—all the tiny moments, pointing towards countless outcomes, that ultimately lead me to the doorstep of Scientology. That story begins when, as a child, my family relocated (for the second time) from San Francisco to Los Angeles, settling into the rustic Hollywood Hills neighborhood of Laurel Canyon— a place filled with mystique long before it earned the title of legendary rock-n-roll neighborhood. So if you've come here to read about Scientology and find yourself instead steeped in the counter-culture of the sixties, indulge me. We'll get there.

—Mitch Brisker, Los Angeles 2023

PREFACE

A CULTURE IS ONLY AS GREAT AS ITS DREAMS,

AND ITS DREAMS ARE DREAMED BY ARTISTS.

—L. RON HUBBARD

A COUPLE OF YEARS AFTER leaving Scientology, I updated my LinkedIn profile to include the following shameless self-promotion:

> If you're looking for someone to blame for directing what some have referred to as perhaps the most successful television advertising campaign in the history of publishing, a campaign that took the book *Dianetics: The Modern Science of Mental Health* from 3 million copies sold to over 13 million in a few short years; if you're looking for someone to blame for making Scientology look appealing; and someone to blame for creating those slick-looking ads Scientology ran during the Super Bowl that caused fans in sports bars across America to air barf, and lit up the Twitterverse with a torrent of "WTF is Scientology doing on my Super Bowl?"—ads that only looked cool to their intended audience of brainwashed Scientologists—and otherwise created visual material intended to buff Scientology's sinking reputation, blame

me! I did that. But, while you're blaming me, keep in
mind, if I can make the Church of Scientology look good,
possibly I can make you look good as well.

Seeing as my resume was mostly a long list of work I'd done
for Scientology, I thought a little humor was in order when
announcing my intention to rejoin a professional community
I had abandoned decades prior.

I'd spent nearly three decades working for the Church
of Scientology creating ad campaigns, writing scripts, and
designing exhibitions. I produced propaganda films and
television ads aimed at polishing Scientology's reputation, or
designed to neutralize its enemies. Most importantly, I directed
a body of films written by the founder of Scientology, for the
purpose of training Scientology practitioners. I was their sole
film director, a position that normally would have been held by
a member of Scientology's secretive monastic order and ultimate
governing authority in Scientology, the "Sea Organization"
(commonly referred to as the Sea Org). Essentially, I was hired
to this position because they had not been able to fill it from
among their own ranks. Sea Org members take pride in their
willingness to perform any needed task. But when it came to
directing films, not one of them ever stepped up who could
actually do the job.

As an expert in persuasion and propaganda, Hubbard knew
well the power of film to hold sway over people's thoughts
and so considered films to be vitally necessary to the survival

and expansion of the religion, whether to train Scientology practitioners in the verbally abusive and mental health-harming procedure known as "Auditing," or to inform the world about Scientology's supposed benefits and achievements. I was never asked to join the Sea Org, nor would I ever have joined if I'd been asked. I saw the Sea Org as an austere culture that eschewed many of the things most people aspire to, such as raising a family and having the freedom to decide to come and go as you choose. Thankfully, many of the Sea Org members I respected eventually escaped, spoke out against Scientology, and went on to claim the lives the Sea Org had denied them. Regardless of how I felt about the Sea Org, I eventually ascended to one of the highest official positions within the Sea Org ever held by a non-Sea Org member.

A carefully maintained firewall exists between public Scientologists (the so-called parishioners) and the Sea Org. Whatever goes on in the Sea Org that is not directly aimed at convincing parishioners to donate ever increasing amounts of time and money, goes on strictly behind closed doors. For professionals such as myself, who were hired to work alongside Sea Org workers at Scientology's secret production facility known as Golden Era Productions, or "Gold," that firewall took the form of a bubble of isolation. While the intention was to keep us isolated from the inner workings of the organization so that we could focus on our jobs, it also kept us isolated from the violent abuses of the Church's leader David Miscavige, who kept his vicious tendencies and violent outbursts in check when I and other non-Sea Org workers were present, creating a truly bizarre codependency between me and the staff who I worked with directly. The staff were dependent on me to produce film projects; in doing so, my presence lessened the impact of Miscavige's abusive leadership style. At the same time, I was dependent on the job for my income, and after some time, for my identity. As a true believer, I was convinced that my eternal future depended on Scientology succeeding and therefore in me succeeding as their film director.

Having been responsible for the successful completion of many major audio-visual Church projects, some of which were ongoing and incomplete for years despite massive efforts, I became invaluable to Miscavige's mission of giving Scientology an attractive veneer. As a result, I lived in a kind of Twilight Zone: well paid, highly respected, and utterly unaware of the violence taking place just outside my view. Eventually, the bubble wore thin and I had a front-row seat to the institutional abuses of the high-control cult known as Scientology.

As time passed, the work I did for Scientology seemed to have much in common with the Stalinist propaganda known as Socialist Realism, which sought to limit thought and emotion by mandating that only a certain type of content, pushing a narrow range of ideas, could be exhibited in artistic works. Soviet workers were idealized as dauntless, purposeful youth heroically striding toward a bright future. In "Scientology

Realism," Scientology practitioners—or torch carrying members of the International Association of Scientologists— were swapped out for the Communist workers. But the effect was the same—control the viewer's emotions, limit their critical reasoning and, most importantly, get everyone focused on the same glorious goal.

For me, exiting Scientology was like watching a slow-motion train wreck. It was the only community, the only structure and the only source of income I'd known for most of my life, and it had become a heap of twisted metal.

It is my hope that my story will help others learn to recognize the true nature of such abusive organizations.

ONE
THE CANYON

Y EARS BEFORE SCIENTOLOGY
conspired to swallow my identity and consume the most
productive years of my career, I was just an awkward kid from
an upper middle-class family coming of age during the drug-
soaked '60s and '70s in the epicenter of the Southern California
counterculture—in a leafy enclave in the West Hollywood
Hills known as Laurel Canyon. My parents bounced back and
forth between San Francisco and Los Angeles, finally settling
in LA just before my eighth birthday in the fall of '57. There are
four canyons that snake their way northward from Beverly Hills
and West Hollywood over the Santa Monica mountains to the
San Fernando Valley. From west to east, they are: Beverly Glen,
Benedict Canyon, Laurel Canyon, and Nichols Canyon. But
of the four canyons, Laurel Canyon was the only one referred
to as "the Canyon"—a sleepy hillside neighborhood of homes
ranging from shacks to mansions.

Traveling west on Hollywood Boulevard, you eventually encounter a sharp curve where the road suddenly collides with the hills, forcing you to turn right onto Laurel Canyon Boulevard. I still recall the first time I rounded that curve to see my new neighborhood, the five of us and two cats stuffed into a white '57 Chevy station wagon. At the base of the canyon, on a cement island in the middle of the boulevard, stood a derelict 76 gas station. In front of the station—like a warning on an old mariner's map that beyond this point there be monsters—there was a hand-painted sandwich board displaying the message, "Last Gas Before the Valley." Such were the times. Today, traversing the twisty canyon road is a minor nuisance.

Before it became the center of the LA music scene in the '60s, Laurel Canyon had been home to silent stars Tom Mix and Clara Bow, writer-actor Noel Coward, the artist Erté, and most famously Harry Houdini (though recent historians claim he never lived there and only visited the guest house of the "Houdini Mansion.") Robert Mitchum lived in the Canyon when, early in his career, he was arrested for marijuana possession and sentenced to two months in a minimum-security Malibu work farm. When the press asked him about his experience at the farm, his reply typified the Canyon's rebellious spirit: "It was like Palm Springs without the riffraff." Rock and Roll Hall of Fame inductee Chris Hillman is credited with being the first rock musician to move to Laurel Canyon when, as a young bluegrass musician from San Diego, he was searching for a cheap place to stay. He would later join Roger McGuinn, David Crosby, Gene Clark, and Michael Clarke to form The Byrds. Today, Laurel Canyon is an enclave for the wealthy seeking to co-opt a piece of the Canyon's mystique as well as young people who yearn for the proto-hippie promise of peace, love and understanding, and who can afford a place in the Canyon.

Back then, Laurel Canyon was a magical place to grow up, a vast network of trails, some leading to the old Houdini estate, where we played in the burnt ruins of the mansion and explored an underground tunnel connecting the Houdini property with the "Log Cabin" (Tom Mix's former home made famous by one-time resident Frank Zappa), along with another nearby mansion that was once the home of Errol Flynn. Supposedly the tunnel had been built so partygoers could travel unseen from one mansion to the other.

I attended Hollywood High my first year of high school. After school we hung out at Stan's drive-in across from the campus, with its decidedly *American Graffiti* vibe. We spent weekends surfing or playing folk music. When the folk-rock scene landed, we traded in our acoustic instruments for electric guitars, grew our hair and gave up surfing. I played in garage bands, and even opened for emerging acts such as Santana and Steppenwolf at venues where you didn't have to be good, you just had to be loud. And we were louder than we were good.

When we moved to the Canyon, the Sunset Strip, located just a mile or so south of our home—referred to as "The Strip" due to its being a narrow strip of unincorporated land within the county of Los Angeles—was populated mainly by mobsters and movie stars. They frequented clubs such as Ciro's, Dino's Lodge, and the Crescendo. Within recent memory, there had been an attempted hit on mob boss Mickey Cohen as he was leaving Sherri's Restaurant on the Strip. I remember being eight years old and getting my haircut at Blackie's Barber Shop, named after the heavyset Italian barber and bookmaker who was always cradling a corded phone, hands-free style, between his cheek and shoulder, speaking in a coded language that I would later come to understand as the patter of a bookie.

As the '60s rolled in, the mobsters and movie stars were displaced by musicians and record moguls. It was then I witnessed first-hand a seismic shift in pop culture—the changing of the guard on the Sunset Strip. What had been an authentic coffee house that once featured bongo-playing, goateed, poetry-reading beatniks and folk singers, Pandora's Box now began featuring local rock acts. Pandora's didn't serve alcohol, so they'd let you in as young as 15. We often walked to Pandora's on Sunday nights to see the Beach Boys, the house band at that time. I recall standing next to a drunken Dennis Wilson in the basement men's room as we each pissed into oversized walk-in urinals—the ones that start at the floor and extend to your chest. Dennis had a pint bottle in a paper bag stuffed into the back pocket of his seawater-bleached jeans, the pattern of that bottle permanently scuffed into that pocket, suggesting it was a constant visitor. I recall how Dennis' Mexican huarache sandals revealed the calcium deposits on the tops of his feet—the badge of a hardcore surfer. Dennis Wilson was, after all, the only Beach Boy who actually surfed. Recognizing we shared elements of the basic surfer uniform—bleached jeans, huaraches, sun-lightened hair, and a hand-dyed Madras shirt—slurring his words, he asked where I'd surfed that day. I answered while dodging his drunkenly careless yellow stream.

Occasionally I'd head over to the far west end of the Strip and sneak into the Whisky a Go Go to see their house band, a new LA group, The Doors. But my most remarkable night as an underage teenager sneaking into clubs occurred in June 1965 when I snuck into Ciro's to see The Byrds.

I'd guilted my father into buying me a motorcycle, a 1965 Suzuki two-cylinder café racer—all shiny chrome, twin pipes, and a sparkling candy-apple red tank. Being that I was fifteen and a half, I was able to get a learner's permit, which allowed me to legally drive the bike during daylight hours. With my folks sound asleep, I carefully rolled the Suzuki out of the garage, hopped on, and coasted until I was at a safe distance, then popped the clutch and the bike roared to life.

When I arrived, Ciro's was mobbed with hopeful fans. The air was electric. The Byrds had performed there many times, but this was their first gig since releasing "Mr. Tambourine Man"—I'd practically worn out my LP copy of the record.

I still remember the day I bought it at Wallach's Music City and the first time I dropped the needle to give it a listen. I'd been listening to Dylan ever since he released the eponymous *Bob Dylan* in 1962. I wondered what he might have thought about The Byrds having such a huge hit with their cover. After all, The Byrds' version of "Mr. Tambourine Man" along with "Turn, Turn, Turn" had both charted at No. 1, while Dylan's first electric hit, "Subterranean Homesick Blues," peaked at No. 37 on the US charts.

I stashed the bike in a darkened corner of the parking lot and headed towards the kitchen door at the rear of the club—a familiar route. Moments later I stood at the back of the club, looking over a sea of people directly at the stage, watching Taj Mahal open the show. At some point during The Byrds' set, Dylan walked onstage to accompany the band as they performed "Mr. Tambourine Man." Any question I had concerning what Dylan may have thought of the cover was answered.

Every generation is defined by a set of factors unique to its time. The time of my generation was set to the soundtrack of the British Invasion, the LA and Bay Area music scenes blended with the background threat of all-out nuclear war with the Soviet Union. The Kennedy assassination was within recent memory, and with the constant threat of being drafted into the Vietnam War, there was plenty to be anxious about.

Perhaps that anxiety, magnified by the teenage search for identity, softened us to the idea of experimenting with

drugs. References celebrating drug use were creeping into
our music. In health class we were shown educational films
produced in the '50s that were meant to teach us about the
dangers of drugs. But the message of those films coming from
the establishment—which was basically anyone over 30 who
wanted to keep our hair short, our dress conservative, and send
us off to die in a foreign land—was just another invitation to
rebel. To us it seemed the world had gone mad, pushing us
to find another path forward, to rip apart the status quo and
make a new world. Or at least to party so hard, get so stoned,
and turn the music up so loud, that the old world could not
survive. Though we didn't know it at the time, a new source
of heroin had begun flooding into America, smuggled in the
caskets of dead soldiers returning from Vietnam. A drug once
relegated to the inner city had found its way to the Canyon.
It was as though a bullet fired in some Southeast Asian jungle
made its way halfway around the world, striking at the heart
of the Canyon.

The first time I tried heroin was in the Summer of '65. I was
15 years old. Even though I managed to disentangle myself from
drugs in my early 20s, and have remained drug-free ever since,
I still struggle to fathom the internal forces that led me to make
the decision to try heroin. I was a well-behaved middle child,
I performed above average in school, was somewhat awkward
at athletics, and showed promise in art and music. By 15, I had
grown tired of being cast as the dutiful middle child who was

made to shoulder the responsibility that would have gone to my older brother had he been more dependable. Prior to the 1960s, the notion of a middle-class junkie didn't exist. By the mid '60s that would dramatically change. From the summer of '65 forward, until I finally escaped its grip, sometimes managing to stay clean for months on end, I would struggle with addiction.

My parents thought their children should have the freedom to dress however they wished and grow their hair to whatever length suited their taste. The dress codes at Hollywood High were not so permissive: no fringed deer-skin boots, no blousy shirts, only above-the-collar haircuts for the boys—the list was long. Growing frustrated with the school's policy of sending students home for dress code violations, my sister and I were sent to a small, progressive, private high school in Beverly Hills where our academic performance was considered to be more important than how we dressed. The socioeconomic background of the student body at our new school varied from the children of professionals— such as my sister and I—to the children of super-wealthy and/or super-famous parents. Dean Martin's three kids, Frank Sinatra's youngest daughter, and Burt Lancaster's daughter were amongst our classmates. We were all friendly in school but when it came to the children of the super-rich and the very famous celebrities, being from an upper middle-class family was like being from the wrong side of the tracks; I never knew West Hollywood could be so far from Beverly

Hills. We were not invited over to their homes after school. I'd never experienced that kind of class mentality. I'd gone to junior high in East Hollywood, which had an economic imbalance as sharply defined as the economic spread from Hollywood to Beverly Hills, but the class distinction was largely ignored when it came to deciding who you were going to hang out with beyond school hours. While the economic divisions were less extreme than between West Hollywood and Beverly Hills, the racial divisions in East Hollywood were strong, specifically between the Mexican kids and the white kids. Most specifically, between the surfers and the so-called "cholos." I recall a time in junior high when I turned around, having just shut my locker door, to be sucker-punched by a Mexican kid, a year younger and four inches shorter than me. Before I could retaliate or run, his three very large cousins appeared, flanking him, and daring me to react. The word was out: they were going to stomp me to a pulp after school. The sound of the 3 o'clock bell, signifying the end of the school day, struck terror in my gut. There was no hiding in a crowd of departing students. A group of a half-dozen "cholos" were making a beeline straight for me when suddenly a canary yellow, 1949 Ford woody station wagon with surfboards stacked on the roof, rushed, very illegally, across the blacktop schoolyard, coming to an abrupt halt between me and the oncoming "cholo" threat. It was my older brother and three of his surfer buddies. The door of the woody swung open. I was hauled in and away we sped. I never found out exactly how the news of my impending doom traveled so quickly, I was just glad that it had.

By the time we got to high school, we were all smoking weed and the sharp racial distinctions mostly dissolved like a puff of marijuana in a gentle breeze, as the surfers and "cholos" passed around a joint.

Fortunately, my days of being an intravenous drug user predated AIDS. Still, there was hepatitis, the highly infectious blood-borne virus that could be passed easily by sharing needles. My high school experience was dramatically interrupted when, a week before graduation, I passed out in Spanish class after contracting the dreaded virus and ended up hospitalized on the day of my graduation ceremony.

TWO

SUMMER OF LOVE

I WAS LAID UP FOR MOST
of the summer following my high school graduation—the one
I'd missed. I spent four days in the hospital followed by six
weeks, mostly in bed, trying to hold down solid food. Hepatitis
is an excruciatingly debilitating disease; the body struggles to
digest fat, your joints ache, and the fatigue is indescribable.
Once I was up and around, there were twice monthly trips to
the doctor for liver panels involving a six-test-tube blood draw.
In those days you could have either hep 'A', hep 'B' or both. I had
neither. I had the mysterious other type of hepatitis which they
simply identified as non-A, non-B. Decades later, when I was in
my thirties, with advances in virus detection, and ultimately the
mapping of the human genome, that mysterious non-A, non-B
hepatitis was designated as Hep-C, also known as *The Silent
Killer* for its ability to remain asymptomatic for an average of
20 years after which I had a 20% chance of developing end

stage liver diseases and dropping dead two weeks later unless I received a liver transplant. I was approaching the twenty-year mark with no symptoms and figured the one-in-five chance of developing end stage liver disease was pretty good odds.

As Fall approached two things were certain—I was going to turn eighteen in September and I was going to head up to the Bay Area to begin College.

All kids love to draw and paint, but that's what I wanted to do when I grew up. I went to art museums and stared at paintings. I spent hours poring through my parents' art books. My mother enrolled me in children's weekend art classes at UCLA and Art Center College of Design. After graduating high school in 1967 (missing the graduation ceremony hadn't disqualified me from receiving a diploma), I had been accepted into the painting program at California College of Arts and Crafts in North Oakland—a professional school of fine art later renamed California College of the Arts. I arrived in the Bay Area during the summer of 1967, along with a hundred thousand or so other young people who converged on San Francisco's Golden Gate Park to enjoy a months-long party that came to be known as the "Summer of Love."

I'd heard many colorful stories about my politically radical parents and their San Francisco friends. Moving to the Bay Area to begin my college career, I got to know some of them, most notably my mother's longtime friend, the British author Jessica Mitford. Jessica helped me to get settled in, made sure

I had groceries, and brought me my amp and bass guitar which my mother had sent up. She lived with her husband in San Francisco. I knew her by her nickname, "Decca," and her married name, "Treuhaft." Her husband, Robert Treuhaft, was a noted civil rights attorney and political analyst. Decca was one of the six aristocratic Mitford Sisters noted for their sharply conflicting politics. Her 1960 memoir, *Daughters and Rebels*, and her 1963 book of social commentary, *The American Way of Death* (one of the inspirations for Tony Richardson's film *The Loved One*) both became classics.

Decca arranged for me to stay with Matthew Hallinan and his younger brother Danny. Their father, Vincent, a prominent San Francisco attorney, had run in the 1952 presidential primary on the Progressive Party ticket. Danny, who was my age, was a student at UC Berkeley, where Matthew taught Southeast Asian studies. In Matthew's home office, on the wall behind a solid wooden desk, was an oversized poster of political activist and Black Panther member Angela Davis—who was soon to appear on the FBI's most wanted list—a gun cabinet, and a large map of Vietnam.

A few days after my arrival, Decca took me on a tour of Telegraph Avenue. Like its counterpart, Haight-Ashbury across the Bay, it was a focal point for the counter-culture but with its own unique history and influences. Famous for her biting wit and piercing observations of American society, Decca was an apt tour guide. She took me to Moe's Books, founded in the Beatnik era by Moe Moskowitz who, among other achievements, had financed albums for the band Country Joe and the Fish. We ate at Cafe Med, a Telegraph Avenue icon where Allen Ginsberg and Jack Kerouac had hung out, and where the Black Panthers held their Berkeley meetings. It was also a favorite of UC Berkeley frat boys and jocks with their short hair and preppy dress. Down the block from Cafe Med was Pepe's Pizza Parlor, frequented by drug-dealing Hells Angels and a younger, artsier, long-haired crowd. As we walked along, Decca pointed out the layers of culture that formed the tribalistic milieu that was Telegraph Avenue in 1967: hippies and beatnik holdovers, musicians, Berkeley intellectuals, art students, bikers, political radicals, and Black Panthers.

Another of the Hallinan clan, Danny and Matthew's older brother Terrence—a young attorney who'd just successfully defended three members of Moby Grape from charges of allegedly corrupting three underage teenage girls—lived across the Bay in San Francisco. Moby Grape was a highly influential San Francisco band considered by many to be the greatest band of the San Francisco music scene that never struck it big. Following a concert one night at the Avalon Ballroom, three of the band members, Jerry Miller, Peter Lewis and Skip Spence, were caught with three underage girls and charged with contributing to the delinquency of minors. The prosecution contended that the girls had no good reason to be secluded with the three musicians. In their defense, the band-mates claimed the girls were interviewing them for their high school paper for an article they were writing on the San Francisco music scene. The prosecution tried to sabotage their alibi by painting the music scene as a drug-fueled, corrupting influence on the youth of America. Terrence Hallinan called acclaimed music critic Ralph Gleeson to testify on the musicians' behalf. Gleeson was a frequent contributor to the *San Francisco Chronicle* and later a founding editor of *Rolling Stone* magazine.

He was also one of the founders of the Monterey Jazz Festival and the only music critic on Nixon's Enemies List. Gleeson's testimony convinced the jury that the San Francisco music scene represented a significant contribution to the history of contemporary music and that the girls had a legitimate academic interest in covering it for their school paper. The charges against the three musicians were dropped.

One night, shortly after the successful conclusion of the Moby Grape case, Danny and I headed into the city to meet Terrence. We parked in front of a classic San Francisco Victorian and walked up to Terrence's second floor apartment. As he let us in, we were hit with the pungent odor of freshly smoked pot. Across the dimly lit room, piled high on a coffee table, sat a large mound of marijuana; a drum set, an amp and a couple of electric guitars sat against the wall. We passed around a joint while Terrence recounted the case, explaining that the band members, being short on cash, had partially paid him with a pound of weed and some musical instruments.

Terrence Hallinan would go on to achieve a storied career in San Francisco politics. A staunch defender of civil rights, he would later briefly defend Patty Hearst and eventually become San Francisco District Attorney. I only met Terrence that one night, but my memory of the encounter has never faded.

I ended up renting an apartment with two other guys, one a fellow student at the Art College and the other a musician who played bass in a Bay Area band. Our apartment was on the lower floor of an old Carpenter Gothic house that had been converted into four separate apartments; it was on Montgomery Street within walking distance of the college. My roommate played bass in a band that had a local following big enough to get them paying gigs on most weekends. Usually, venues like the Avalon Ballroom, the Fillmore West, and Winterland, would have a three-act lineup. My roommate's band would appear first up on a bill with some of most iconic bands of the '60s. I would often tag along with him, which afforded me an opportunity to see some unforgettable performances. Without a doubt, nothing equals the night Jimi Hendrix appeared at Winterland with Albert King. Hendrix walked onstage in the middle of King's set, picked up one of King's legendary Gibson flying "V" guitars, and began to play along. It was pure magic. Not even seeing Hendrix set fire to his white Stratocaster came close.

My bass-playing roommate also shared my interest in heroin. Not long after I arrived in Oakland, we were at Pepe's scoring dope from the Angels. The covered patio in front of Pepe's had four picnic-style tables. The thickly bearded Angel with his club "colors" sewn to the back of a greasy denim vest would sit on a bench in the far corner, giving him an unobstructed view of anyone coming or going. Somehow, we had obtained the necessary credentials to be accepted as legit customers. As far as I could tell, the Angels controlled the illicit drug trade in the Bay Area at that time, especially heroin. It wasn't long before I had a "kit"—a syringe, a bent spoon, and a cotton ball—stashed in my art tackle box. I wasn't using every day, but often enough that it was a problem.

On balance, the semester I spent at the Art Institute was well worth it. I'd survived hundreds of hours of drawing, painting, and design exercises. I'd studied the basics of color theory and composition and I'd received the kind of famously scathing criticism from a life drawing instructor that is apparently a rite of passage for all fine arts students, wherein your instructor rips your work from your easel and tears it to shreds in front of the entire class proclaiming that only one in a million art students will ever make a dime creating art and that you aren't one of them. Some of my work had been praised by the head of the painting department in which he stated that while technically lacking, it showed enough originality of viewpoint that he urged me to return the following semester.

By the end of the semester I had survived wild nights in The City or weekends camping on the sand at Big Sur's Pfeiffer State Park and Stinson Beach in Marin; but regardless of the friends I'd made and the adventure of living on my own for the first time, I felt displaced in the city of my birth—disillusioned and burned out, and I was homesick for LA. Wanting to avoid the criticism from the locals, who freely expressed their negative opinions of Southern California, especially Los Angeles, I had to conceal the fact that I wanted to return to LA. To give you an idea of how great the Bay Area's disdain for LA was, when Jefferson Airplane signed with LA's RCA Records in 1965, they were considered sell-outs by Bay Area fans. By 1968, the rivalry between the San Francisco and LA music scenes had dissipated, helped in large part by the emergence of LA bands like Crosby, Stills, Nash & Young and The Doors. But in 1967, with the rivalry between Northern and Southern California still strong, I kept quiet about being homesick for LA with no plans to return to Oakland in the Fall.

On the final day of the semester, students mingled on the quad enjoying the dawning summer and the end of the pressure to churn out the seemingly endless assignments that come with being a fine arts student. My recollection of that day is a hazy blur of bright colors and the faces of strangers—faded as though the passage of time was a mist that rolled in obscuring the past. So many people I never got to know and never would. But for no logical reason, one image remains clear in my memory. At the top of the stairs leading down to the quad, a student was recording the scene with a 16mm movie camera. Something about that image struck me. I'd never considered filmmaking as an art form. I had never considered it to not be an art form; I just never considered it something I would pursue. But that image of the young man panning that movie camera across the crowd of students stuck in my mind. I felt a twinge of disillusionment with my current field of study—painting, the kind of momentary disappointment you might feel when catching an unflattering glimpse of a lover—a pit of doubt we sometimes stumble into. Maybe it was the allure of new technology. After all, the last big technological breakthrough in painting was literally back in 1840 when Winsor & Newton introduced oil paint in tubes, giving the revolutionary Impressionists the freedom to paint outdoors. But whatever it was, that image of the young man with the movie camera, with its hint of possibility lodged itself in my memory.

By 1968, the cultural mood had shifted dramatically. If 1967 was the summer of love, then '68 was the summer of hate. The Vietnam War was at its height. Martin Luther King, Jr. was assassinated in April, followed by Robert Kennedy in June. Protests at the Chicago Democratic Convention turned bloody, and Richard Nixon was elected president. The counter-culture movement was awash in drugs, with heroin rearing its ugly head across all socioeconomic boundaries.

To avoid the draft, I'd need to remain enrolled in school. With no plans to return to school in the Bay Area, my plan was to attend LA City College and get some undergraduate requirements out of the way while I looked for an art school closer to home. I enrolled in science and English classes, both of which would be needed to fulfill graduation requirements wherever I ended up next. Scanning the college catalog, I noticed the newly founded Cinema/Television Department and that memory of the young man with the film camera sprang into view. Thinking I should balance my curriculum with something creative, I signed up for a course in film history and a film production workshop. The workshop was taught by veteran Hollywood cameraman Peter Gibbons, who at the time was head of the camera department at CBS Studio Center and would later become the head of Cinematography at USC Film School. Studying with Peter Gibbons altered my artistic trajectory. You could not spend any time studying with him without becoming passionate about filmmaking. I was now intent on getting into film school.

My mother, who taught design at Cal State Long Beach, and was on the board that oversaw the accreditation of the professional art schools of America, was aware of a new school being formed with a 50 million-dollar endowment from Walt Disney. It was a dream of Disney's to establish a multidisciplinary school offering programs in art, design, film, music, theater, and dance. The new school was called

California Institute of the Arts or CalArts. I applied and was accepted. Having no previous film experience, I was admitted to the design school and told I could switch to the film school after one semester. It was 1969. With construction of the new campus underway, CalArts would not open its doors for another year.

For that next year I continued taking courses at LACC, playing bass in a band, and attempting, mostly unsuccessfully, to avoid heroin.

THREE
HONEY DRIVE

Our family home in Laurel Canyon was at the top of a short street named Honey Drive, connected to a one-way access road referred to as "Little Laurel Canyon." The access road began just before Hollywood Boulevard and ended at The Canyon Country Store, a quaint neighborhood market where I'd briefly held a summer job when I was twelve. The apartment house directly across the street from our home consisted of twenty or so units—an anomaly in the Canyon, where zoning laws only allowed for single-family and duplex structures. The apartment had been built in the 1920s as a brothel run by one of the film studios long before zoning laws were enacted. It was an L-shaped, two-story stucco structure. The corner of the "L" where you entered the parking lot was a sweeping curve overlooking the driveway. Anyone entering would have to pass under a one-bedroom apartment, giving the brothel's madam a view of whoever was coming or going. All the other units consisted of a small living room with an exterior entrance, a bedroom with its own exterior entrance, a kitchen, and a bathroom. This layout meant that one customer could wait in the living room while another could exit through the bedroom's exterior door without either one bumping into the other. The wiring from the buzzer system that connected the bedrooms to the madam's room, covered in decades-old layers of paint, had never been removed.

Where the end of Honey Drive turned into a short dirt road, you'd find the weathered residence of Mr. DeWinter, an elderly recluse straight out of a Stephen King novel, who kept bees and restored oil paintings for a living. Perhaps the name Honey Drive was inspired by Mr. DeWinter's beehives, but with a brothel being one of the first structures to appear on the street, one had to wonder if "Honey Drive" wasn't a euphemism for a different kind of honey.

Over the years, I made friends with some of the residents of the Honey Drive apartments. Jazz bassist Henry Franklin, who played on Hugh Masekela's 1968 number-one single "Grazing in the Grass," lived in the former madam's single bedroom unit for a time. Henry took me into his circle of jazz musician friends. We'd smoke weed, listen to music, and sometimes he'd give me a bass lesson.

The ground floor apartment directly across from the entrance to our house, was occupied by a graphic artist who mostly worked in an intricate pen-and-ink style creating psychedelic posters for LA rock venues as well as his own fine art. On a warm summer day in 1969 I was walking up Honey Drive, headed home. The graphic artist had recently moved out and, as I passed by his now vacant apartment, something caught my attention. Through an open kitchen window, with the sun blasting onto the window screen obscuring the background, I could barely make out the figure of a young woman, wearing only a sheer black bra, lifting a freshly dipped paint brush and then reaching above the window to apply the paint. I watched her for a moment, then got up the courage to knock on her door. The girl who appeared, now wearing a vintage silk robe, stood there in the sunlight, ringlets of shimmering golden hair halfway down her back, piercing green eyes and porcelain skin, looking like she'd stepped out of a Pre-Raphaelite painting—a style of art, as I was soon to discover, for which she had a great fondness. I couldn't simply walk up to her door and say, "Hey I just saw you half-naked in your kitchen window and thought I'd drop by," so instead, I asked for the previous tenant, pretending I didn't know he'd moved out. She explained he no longer lived there. We struck up a conversation. She invited me in.

Her name was Beverly. She grew up in Canoga Park, a wrong-side-of-the-tracks section of San Fernando Valley. Occasionally, her mother sent her to live with relatives in Las Vegas to escape her physically abusive alcoholic father. With her connections to the LA rock music scene, she was a natural to end up living in the Canyon. Her close friend and fellow San Fernando Valley native, Pamela Miller, was a member of the GTOs (Girls Together Outrageously), an experimental music group produced by Frank Zappa. Beverly was an unofficial GTO and occasionally performed with them. "Miss Pamela" (all the GTOs were referred to as "Miss") would later marry rock musician Michael Des Barres. Pamela Des Barres is best known for her 1987 memoir, *I'm with the Band: Confessions of a Groupie*, in which she devoted a passage to the night she met Beverly while "gliding along" the Sunset Strip. She describes her as the most ravishing beauty ever born and how the two of them formed a bond so deep they married each other in a mock ceremony that was never consummated.

Beverly and I had many interests in common. Unfortunately, one of them was drugs. It was not long before heroin became the focal point of our relationship. We never considered ourselves drug addicts—we didn't fit the inner-city profile. Rather, we thought of ourselves as a pair of Kerouac-esque misfits—non-conformists living on the fringes.

We would go on wild adventures to escape the pull of heroin. We once drove all night to attend the 1969 Big Sur Folk festival, held annually from 1964 to 1971 at the Esalen Institute, which had a sweeping view of the Big Sur coastline that literally took your breath away. We slept in the back of her VW Bug on a cliff overlooking the Pacific and arrived just in time for the first act. We spent the weekend, dopesick, sitting within spitting distance of Crosby, Stills, Nash & Young, Joan Baez, Joni Mitchell, John Sebastian and a host of other performers. We never complained about the physical pain we were experiencing. Neither of us suggested we should go back to LA and get high. We stuck it out. We had each other and the magical space of the Big Sur coastline and that got us through the weekend, but the future was another matter. We needed a more permanent solution to our drug problem than running off to spend a few days not doing drugs at a music festival in Big Sur.

In response to the growing drug problem, rehab programs seemed to be popping up around the LA area faster than California poppies in the springtime, probably driven by the success of Synanon, the infamous drug rehab program located on the beach in Santa Monica. Synanon became a cultural phenomenon that went from being a celebrity-socialite-darling, to a religion, to an armed cult known for attempting to murder a detractor by slipping a rattlesnake through his mail slot. I had friends who'd gone to Synanon. Ironically, the rumors that it was a cult steered me away from Synanon and towards a garden-variety, generic rehab in Sylmar, California.

Sylmar, a mostly suburban section of the San Fernando Valley, is the northernmost neighborhood within the City of Los Angeles, the kind of place you refer to as "the outskirts"— a place you drive through on your way to somewhere else. It was a place comprising mostly of unkempt open spaces, chicken farms, and stables in disrepair that housed unhappy horses. In the residential part of Sylmar, it was not uncommon to see an old Chevy up on blocks in the front yard. I was on my way to Sylmar to check into rehab, committing once again to getting clean. While I was in rehab, Beverly was toughing it out on her own.

Near the end of my month-long stay, the owner of the rehab told me he'd received a call from a production office looking for recovering addicts to appear in an upcoming film about young heroin users in LA. Specifically they were looking for an attractive young couple, and he had suggested Beverly and me. We were driven to the production office located on the CBS Studio Center lot in Studio City. A few minutes after walking in the door of the production office, we were cast to play the title roles in *Dusty and Sweets McGee*. The director, Floyd Mutrux, envisioned a faux cinema-vérité romp through LA following a mix of ex-addicts playing addicts and a couple of actors playing addicts and drug dealers. It was sort of a drug-fueled *American Graffiti*. We were told we'd be playing fictional characters drawing on our personal experiences. Floyd shot the film from an outline which described the plot with much of the dialogue and action being improvised. As a film student, it was a great experience. As a recovering addict, it was a disaster.

I needed to get away from the drug scene. I needed to get myself cleaned up and ready to start CalArts in the fall. I did not need to be portraying one half of a drug-addicted, drug-dealing married couple running from the cops on the streets of LA. By the time we completed the film, we were both using again. For me, heroin proved to be an on-again, off-again dance with the devil that was not going to stand in the way of my getting into film school and pursuing my goals. By the time CalArts opened its doors, I hadn't used in months.

With the new CalArts campus still under construction, the inaugural year (1970-1971) was temporarily held at Villa Cabrini, a Catholic girls' school in Burbank that had closed due to a lack of religious workers. The school featured a swimming pool, which the students deemed "clothing optional," and a chapel that became the perfect setting for the final scene of a student vampire film. As the chapel was still considered sacred ground, the nuns were obliged to pay a monthly visit. Needless to say, the nude students in the swimming pool and burnt offering on the chapel's altar, left over from the vampire film, did not go over well with the nuns. Subsequently, nude swimming was banned, and the chapel was declared out of bounds.

That first semester at CalArts was one for the history books. Legendary musician Ravi Shankar, who had taught George Harrison to play the Sitar and was teaching in the music department, gave lunchtime concerts on the lawn each Wednesday. Buckminster Fuller, inventor of the geodesic dome, taught in the design school. The faculty at CalArts that first year, and into the future, comprised an impressive list of painters, designers, choreographers, musicians, authors, and filmmakers.

When *Dusty and Sweets McGee* opened on July 14, 1971, I was in Arco, Idaho, sitting in a rustic diner eating a T-bone steak that hung over the edges of a large oval dinner plate, barely leaving enough room for a baked potato the size of a kid's nerf football—standard portions for Idaho. Sitting amongst the truck drivers and ranch hands, *Dusty and Sweets McGee* seemed a million miles away. At that moment I was contemplating what it must have been like back on July 17, 1955, when a technician fired up the nuclear reactor at the nearby National Reactor Testing Station, and for the next hour or so, Arco became the first community in the world with electricity generated by nuclear power. The lights in Arco blinked. An hour or so later they blinked again. From that point forward, the tiny city of less than 1,000 would be known as "The Atomic City."

Arco was also the gateway to Craters of the Moon National Park and Preserve, a breathtakingly beautiful landscape formed by lava flows dating back thousands of years. It was once used to train Apollo astronauts in preparation for the first moon walk. It was also the perfect location for the low-budget sci-fi film being produced by Peter Fonda's Pando Company, and on which I'd been hired as a production assistant—which is how I came to be having a steak dinner in that Idaho diner. I'd returned to LA a few times ferrying equipment and people back and forth for the film, and once to appear in publicity photos for *Dusty and Sweets McGee*. On one of those trips home, I happened to see the large billboard announcing the film's upcoming opening, strategically located in a prime spot on the Sunset Strip. The billboard featured an image of Beverly and me as the title characters. When I saw it, I felt strangely dissociated. I never aspired to appear on a billboard on the Strip, yet there it was, right in the neighborhood where I grew up.

By the next time I returned to LA, the film had held the number-one spot at the box office for two weeks, after which it was bumped by Jane Fonda's *Klute*, for which she won a best actress Oscar.

When I finally got a chance to see the film, I felt like I was being torn in two directions. It was as though someone who looked just like me was playing a fictitious character that I had a lot in common with. The film had been publicized as a documentary—that the fictional characters we played were not fictional at all, but Beverly and Mitch in real life. Mutrux, the director, had spun that narrative to help bolster the film's credibility. He wanted to be recognized as having delivered an authentic experience, hoping to create the impression that he'd followed us around with a camera crew, capturing our self-motivated activity. While some of the players in the film were willingly portraying themselves using their real names as their character names, that was not the case with us. We had unwittingly participated in Floyd's quest to produce his cinémaverité "masterpiece," or maybe that was just how they decided to market it after the fact. But in any case, the impression we had been given was that our past drug experiences, coupled with our screen-ready good looks, qualified us to play the fictional title characters. It was never, "Oh yeah, you'll be playing yourselves but not yourselves, because everything you do in the film will be fictional, but we'll present it to the audience as a documentary and not tell you." They even went so far as to make up phony bios that appeared in the end credits, about what happened to us after the film was made.

In the Fall of '71 CalArts was fully open, with the new campus located in Valencia, California. I can still recall walking into the main gallery and smelling the fresh paint and floor sealer. Beverly and I had drifted apart. I was focused on school, and she was doing whatever she was doing.

My relationship with Beverly seemed to be driven by a kind of fatalistic imperative—no matter what circumstances conspired to draw us apart, an equal and opposite force would always draw us back together. And such it was six months later when we moved into an apartment on Crescent Heights in West Hollywood not far from the base of Laurel Canyon and slowly started to transform into the characters we'd played in *Dusty and Sweets McGee*—constantly looking to score dope, connecting with small-time dealers who'd front us dope to sell, and worrying about being busted. It was a desperate scene. Where I once felt like a tourist visiting the land of hardcore drug use, I now started to feel like a permanent resident.

On December 16, 1972, Beverly sat cross-legged on the floor of the living room in our small apartment making handmade Christmas cards from scraps of art she'd collected—mostly images of Pre-Raphaelite angels and cherubs, and fanciful depictions of frogs dressed in Shakespearean costumes. I stared at her for a moment, sitting there in a tie-died velvet robe skillfully assembling the bits of paper. We'd planned on entering a drug treatment program the first week of January and, from there, getting fully off drugs for good to start a new life together. The program was in Santa Monica. We'd spoken with them. The arrangements were made. On Saturday the 16th we got high and went to sleep early. Sunday morning, I bolted awake, walked to the kitchen and found her lying on the floor. Sometime in the early hours of the morning she'd gotten up, gone into the kitchen, and died of an overdose. She was 25 years old.

I don't remember calling the police. A homicide detective interviewed me at our small kitchen table while in the background the coroner's office removed her remains. Satisfied no crime had been committed, the detective closed his notepad, gave me a look signifying "I'll probably be back for you later," and walked off.

We each recall our lives as having happened before or after key events: before/after graduating college, before/after getting married, before/after having children. We organize our personal timeline around such events. They are the points at which some profound change alters our trajectory. My timeline, now and moving forward, would include the before and after Beverly died. My life, after that Sunday, would never be the same.

FOUR

FINDING SCIENTOLOGY

A FEW DAYS LATER, FLOYD Mutrux, the director of *Dusty and Sweets McGee*, invited me to meet him for dinner at Over the Rainbow on the Sunset Strip—a very exclusive small cafe and bar above the rock-centric hangout "Rainbow Bar & Grill." If the Stones or The Who or Elton John were in town, at some point they'd be hanging out at Over the Rainbow. Floyd and his new girlfriend, an actress who'd recently introduced him to Scientology, were sitting at a quiet corner booth. His girlfriend expressed her condolences over Beverly's death and quipped, "At least she died on my birthday. I hate my birthday and her death distracted everyone away from it," as if it had anything to do with her. During the conversation, Floyd told me he'd started taking a course at the Scientology Celebrity Centre. He thought Scientology might help me get off drugs and arranged an appointment for me to go there.

SCIENTOLOGY - THE BIG LIE

The original Celebrity Centre was on 8th Street just west of downtown LA, located in a building that had previously been a furniture shop. The streets in that area reminded me of trips I'd taken with my parents deep into Mexico: Mariachi bands, street vendors, the smell of grilled beef and chicken, and the foreign, yet familiar and emotionally satisfying aroma of handmade tortillas.

Walking into Celebrity Centre, Floyd and I were greeted by a smiling receptionist. The place looked like it had been decorated with leftover carpet remnants, garage sale furniture, and thrift store knickknacks. In a brightly lit corner of the room there was a large bronze bust of L. Ron Hubbard mounted to a freestanding base; an oversized black and white framed photo of him hung on an adjacent wall. I recall the walls in reception were mostly burgundy, though my color memory is often in error. The reception area was spacious enough to hold intimate events, and a small stage was located off to the left of the reception desk. The course rooms were spacious. There was one room for the Communications Course, or Comm Course as it was known—a two-week course giving an introduction to Scientology communication skills. On the east side of the building a large room with a high ceiling was separated into different designated zones depending on the course you were on. Essentially, all the students on any one course sat together in one large room—usually about five different courses were located in that one space making roll call a boisterous event.

36

And naturally, being the '70s, there were a variety of clay pots suspended in macrame hangers, dripping strands of ivy.

Most of the staff at Celebrity Centre were members of the "Sea Organization" or Sea Org. The Sea Org holds the ultimate authority within the Scientology Organizations. Sea Org members commit to a billion years of service. They work together, live together, and are only allowed to marry within their own ranks. A young woman appeared, about my age, and ushered me into a small room for an interview. She was an "Ethics Officer," a member of a division that exists in every Scientology Organization that handles security matters and oversees the execution of Hubbard's arcane system of ethics and justice. As I would discover later, Ethics Officers are generally the most fanatical members within the organization—they are famously feared for making people's lives miserable. In this case, the Ethics Officer was an inexperienced, twenty-two-year-old woman named Kathy. Newly into Scientology and the Sea Org, whatever vile spell overtook ethics officers in general, had not fully invaded Kathy's demeanor. She seemed friendly and helpful. I explained my situation. She then introduced me to another young woman, the "Medical Liaison Officer" or MLO, who coordinated medical needs for the staff, as the staff were not allowed to seek medical help without first going through the MLO's office. Every aspect of a Sea Org member's life is tightly controlled by the organization, including access to health care. If a Sea Org member needs any kind of healthcare, it must be approved by the MLO. The Sea Org does not provide health insurance for its employees. They do everything on a strictly cash basis. If someone needs to go to the doctor, the funds to pay for it must first be sought by written proposal and only once funds are approved is the person allowed to see a doctor. All staff going to the doctor are accompanied by someone from the MLO's office, who will remain present during examination. The offer of help extended to me by the MLO, a former nurse with a professional manner, seemed sincere. She convinced me that with Scientology I could free myself of drugs. I was sold an inexpensive communications course and promised to return the following day. I had no idea, or any hope whatsoever, if Scientology could possibly help me.

I was going to be starting The Communication Course. How taking that course connected with the loss and pain I was suffering, I had no idea. I was severely drug dependent, yet I was handled like anyone else who walked in the door. One would think I would have been a candidate for the Scientology sponsored Drug Rehab program, Narconon. However, Narconon was barely a blip on the map back then, and according to the MLO, "Narconon was just for criminals. We would never send you there." Narconon was originally founded by a prison inmate by the name of William Benitez who was inspired to create the program after reading Hubbard in prison. He later wrote to Hubbard who gave the program his blessing.

Eventually Narconon would expand into an international network of Scientology sponsored drug rehab facilities, and William Benitez's name would be expunged from the official record. But that day I walked into Celebrity Centre, there was one Narconon facility in Los Angeles, catering exclusively to ex-convicts.

The Purification Program, Scientology's sauna-nutrition based detox procedure, which would become a fundamental element of the Narconon program, had not yet been released. So, regardless of my being an emaciated 125 pounds sweating profusely from heroin withdrawals, as a fledgling film student brought in by a celebrity film director, I was deemed to be a good fit for Celebrity Centre.

The day after I signed up for the course at Celebrity Centre—the day I'd promised to return—I was standing in my parents' driveway at the top of Honey Drive watching a garishly adorned, late model, Cadillac Eldorado glide slowly up the street. Behind the wheel was the dealer Beverly and I had been buying from just prior to her death. He fashioned himself after the main character in the classic blaxploitation film, *Superfly*. He drove a garishly ornamented Cadillac Eldorado, wore a leather trench coat with a fur collar, and sported lots of gold jewelry. Under his wide-brimmed hat was a coiffed hairdo that looked like it used enough chemical hair straightener to kill half the fish in the Santa Monica Bay. As Beverly was particularly prone to overdose, I had always had to keep an eye on her, never

SCIENTOLOGY - THE BIG LIE

letting her keep her own dope or shoot up alone. Apparently, when I wasn't looking, Superfly slipped her the bag of heroin that killed her.

Instead of keeping my promise I watched Superfly's Eldorado roll to a stop and met the drug dealer who'd gifted my girlfriend with a lethal dose of smack. He got out of the car and, in a low gravelly voice, expressed his condolences. "Here," he said, handing me a baggie containing about an ounce of heroin, "Take this and pay me when you can." As he drove off I said to myself "Pay you? How about, 'Fuck you!'" I never liked the guy that much to begin with. He was a means to an end. As far as I was concerned, by giving Beverly a stash of heroin without telling anyone, he was responsible for her death. The bag I held in my hand was a way to escape the chaos, and for the next week that's exactly what I did.

I went through that baggie of heroin like there was no tomorrow. It's a miracle I survived. I was so strung out it made every other episode of heroin use look like I was a weekend "chipper"—someone who chips away at a habit but never really gets strung out. My parents were frantic seeing me deteriorate that way. I was on the verge of being thrown out onto the streets with no place to live when, out of desperation, I agreed to check myself into a locked hospital ward to dry out. The nurses provided methadone to help with the withdrawal symptoms. Still bent on self-destruction, I persuaded a friend to retrieve a small amount of heroin I'd stashed in my parents' garage before

I left for the hospital and toss it over the hospital fence onto a small patio. I retrieved the heroin and stole a syringe from the nurse's station. I'd hit rock bottom, the point at which addiction specialists say addicts must find themselves before they can begin to recover. Smuggling heroin into a locked hospital ward where you signed yourself in to get off heroin—that was the bottom rung of the ladder to rock bottom.

A few days into my hospital stay, the Medical Officer from Celebrity Centre burst in demanding that the nurse bring me to her at once, and to bring her the discharge papers. She then thrust a metal clipboard at me, handed me a pen and pointed where to sign the form. I was checking myself out against medical advice and so had to sign out of the hospital. The MLO gave the clipboard back to the nurse, turned to me and said, "You're coming with me." A small crowd of hospital staff stood stunned as I was ushered out of the locked ward. I had no idea what lay ahead. All I knew was, if I had not gone with her, I would have been discharged from the hospital within a week or so, then back on the streets, and likely dead a few weeks later. At the time, it felt as though my fast track to oblivion had been disrupted, and I was going along for the ride.

On the way to the Celebrity Centre Staff House, the MLO explained that when I hadn't shown up for my course, she'd become concerned and contacted my father. She offered to take me out of the short-term hospital treatment and put me on a longer program to get off drugs permanently. He agreed to pay the small sum of $250 a week for room and board plus whatever it cost for courses, which in those days was not much. This had never happened in the history of Scientology, and would never happen again: a non-Sea Org member, one with a drug habit no less, being taken in to live in Sea Org quarters in order to help the person get off drugs. I've always considered that the MLO who busted me out of the hospital literally saved my life. We were friends for years. She and her husband eventually left the Sea Org and started a family and a successful business. Regardless of the abuse I would eventually experience in Scientology, I would be forever grateful that this person, to whom I was a total stranger, pulled me out of that hospital and dedicated her time to helping me get clean, driven by nothing more than her idealism and desire to be of service to others.

I came to realize many years later that *idealism* is a common thread running through what attracts people to join cults. But her actions, and her low pressure tactics that allowed me to make a thoughtful decision, in my own time, as to whether or not I wanted to stay in Scientology, were absolutely in violation of Scientology policy, which dictates that by any measure, due to my drug dependence, I never should have been let in the door, let alone signed up for a course and allowed to live with the staff. Once someone is let in the door, they are signed up for blood with high pressure sales tactics—something I did not experience until later.

Celebrity Centre staff lived in what was referred to as the

"staff house," located a few short blocks from Celebrity Centre in a sprawling 1920s Craftsman-style mansion left over from a glamorous era before the wealthiest neighborhoods in LA had begun their westward migration from Boyle Heights in East LA to Beverly Hills on the West Side. Back in the day, that house was the equivalent of a luxurious West Side mansion, but by the time I arrived, courtesy of the MLO, even on a moonless night you could see it was long past needing a new coat of paint. As well, the lawns were brown, and the landscaping was sparse. The warmly lit interior and the pastiche of mismatched furniture gave it a homey feel. I could hear children laughing in the distance. It was like an enormous hippie crash pad housing perhaps fifty staff. Once crossing the spacious front porch, you'd enter to find a grand stairway leading to the second floor where most of the bedrooms were located. Every room with a door had been converted into sleeping quarters, including the attic. The only non-sleeping spaces were the kitchen, large living room, and huge basement dining room. When I arrived, most of the staff had just returned from their duties at the Org. I was greeted enthusiastically; everyone seemed genuinely happy that I was there.

I settled in as best I could, spending long hours in the Scientology course room, suffering from flu-like withdrawal symptoms and occasionally passing out. When not in the course room I worked in the kitchen, cleaned floors, and assisted in the nursery with some of the married staff's children.

In the future, under David Miscavige's reign, Sea Org members were forbidden to have children—they were considered an expensive, time-consuming distraction from one's core mission, so the Sea Org phased out parenting. Once Miscavige forbade children in the Sea Org, pregnancies were frowned upon, and abortion was heavily promoted as the solution. But when I arrived, there were lots of small children and a few infants. All of these activities, including polishing the linoleum floors with a heavy floor polisher, were a welcome distraction from the discomfort of withdrawals, and the crew certainly didn't mind having someone to handle their "cleaning stations."

Charlie Chaplin was said to have been a former resident of the house now occupied by the staff of Celebrity Centre. But like so many things in Scientology, the truth never stood in the way of a good story. Charlie Chaplin never lived in that house, let alone in that neighborhood. And, as with much of Scientology history, as I'd later come to learn, the house was not without at least one human tragedy. I don't recall her name, but she was a young mother with a small child who worked as a cook when not at the Org studying Scientology. She was there when I first arrived, and I helped care for her little girl in the nursery and spoke with her every day when helping in the kitchen. Then one day, suddenly, she was gone. I inadvertently found out there had been an accident. A commercial-sized stock pot of boiling liquid had tipped over and landed on her. She died of her injuries a few days later.

No one spoke of it for fear of spreading bad news—something which was viewed in Scientology as a nearly criminal activity. To let anyone know she had died would be spreading bad news or "Entheta." Entheta is a portmanteau of the Scientology words *enturbulated* and *theta*. *Theta = life force. Enturbulated = agitated or confused*. Thus *entheta*, means agitated or confused life force. Scientologists believe that spreading entheta lowers the emotional tone of anyone on the receiving end, thus, to some degree, lessening their potential to survive. But to me, the lack of transparency regarding the tragic death of the young mother seemed cold and callous, as if no one cared enough about her to mark her passing, and so created a mystery surrounding her disappearance. Acknowledging a person's passing shows respect and allows mourning to occur. Keeping death a secret implies shame or complicity. It seems strange to me now that at the time I simply thought that's how they did things so I went with the flow, respected the local customs, and didn't ask questions. Inwardly, I was devastated at the news of her passing. I liked her and valued our friendship. Years later I realized that limiting information of that sort is part of what a high-control group does—they decide what you should and should not know about what's going on around you and how you should feel about it.

In 1973, there was no shortage of colorful individuals at Celebrity Centre. Though staffed by Sea Org members who'd signed a pledge to dedicate their lives to the Church for a billion years, unlike today, they did not wear the standard, hospitality-inspired uniforms that are currently de rigueur at Scientology Orgs—in fact they wore no uniforms at all but dressed in the casual hippy garb of the day, jeans, fringed leather jackets, blousy shirts, and lots of tie-died colorful fabrics. Celebrity Centre felt more like a hippy commune without the drugs than it did a church.

Hubbard's obsession with bringing celebrities into his movement began in 1955, when his article titled *Project Celebrity* appeared in *Ability*, a newsletter sent to Scientology members. The article contained a list of 63 well-known celebrities: athletes, actors, artists, writers, and singers, including the likes of Walt Disney and Sammy Davis, Jr. The Scientologists who received the newsletter were invited to pick a celebrity from the list and pursue them like prey.

> These Celebrities are well guarded, well barricaded, over-worked, aloof quarry...
>
> If you want one of these celebrities as your game, write us at once so the notable will be yours to hunt without interference.
>
> If you bring one of them home you will get a small plaque as your reward.
>
> —L. Ron Hubbard, from *Ability* newsletter

Yvonne Gillham Jentszch, the Commanding Officer of Celebrity Centre, was an Australian citizen with a sunny disposition. She joined the Sea Org upon its inception, serving first on the Sea Org vessel *Avon River* and then the *Royal Scotman* (misspelling due to a transcription error when the ship's name was registered) which later became the flag ship *Apollo*, Hubbard's seagoing refuge from government scrutiny. Nearly 15 years after Hubbard wrote *Project Celebrity*, Yvonne took up the cause of celebrity recruitment leaving the *Apollo* to establish Celebrity Centre in Los Angeles; its stated intention was to assist celebrities with their careers. Within a few years, Celebrity Centre evolved to become a full-blown Church of Scientology, focused on recruiting celebrities, their families, and their entourages, and delivering Scientology training and counseling. Eventually other Celebrity Centres were established in the US, Great Britain, and Europe. Yvonne practically worked herself to death, surviving on a few hours of sleep a night, though it never showed through her cheerful and caring manner. She was the heart and soul of Celebrity Centre, and one of the most popular and beloved figures in all of Scientology. Eventually her popularity and her ability to manage Scientology's many relationships with government officials began to be seen as a threat to individuals in the Guardian's Office—Scientology's intelligence bureau— who felt she was encroaching on their turf. As a result, Hubbard mysteriously dismissed her from running Celebrity Centre. Tragically, she died of a brain tumor not long after.

Ray Mithoff was the Senior Case Supervisor or C/S. The C/S is perhaps the most revered position in any Scientology Church, as they are the person responsible for supervising delivery of the Scientology activity known as "Auditing," a specialized version of the word taken from its Latin root word "audire," which means "to listen." In Scientology, an Auditor is one who listens. To a Scientologist nothing is more important than freeing oneself from one's "Case" which is defined as the negative effect of the accumulation of the upset, pain, and failure one has experienced throughout one's entire existence. These negative effects manifest as the thoughts, considerations, and conclusions related to those experiences. Whether you are receiving counseling, known as "Auditing," or taking training courses in Scientology, handling your "case" is your top priority. From the point when you decide to move forward in Scientology, your most important life decisions, right down to whether you should take prescribed medication for a medical condition, can only be made with approval from the C/S. This is one of the many ways Scientology takes over your life. You go along with it because you believe the C/S has your best interests at heart. In the pursuit of handling your case, you will fork over your money and turn over your personal agency to Scientology.

Ray Mithoff, the lanky, easygoing C/S at Celebrity Centre, was rarely seen around the Org, as C/Ss mainly toiled away at their solitary jobs in offices referred to as the "Ivory Tower." They were never to be disturbed while at work. When we did see Ray at meals or mingling with parishioners, he would often be dressed in cowboy attire, a holstered replica six-shooter slung at his side. It was more costume than authentic—all in fun, nothing threatening about it. Ray Mithoff was one of the nicest, most unthreatening people I'd ever met. I took the cowboy garb to be a statement on the fluid nature of personal identity, something which Hubbard believed you could change or "mock up" as you pleased, like a costume donned for a play or a uniform for a game.

In the early 1980s Ray was assigned to the post of Senior C/S International, responsible for delivery of all Scientology Auditing across the globe. He became L. Ron Hubbard's personal auditor, attending to him at his death in January, 1986. By the '90s, Ray was a frequent spokesperson at international events and was admired by Scientologists the world over. I felt fortunate at the time for having known Ray when I first got into Scientology in my drug-addled period, and then to see him again, and even receive auditing from him, when I arrived at the International Base in 1990.

Yvonne Jentzch's husband, Heber Jentzsch, was once a working actor and an accomplished singer. Recognized for their work establishing Celebrity Centre and their kind and caring manner, Yvonne and Heber were amongst the most beloved people in Scientology. Heber Jentzsch, an ex-Mormon from a polygamist family, would go on to become the President of the Church Scientology International, a well-known spokesperson and one of the Church's most ardent defenders. In 1988, Heber was jailed in Spain along with 69 other Scientologists, charged with "illegal association" and various other crimes including tax fraud and endangering public health. Three weeks later, he was released on bond, and fled to the United States.

But to me, like Ray Mithoff, as far as I was concerned, Heber would always be one of the staff who welcomed me so graciously the day I landed at Celebrity Centre, strung out and desperate for change.

In spite of the looming threat of the dangerous cult that lay just beneath the surface of Celebrity Centre, daily life at the "Org" (Scientology term for organization) felt electrifying. Course rooms were near capacity during the day and packed to overflowing at night. The place was literally buzzing with activity. When the courses ended at 9 PM, most everyone stayed. There was always something going on afterwards. Often there would be performances given by any number of the talented actors and musicians taking courses. You might see jazz legend Chick Corea playing piano, or sketch comedy from the Celebrity Centre-based theater troupe headlined by Karen Black and Geoffrey Lewis. Everyone was on equal footing; there was no VIP attitude.

My schedule consisted of walking the few blocks to the Centre after breakfast, followed by an entire day spent studying basic Scientology principles. I was told that all of these activities were designed to put a person in better communication with their environment and themselves, and that the pain I was experiencing was due to my being out of communication with my body.

Among my daily activities were so-called "Assists" referred to as "spiritual first aid." Scientology claims that assists help the individual overcome the effects of loss, shock and trauma and speed recovery by addressing the spiritual and emotional factors that they say are related to illness and injury.

Some of these assists consisted of being directed by another person to move about the room touching things as they were pointed out. Common assists for alleviating pain consisted of sitting in a chair while someone repeatedly touched different parts of one's body while saying "Feel my finger," or lying down while someone pressed their hands on various points on one's body while stating "Feel my hands." I later learned that such activities had led to cases of sexual abuse. I was told that my withdrawal symptoms would increase or "turn on" during the assists and that if I "confronted" what I was feeling, it would "turn off." In this way, they were assuring me I could get through the withdrawals in the shortest possible time.

Strangely, it worked. Likely because it was a kind of poor man's version of "Exposure Therapy"—a therapeutic technique popular when Hubbard developed Dianetics, involving patients facing their fears and phobias. But having something specific to focus on did help to get through the pain.

Hubbard's mantra repeated by every Scientologist, "The way

out is the way through" is also, I discovered later, a sentiment found in the writings of Robert Frost and the teachings of The Buddha. But in Scientology it is used as a thought-terminating cliché—a term popularized by Robert Jay Lifton in his 1961 book *Thought Reform and the Psychology of Totalism*—intended to stifle further conversation and to keep one at whatever challenging activity in which one is engaged. I heard that mantra often. But, in any event, at least I was in an environment with people who shunned drugs and supported my recovery. On balance, it had a positive effect.

Nights were the roughest. Sleep was elusive. A few days in, I phoned a sympathetic doctor I'd previously seen and asked for a sleep aid. He prescribed the ever-popular '70s sleep aid, Quaalude. On some pretense I convinced the supervisor of the course I was taking to lend me his car. That night I fell asleep in a Quaalude stupor. The next night, I decided to pop one on the walk home from the Org. I stopped off in a coffee shop for a quick bite and promptly passed out in a plate of fries. Fortunately, a couple of students from the Org recognized me and somehow guided me the rest of the way to the Staff House. Yvonne greeted us at the door. She gently placed her arm around me and said, "Let's get you to bed, Dearie." It is a mystery how she effortlessly guided me up a flight of stairs.

The following day, no one mentioned the events of the previous night. It was as though it never happened. I was sharing a room with a Sea Org member by the name of Wings

Livinryte. Wings, a talented singer/songwriter who often performed at Celebrity Centre and thought being in the Sea Org wouldn't interfere with his recording career, had been asked to take me aside and get me to hand over the drugs. I did so and that was that. Never to be mentioned again. This was in stark contrast to what Scientology would morph into over the years: a vengeful organization with a fetish for punishment, victim shaming, and humiliation. In the Scientology of the future, I would have been paraded in front of my fellow Scientologists, staff and public, had my "crimes" read out, and then been forced to scrub toilets with a toothbrush or perform some other humiliating amends. But the way Yvonne and the crew handled the situation won me over. Their compassion and non-judgmental manner convinced me that their offer of help was sincere and that I had found a home in which to heal. The seemingly selfless and caring group I had fallen into, with its mission to create a new civilization, would eventually become a fundamentalist religious movement driven by money, wielding soul-crushing control over its members. So many of the people I knew from Celebrity Centre, both students and staff, would later leave Scientology. Wings eventually left the Sea Org and Scientology, took on his birth name Wings Hauser, and went on to make a name for himself as a film actor.

Six weeks after arriving at the Staff House, I was drug free, I'd gained 40 pounds, I was sleeping like a baby, and was convinced that Scientology had saved my life. Living at the Staff House and spending my days studying Scientology had disrupted the cycle of drug use and enabled me to exert enough control to stay clean. Unlike those who considered themselves addicts for life, attending 12-step meetings, introducing themselves by giving their names and stating they were an addict, I simply no longer had any interest or desire to do drugs, so there was no reason to state otherwise.

By the time I left the Staff House, I had become born again as a Scientologist. I believed I was an immortal spiritual being, trapped in a physical realm from which there is no escape save for the teachings of Scientology. I believed that L. Ron Hubbard was the only person to have ever discovered a way out of the amnesia—the inability to retain the memory of your previous lives. Only with Scientology could you ascend the Bridge to Total Freedom, ultimately regaining your "native state" in which you could recall your entire existence over countless eons, gain the ability to be exterior to your body at will with full perception, and be able to control matter, energy, space, and time.

The "Basic Books," the body of Hubbard's written works intended to introduce the public to Scientology, are composed of seemingly common-sense ideas marketed as useful tools for improving your life, as well as methods for removing barriers preventing you from attaining your goals and achieving your full potential. For the most part, these were not new ideas, but had been repackaged from other sources, parsed, and reworded to make it appear as though the ideas were new. Having just gotten off heroin, I was very receptive to any ideas that would help me to become a better version of myself. Scientology presented itself as exactly that. The bait was irresistible.

A few nights into my course at Celebrity Centre I came across my first basic Scientology principle—the ARC triangle, an acronym standing for Affinity, Reality and Communication. (Pronounced by voicing the letters A-R-C, they are thought to be the components of understanding.) Hubbard presents the ARC triangle as a tool with which one can increase one's understanding of anything in life. By increasing any one of the components (corners of the triangle), you can increase the others. For example, by communicating with someone you can become aware of common interests (reality) and thus raise your affinity for them. I thought, "This is remarkable. I can use this." And so began my indoctrination into Scientology.

Many years later and after thousands of hours of study, I began to see inconsistencies in those principles and to realize that the principles I had accepted as profoundly true and had put into practice were actually a form of reductionism—a belief that the whole of reality consists of a minimal number of parts. There were many inconsistencies. For example, at times I encountered individuals or subjects and by increasing my communication discovered my affinity for them had lowered—and for good reason. All of Scientology is built on such reductionist principles. It's a brilliant tactic for drawing people into a cult. Once an adherent believes in a simple set of principles that explain everything, they believe they have a deeper grasp of reality. With that, they immediately put themselves above those who do not possess an awareness of those principles. They no longer need to be curious about existence because they already know everything there is to know about the mind, life, the physical universe and humankind's spiritual nature. All subsequent study in Scientology will encompass those basic principles in a closed system that shuts out critical thinking. Once that happens, you are ready to advance up the "Bridge to Total Freedom." The "Bridge" was Hubbard's analogy for the various detailed steps one would need to accomplish in order to achieve spiritual freedom. He likened it to a bridge across a deep chasm, from a lower plane of existence to a higher one. Hence, The Bridge to Total Freedom—though it is more of a ladder than a bridge.

The MLO reaffirmed her promise that once I got off drugs, continuing on in Scientology was up to me. I had no obligation to stick around. My decision was to stay in Scientology and to get some Auditing. Around that time, my academic leave from CalArts was ending. The Admissions Office tracked me down and informed me if I didn't return by the start of the next semester I'd have to reapply. CalArts was extremely difficult to get into, so with my vitality restored and my newly found beliefs, I made a headlong charge at earning a degree in cinema.

FIVE

GLORY DAYS

IGRADUATED FROM CALARTS
in 1974 right in the middle of one of the worst recessions
in modern times. Any job was hard to come by, and jobs
in the film industry, usually requiring you to be connected
to someone in the business, were particularly scarce. With
a short film in hand, I started making calls and going to
appointments.

Following graduation, I got an entry-level job with the
newly formed commercial production company, Robert Able
and Associates that would grow to international acclaim for
its pioneering work in film graphics and visual effects, playing
a vital role in ushering in the era of digital effects. I worked
on numerous commercials for domestic and international
clients, on-air promotional campaigns for major networks,
and ultimately became the creative director of the company,
a position I held for five years before being ousted in a power

57

play by individuals who, while intending to restructure the company's financials, led it off a cliff into bankruptcy.

After leaving Robert Able and Associates, I formed my own production company and continued directing commercials while studying Scientology part-time at Celebrity Centre in Hollywood.

I also began focusing on my core goals as a filmmaker; to make my own projects and no longer survive as a hired hand promoting products and ideas I didn't necessarily believe in. I was also intent on furthering my writing skills and enrolled in writing workshops for directors sponsored by the Directors Guild of America. It was during this time that I received a call from a The Public Exec Sec at Celebrity asking that I arrange to come in and meet with a Scientology executive. The next day I met with Caroline Mustard, the executive overseeing all marketing for the Church of Scientology. Caroline explained they were looking for a commercial director to work on a new TV campaign for the book *Dianetics: The Modern Science of Mental Health*, which Scientologists held as the foundational work underpinning their entire belief system—a foundation upon which Hubbard would later build the entire cult of Scientology.

I subsequently met with Jeff Hawkins at the old Cedars of Lebanon hospital—that garishly blue painted building in East Hollywood. Cedars, a landmark destined for demolition, had been purchased by the Church for office and living space. Jeff had established the Strategic Book Marketing Unit (SBMU), later absorbed into Scientology's overall marketing machine, The Central Marketing Unit (CMU). Jeff was a veteran Sea Org marketing executive and had launched the extremely successful Dianetics campaign in the early '80s. Subsequently, Caroline and Jeff put together a core team of professionals; Rick Rogers, an experienced ad agency creative director; Jan Gildersleeve, a pioneer in media buying for the emerging cable TV platform; and me.

It was Jeff, perhaps more than any other person, who had the vision and insight to bring Dianetics and Scientology marketing out of the dark ages.

The goal of the Dianetics campaign was to increase the sales of Hubbard's book *Dianetics: The Modern Science of Mental Health* (referred to internally as *DMSMH*), originally published on May 9, 1950, a date celebrated with reverence by Scientologists. In fact, the book is considered so fundamental that it is referred to as "Book One." Following its 1950 release, *Dianetics* created a media frenzy and spawned a self-help movement. The book contains Hubbard's theories on the mind as well as his proposed method anyone could use to free themselves from past trauma. In *Dianetics*, Hubbard describes the mind as being composed of two main parts: the "Analytical Mind" and the "Reactive Mind." As the theory goes, you use the analytical mind to think with and solve problems, and to imagine and to envision the future. Hubbard described the analytical mind as having the potential to operate like a perfect computer, never making a mistake, except of course when erroneous data is fed to it by the other part of the mind, the reactive mind. According to his theory, whenever you experience pain or unconsciousness, the analytical mind shuts down and the reactive mind kicks in, recording every detail as three-dimensional mental image pictures he called "Engrams." In fact, the term engram was originally introduced by German zoologist Richard Semon in 1904 and later incorporated into neuropsychology. Hubbard regularly purloined terms from established fields of study, giving them new definitions while never giving credit to the original source material. Hubbard's engrams are supposedly stored below one's level of awareness and are considered to be composed of negative energy. At any time in the future, any of the details recorded in the engram may become present again in the current environment, triggering the content of the engram to spring into action, causing you to think and act irrationally without knowing why. For example, according to Dianetics, if as a child you fell off your bike and blacked out and a dog was barking in the background, in the future, whenever you hear a dog bark, you may feel threatened and get a headache. Hubbard claims engrams are the sole cause of all irrational fears, negative thoughts, destructive behavior, and psychosomatic illness. Using Dianetics procedure, Hubbard asserted, a person could become free of the negative energy stored in the reactive mind, ultimately achieving the state of "Clear"—a state in which one is thought to have been freed or "cleared" of the reactive mind's negative effects.

Hubbard claimed engrams acted on a person in the same way a stage hypnotist, giving a post-hypnotic suggestion to a volunteer, could cause the person to act against their will. In the book, *Dianetics: The Original Thesis*, published the year after *Dianetics: The Modern Science of Mental Health*, Hubbard gives the example of a hypnotist telling a hypnotized volunteer that whenever the hypnotist touches his tie, the volunteer will take off his coat. When he touches it again, the volunteer will put his coat back on. The hypnotist informs the volunteer he will have no recollection of having been told this. The volunteer faithfully complies, even justifying taking off his coat when asked why he did so, by saying the room is too warm.

Hypnotism was all the rage when *Dianetics: The Modern Science of Mental Health* was first published in 1950. As the decades rolled on, more and more skeptics joined a growing chorus of hypnosis deniers. Most notably, after working as a stage hypnotist and magician for nearly two decades, the renowned stage performer Kreskin became a skeptic and whistleblower from within the stage hypnosis field.

Stage hypnotism and professional wrestling have a lot in common. They both require unique talents, some knowledge of stagecraft, and a willingness on the part of the audience to believe that what they are seeing is actually happening. And in both cases it's just a show. Thus, the principles upon which the entire subject of Dianetics relies have no more basis in reality than stage hypnotism or professional wrestling.

But what about the use of hypnosis in psychotherapy? Studies have shown that hypnotherapy can be effective in helping people cope with pain, stress, and anxiety, though it is not considered a first-line treatment such as cognitive behavioral therapy.

Hubbard proclaimed Dianetics to be a breakthrough unlike anything in history. Gossip columnist Walter Winchell (best known for his attempts to destroy the careers of his political and personal enemies) proclaimed Dianetics to be more important than the discovery of fire. However, a reality-based analysis of Dianetics places it as a mild form of Exposure Therapy at best.

The idea that guiding a person through their past trauma can be therapeutic dates back before Dianetics to a form of therapy known as "Abreaction Therapy," which was popular when Hubbard first released *Dianetics: The Modern Science of Mental Health*. Abreaction is a psychoanalytical term defined as "bringing to consciousness." With Dianetics, Hubbard claimed to have created the first psychotherapy to address traumatic experiences. In fact, *Dianetics: The Modern Science of Mental Health* was likely Hubbard's attempt to cash in on the new therapy craze. It was not a new idea, for Dianetics procedure falls into what is known as the "in vivo" category of exposure therapy in that it involves a guided session and the use of one's ability to visualize (imagine) past incidents.

The person receiving Dianetics procedure, the "Preclear" or "PC" (a person who is not yet Clear) is told to close their eyes. Then, with their attention on the person's voice, they fall into a light trance. The preclear and auditor sit facing one another in chairs a comfortable distance apart. The auditor (the person giving the session) asks the preclear to locate a moment of pain and unconsciousness. With that, the person is told to go to the beginning of the incident and tell the auditor when they are there. To reinforce the hypnotic effect, they are instructed to move through the incident describing what's happening as though it's happening in the present. (For example, if the preclear is describing falling out of a tree, they would begin by saying something like "I'm climbing a tree" and not "I climbed a tree.") This is repeated over and over until the person becomes cheerful, and if they don't, the auditor asks for an earlier similar time the person experienced pain and unconsciousness, and so on. In this way with each recounting, in a manner exactly like exposure therapy, the traumatic experience is given a new context and the person becomes more and more desensitized to the trauma of their past experience. The results are often short-term. With Dianetics, Hubbard proclaimed, "The hidden source of all psychosomatic ills and human aberration [a deviation from what is considered normal, usual, or expected] has been discovered and skills have been developed for their invariable cure."

By Hubbard's logic, everyone on Earth is chained to their reactive mind—each one a ticking time bomb waiting to be triggered whenever some aspect of the contents of an engram resurfaces in the person's present-time environment. Adding to the urgency of eradicating the reactive mind, Hubbard called upon his favorite Cold War trope, the fear of total nuclear annihilation, boldly proclaiming in the opening chapter of the Dianetics book, "And down in the arsenal is an atom bomb, its hopeful nose full-armed in ignorance of it [Dianetics]."

That's how high the stakes were; it was Dianetics or oblivion. The reactive mind (or "bank" as it is colloquially referred to) was the boogie man, the monster under the bed, the ghoul hiding in the closet, and it could only be vanquished using Dianetics—cash, checks, and credit cards accepted.

The headlines read, "Dianetics Takes The Country By Storm." Soon Hubbard was crisscrossing America giving lectures, holding Dianetics workshops, and establishing a Dianetics foundation. Within a few years, and following a series of financial missteps, Hubbard went bankrupt, and the Dianetics book publishing rights were acquired by Don Purcell, a wealthy real estate developer in Wichita, Kansas. Losing the rights to publish *Dianetics*, Hubbard moved on to develop Scientology—a brand-new subject he could own and control.

As adherents plumbed the depths of the reactive mind,

uncovering earlier and earlier engrams, they began reporting incidents that could only be explained as either imagination or experiences predating their current lifetime. Opting for the latter explanation, these "past-life" experiences served to confirm for them the existence of the spirit or soul as being independent from the body. The reasoning was along the lines of, if you can imagine having lived before this life, then you must have. And with that, Scientology was born.

There is a key philosophical difference between Dianetics and Scientology. Dianetics considers you to be a product of everything that has ever been done *to* you. In Dianetics, nothing was your fault. With Scientology you are considered to be a product of everything *you* ever did; as such, everything is your fault (or at least your responsibility). That distinction, deeply embedded in Scientology's DNA, is a keystone of Scientology's thought reform system; for no matter what happens to you under such a system of thinking, you must have done something to have caused it to happen—to have, in Scientology terminology, "pulled it in." While the idea of taking personal responsibility for anything that happens to you can be empowering if self-elected; but when one person forces it upon another, or a group enforces it on its members, it becomes a form of emotional abuse in which the victim is always at fault. Every Scientologist has been (or will be) put in a position where they sought help with a problem and were met with the demand to cough up what they had done to make that problem happen.

To help locate what you did to make that "problem" happen, Hubbard introduced the E-meter, an electronic device for use in auditing. The preclear, or PC, holds a pair of electrodes, (essentially custom-made tin cans, similar to soup cans) that are connected to the meter via wires. The meter passes a tiny, imperceptible electrical current through the PC's body and back to the meter. Hubbard claimed that any changes in the PC's reactive mind would affect the flow of electrical current, causing a needle on the meter to move. The needle movements are interpreted by the auditor to assist the person in addressing the source of their problems—at least that's the theory. Other theories, such as biofeedback, or fluctuating electrical resistance in the person's skin, offer more sensible and scientific explanations to account for the movement of the E-meter needle. But whatever the explanation, the real problem with the E-meter is that in Scientology, it is considered the final arbiter of the individual's reality. It doesn't matter what anyone believes; if the needle moves, it's real and it's true—your own thoughts, conclusions, and emotions be damned. The E-meter takes precedence over the individual's self-determinism.

With the advent of Scientology, the reactive mind still remained *the* thing to be handled. The E-meter was promoted as providing a more efficient way of accessing the reactive mind.

But our mission at the moment was not to sell Scientology. Our mission was to sell Dianetics, and from there—in a grand scheme of bait and switch—Dianetics book buyers could be sold on a more efficient, and expensive, method of going Clear, Scientology!

By 1967 Hubbard was able to regain the rights to publish *Dianetics: The Modern Science of Mental Health*. By the early 1980s, over thirty years after its original publication date, it had only sold a disappointing three million copies, while sales of some other books in the self-help category had sold tens of millions. At that time Dianetics was Scientology's Trojan horse—a way to attract new members without exposing them to the liability of Scientology's perception as a fringe movement. Not to mention its reputation being tarnished by years of controversy stemming from having been outlawed for a time in both Australia and Great Britain, having had its offices in Washington, D.C. raided by the FDA over mislabeling E-meters as medical devices, and having seen eleven of its officials, including Hubbard's own wife, imprisoned for infiltrating government agencies in order to remove documents related to Scientology.

Public surveys done in the 1980s showed that Dianetics did not share Scientology's negative reputation. On the contrary, more people had heard of Dianetics than Scientology; Hubbard's name was more often associated with Dianetics than with Scientology and that association was, for the most part, positive to neutral: what was old had become new again. In the 1980s, Hubbard wrote about the importance of selling his books as the way to introduce new people to Scientology. He proclaimed, "Books Make Booms," stressing that "Book

One," as the *Dianetics* book was colloquially known, should be marketed on a continuous basis in perpetuity, conjuring up such images from the buzz created by the original release of *Dianetics* as "brush fire" and "groundswell." But until Jeff Hawkins launched the *Dianetics* campaign in the early '80s, there had not been any broad public marketing of *Dianetics*.

The plan was to put *Dianetics* book ads on television, at the time a speculative move, as book ads were never seen on TV. Jeff had produced a series of testimonial spots, including ads featuring an actor playing a marine biologist and San Francisco 49ers star quarterback John Brodie, who received Dianetics Auditing after a near career-ending automobile accident. There was nothing particularly innovative about a spokesperson giving a testimonial. It had been done for everything from laundry detergent to frozen foods, while in contrast, the advertising for brands such as Nike and Apple was breaking new ground. While the *Dianetics* book ads may have been somewhat conventional, the idea of producing ads for TV, from media buying to cooperative marketing programs done in conjunction with book distributors and retail book sellers, had never been done before in the annals of book publishing.

The first *Dianetics* ad I directed was called "Stunt Pilot." As the story goes, when *Astounding Science Fiction* magazine featured an excerpt from *Dianetics*, there was, supposedly, a flurry of interest from test pilots who were attracted to Dianetics for its claims of reducing reaction time. Scientology, like its founder, had a penchant for hyperbole and so the often-repeated "fact" that test pilots signed up for Dianetics seminars in droves became a mainstay of Dianetics lore. In the final analysis, the "Stunt Pilot" ad was just another conventional TV commercial, concluding with an actor holding up a product, looking into the camera and smiling. What was needed was a concept that was in keeping with the significance Hubbard assigned to the *Dianetics* book, something that was not similar to another ad but was unique to the product, in this particular case, the *Dianetics* book. After all, Hubbard claimed the book was going to cure all psychosomatic illness, eradicate the source of all negative thoughts, irrational fears, nightmares, and neurosis, and ultimately raise the intelligence of Earth's population, thus averting nuclear war—yet its TV ads were in the same vein of those produced for countless other products.

Rick Rogers, our creative director, came up with the brilliantly simple idea to make a series of ads using only text on screen with computer-generated animation at the end. Three questions would appear, one after the other, in white text on a black screen. Red numbers appeared in the bottom right corner which corresponded to the page numbers in the book where answers to each question could be found. The questions included things like, "Do you have to live with pain?" "Why are some people attracted to the wrong kind of partner?," or "Is child abuse hereditary?" These ads could be produced at very low expense and, with all the possible variations of questions available, new ones could be swapped out as often as McDonald's swapped out their burger ads. McDonald's had a policy for its TV ads featuring food items; such ads could only run for a week, as the audience seeing the same burger over and over perceives the food as stale. Whether intentional or not, the Dianetics questions ads followed the McDonald's model. The questions were swapped out often enough to never go stale.

By any measure, the Dianetics questions ads were a huge success, perhaps the most successful and memorable campaign in book publishing history. The design of the ads set a trend in television commercials in which text appeared as a main component, not just for titles and small print disclaimers. Rick's idea introduced text as the star, and other advertisers followed suit. Over the next three years, *Dianetics* book sales skyrocketed from three million to thirteen million. The music for the ad, inspired by the musical tag Intel was running on its ads at the time, became as ubiquitous and recognizable as the Alka Seltzer "Plop, Plop, Fizz, Fizz" jingle. Over a decade later, when the Dianetics theme was played to focus groups, when asked if they had ever heard it before, participants unanimously answered yes. When asked what they associated it with, they all said Dianetics—an unprecedented case of brand recognition.

By the late '80s, Jeff Hawkins and his marketing unit were relocated to Scientology's International Base in Southern California. The exact location of the International Base, called Int for short, was a well kept secret. I suspected it was within a few hours drive of Los Angeles, but did not actually know in which direction. All I knew for certain—at least at that moment—was that with the Marketing Unit moving to Int, my involvement with the Dianetics campaign had come to an end.

No doubt the success of the Dianetics campaign loomed large on the radar of the Church's iron-fisted leader David Miscavige, the Chairman of the Board of the Religious Technology Centre—or RTC—headquartered at the secretive International Base. RTC controlled the trademarks of Dianetics and Scientology, and with Miscavige at the helm of RTC, he was the most powerful executive in all of Scientology. All planning and management in all of Scientology could only be done with his approval. With no direct participation for approval from Miscavige, the Marketing Unit in LA had hit a home run with the Dianetics campaign, producing visual material at a level that the Church had been unable to achieve in spite of the crucial importance Hubbard had placed on it doing so. The Marketing Unit in LA had bombarded television sets across the nation with well-produced, clever Dianetics ads that put a 30 year old self-help book back on the New York Times Best Sellers list, while all other attempts by the Church to produce any type of visual material were an utter failure. We had succeeded in making the Dianetics book look good. We had also, unintentionally, succeeded in making David Miscavige look bad—or at least ineffectual, simply because we had achieved a landmark success with Dianetics that he could not take credit for, and that was accomplished beyond his purview. To remedy the situation, Miscavige ordered the Marketing Unit to relocate to the International Base and with that, The *Dianetics* campaign would never again achieve that same level of success or anything near it. When the operation was relocated to Int and put under Miscavige's direct supervision, whatever had driven it to achieve those spectacular results, was killed off. But the big prize he was after was a film director who could take over the Hubbard scripted technical training films consisting of twenty-six films of which only ten had been produced by Hubbard's death. Hubbard considered these films so crucial that he proclaimed Scientology could not survive without them. Without my knowing it, Miscavige had set his sights on me as the solution to completing the sacred Scientology Technical Training Films.

Shortly after the success of the Dianetics campaign, I was approached by the Scientology-sponsored Citizen's Commission on Human Rights ("CCHR") to produce a public service announcement. CCHR's public-facing mission statement calls for the eradication of abuse in the field of mental health. However, internally CCHR's fundraising mission is the eradication of the entire field of psychiatry, a sentiment cheered on by all Scientologists. Hubbard reportedly began to express his abhorrence of the mental health field shortly after Dianetics was—according to Hubbard—rejected by the American

Psychiatric Association (APA) back when he'd offered it to them prior to the book being published. More likely his disdain was motivated by the horrific reviews Dianetics received upon its release. Needing someone to blame, he blamed the mental health industry. In the Scientology universe, Hubbard claimed psychiatrists, or "psychs," were behind all the evil on Earth and are considered to have been the plague of mankind for eons. Yes, eons. In Scientology, psychiatry is considered to have originated a long time ago in a galaxy far, far away, not unlike the evil Sith Lords in *Star Wars*.

The CCHR ad, titled *Assassins*, consisted of a series of photographs of violent criminals such as Charles Manson, Mark David Chapman and John Hinckley Jr. set to a voiceover explaining how all these perpetrators had been in psychiatric care prior to committing their crimes. The correlation suggested that psychiatrists had turned these individuals into killers. CCHR provided a very small budget of $2,500 to produce the ad, a challenging amount which I accepted as I believed in the mission and wanted to help. They planned to use the ad to raise funds to pay for the production costs and to purchase airtime on local cable stations. This was my first exposure to the fraudulent tactics Scientology uses in order to raise donations. One of the executives at CCHR boasted how she had called up potential donors and asked them each to donate $2,500 to produce the ad. It was a successful ploy which convinced quite a few of the Scientologists they had single-handedly paid for the entire cost of the ad. They converted "Paying for the ad" into an abstract commodity that could be sold over and over. "You can't just ask for money. You have to sell them 'something,'" she explained. But sell the same thing over and over to different people convincing each they were the angels that had singlehandedly paid the production costs for the ad?

CCHR's efforts to impugn the field of mental health is complicated by unfounded assertions. For instance, their vigorous stance on the correlation between psychiatric medication and gun violence misdirects the argument away from much-needed gun control. They claim that behind every school shooting is a perpetrator who was currently or recently on psychiatric medication; thus, the cause of gun violence becomes misidentified as medication. Yet there has never been an autopsy or any medical testing to support this assertion.

Following my work on the Dianetics campaign and for CCHR, I received a call from Norman Starkey, an executive at Author Services, Inc. (ASI), to discuss a music video featuring rock legend Edgar Winter—who at the time was a practicing Scientologist. Established as the literary agency for the non-fiction works of L. Ron Hubbard, ASI holds a unique position in the corporate structure of Scientology. While ASI plays no official role in Church operations, when David Miscavige was the Chairman of the Board of ASI, it was the shadowy seat of power for all of Scientology management. It was from that

position that he later rose to ultimate power as the Chairman
of the Board of the Religious Technology Centre, or COB, as
he insists on being called.

Ostensibly, ASI is responsible for promoting the entire
library of Hubbard's fiction writing, from his dime novels to
his ponderous science fiction stories. ASI is also tasked with
raising donations to fund the "preservation of the tech," a
decades-long Hubbard-mandated program established to
convert his works into indestructible archival formats to be
stored in nuke-proof underground vaults situated in remote
locations. Though Scientology is not a doomsday cult, with
respect to the preservation of its "tech" it acts like one,
fundraising millions to preserve the works of its founder against
the inevitable natural or man-made catastrophe that Hubbard
predicted would eventually send life on Earth back to the
Stone Age. Somehow, the thinking goes that the survivors of
that catastrophe, who of course all speak English, will find the
vaults, figure out how to open them and take advantage of the
contents, kick-starting Scientology all over again. No electricity
after the apocalypse? No problem. Hubbard's lectures have
been preserved on gold-plated, stainless steel discs. A solar
powered disc player is included. Hubbard was narcissistic
enough to think his technology needed to be safeguarded for
the benefit of future, post-apocalyptic survivors, who, upon
discovering the nuke-proof vaults containing Scientology
"scripture," would kick-start a Scientology rebirth. There's

about as much chance of that happening as there was of kick-starting a resurgence in the worship of Egyptian Gods with the discovery of ancient Egyptian tombs. More than likely if the vaults containing Hubbard's work are to be discovered by a future civilization, the contents would most probably wind up in a museum of oddities and be laughed at by children. Or if found by primitive people, they would be worshiped as idols or fashioned into weapons.

Norman Starkey, who led the "Cry Out" music video project, was a South African with a commanding presence, as well-mannered as he was intense. Norman was a founding Sea Org member, meaning he'd been there from the outset and had served as Hubbard's captain on the flagship of Hubbard's seagoing navy, the *Apollo*. When I first met him, he was a designated trustee of Hubbard's estate, a financial instrument established to protect Hubbard's assets after his death.

While leaving no known plans for the succession of Church leadership after his death, Hubbard did leave detailed instructions for a record album to be interpreted from his science fiction epic *Mission Earth*, a sweeping, ten-volume saga in which Hubbard sarcastically features governments, psychiatrists, drug companies, and most notably trans people, in the role of villains, with healthy portions of rapists, and child molesters rounding out the cast of characters in a plot to take over the Earth by addicting its population to opiates. The story's hero is white savior Jettero Heller, described as a character of perfection, incorruptibility, and astonishing ability, assigned to save Earth from the Earthlings. The album, with a lineup led by Edgar Winter, was produced at Scientology's music recording studio located at Golden Era Productions and released sometime between '86 and '89. The first track on the 'B' side, titled "Cry Out," was intended as an anthem in support of environmental activism. ASI was hoping a music video would help with the album's sagging sales numbers; by specifically choosing the song "Cry Out," they hoped to drum up partnerships with environmental groups that might help to buff their image and give them something positive to crow about. I agreed to direct the video with shooting slated to take place at various locations around LA.

Norman often visited the set. He had been on the original LRH film crew with David Miscavige and was well versed in the LRH school of filmmaking, which included the use of multiple light meters employed in a time-consuming ritual when measuring the lighting. In contrast, the technique used by the Emmy Award-winning cinematographer Tom Del Ruth, whom I had hired to shoot the music video, only took a few seconds or so. While Tom had a reputation for obtaining perfect exposures, his quick-draw use of the light meter, while it contributed to keeping production flowing, made Norman so nervous that I had to open a film lab after hours to show him the footage. Norman was convinced the guy didn't know what he was doing. The lab technician commented that he'd never seen such consistent exposures. I subsequently asked the cinematographer to be very deliberate when looking at his light meter whenever Norman was around. No amount of explaining to Norman would do. Plus, he was my client, and if I had learned anything from directing commercials, it was to always be respectful to the guy writing the check. In Norman's view, the cinematographer's use of the light meter was "off source," Scientology-speak for not standard—not the way Hubbard (who referred to himself as "Source") would do it—and therefore must be wrong. So strong was Hubbard's hold over his devotees' thinking—in all things—from how to wash a car, to how to raise children, to the proper use of a light meter and myriad other tasks, that they believed these could only be correctly accomplished by following Hubbard's directions. It's a wonder the human race survived before Hubbard came along. In spite of any contrary evidence, the founder's teachings were followed without question. Such black-and-white thinking is common throughout Scientology, as well as in thought-control cults in general. In Scientology, when faced with any kind of challenge, the correct thing to do was to always ask yourself, "What would Ron do?"

Ultimately, the video had no impact on the environmental movement. It didn't get played on Earth Day or on MTV, or inspire partnerships with environmental activists. At best it was an example of Scientology virtue-signaling that it cared about the environment, while at the same time spending millions of dollars to preserve its religious documents against an imagined future catastrophe while doing nothing for the current state of the environment.

Meanwhile, back at the ranch, or I should say the International Base, David Miscavige was formulating his plan to catch his high-valued prize—a professional film director who could make a high quality technical training film, something the Church had never been able to accomplish.

SIX

THE TECHNICAL TRAINING FILMS

T HE EDUCATIONAL MATERIALS used for training Scientology auditors includes 26 films known as the Technical Training Films.

All of Hubbard's written works, films, and recorded lectures on the subject of Scientology are referred to as "Technology." To be precise, "Spiritual Technology." The idea that Scientology is a technology is a major factor in how Hubbard packaged the con. He was obsessed with being perceived as a brilliant scientist, engineer, and discoverer of the basic principles underlying life and the physical universe. Not to mention, of course, his many claimed accomplishments in the arts, humanities, aviation, and maritime technology. Scientologists refer to the spiritual technology of Scientology as "the Tech." If it were possible for an abstract idea to be revered, followed, and cared for as a God, that would be the Tech—almighty and all knowing—to be treasured, adhered to, and cared for at any cost.

At the core of that "technology" are the Technical Training Films, proclaimed by Hubbard to be the key to Scientology's survival and expansion. Only ten of these films had been completed as of Hubbard's death in 1986, with a few more having been made by 1990. A few of these films were directed by Hubbard himself. The remainder were directed by underlings and supervised remotely by Hubbard, or by others after his death. But regardless of who directed them, they all had one thing in common—an embarrassingly low standard of quality.

I had seen a number of these films while on auditor training courses at Celebrity Centre, at least the ones they'd managed to complete before Hubbard departed this Earth. Unbeknownst to auditor trainees, 7 of the 26 films Hubbard deemed vital for the successful training of Scientology auditors had never been produced. It's difficult to describe how bad the films were. There is no comparison. There was the occasional charming moment, not unlike when children put on a play, but mostly the films were composed of cringeworthy overacting that seemed to be modeled after the school that gave us the mustache-twirling villains and fainting maidens from the silent era—but with stilted dialogue. The sets were shoddy and always appeared to be kludged together from scraps stolen off a construction site. The main shooting space was an old warehouse, a date packing plant located within the desert compound Hubbard had purchased in La Quinta, California. It had a low ceiling, making it impossible to position lights at the required distance away from the set. The space was interrupted by a couple of rows of round 6-inch pipes, pillars that held the weight of the ceiling, and were usually wrapped with aluminum foil or some other material to try and integrate them into the set design. The painted backdrops seen outside the fake windows were crude and primitive looking pastoral settings. The lighting was garish—always too bright or too dim. Hubbard fancied himself to be an expert cinematographer, but the shots in these films were badly composed and the camera moves were shaky. But the most blatantly atrocious element of all was the costumes. Hubbard was adamant that the tech films were to appear "timeless." In an Executive Directive, known as an ED—in this case, a Cine ED (as in cinematography)—he proclaimed that they are to take place "in the year zilch." In one example, what they wound up with were costumes that looked like rejects from a '70s *Star Trek* parody: odd fitting Nehru-like jackets, blousy satin shirts in bright primary colors with sashes tied around their waists pirate style. And that was just for one film.

Suffice it to say, as a student studying Scientology, you held your nose and focused on the information you needed to glean from the film to progress on your course. That was likely the universal experience of all Scientology auditor trainees upon seeing any of these films. There was, however, plenty of motivation on the part of the students to overlook the low quality. The importance they placed on the content, and their respect for Hubbard as the source of the only means to save the world, far outweighed the blatantly poor quality. That, and the fear that anyone remarking negatively about any aspect of a tech film would end up in ethics trouble and an invasive interrogation known as a Security Check (shortened in Scientology terminology to "sec check") where you would be expected to confess what you had done or had experienced that made you think the low-quality films were in fact low quality.

So highly did Hubbard regard the tech films, which were only available to be seen on auditor training courses, while overlooking (or failing to see) their embarrassingly bad quality, he proclaimed students would rush to sign up for auditor training just so they could qualify to watch the films.

Hubbard decreed that the tech films were so vital to Scientology's mission that without them, auditor training, and therefore Scientology itself, would fail. The Church had been unable to complete the films in the years since Hubbard embarked on the project; despite investing great effort, their production remained an unsolvable problem.

Hubbard first stressed the need for visual education back in 1963 when, as Executive Director of Scientology International in Saint Hill, England, then the worldwide headquarters of Scientology, he gave a short, filmed lecture titled *An Afternoon at Saint Hill*. The lecture opens with the camera angled at the rear patio entrance of his stately country manor, amidst a perfectly groomed rose garden. Playing the part of the landed-gentry English gentleman replete with leather elbow-patched tweed jacket, matching hat, and perfectly pressed pleated wool trousers, Hubbard strutted up to a short wall, swung a foot up onto it, learned forward with an elbow on his knee and began to speak. He described how Scientology would only go as far as it was correctly taught, and that it could only be correctly taught if you could see how it was done. To accomplish that, you needed films. It was at that moment that Hubbard announced to his followers that Scientology would not succeed without visual instruction, presaging two of his favorite hobby horses—still photography and filmmaking—and though he would never rise above the level of rank amateur in either of these avocations, despite acquiring a world-class camera collection, and despite having his organization and followers laud his artistic achievements, his photography and his films remained laughably bad.

In the early '70s, in an effort to evade being served in lawsuits, Hubbard relocated to the remote Southern California desert town of La Quinta, establishing a film studio in an abandoned date packing plant located on a recently purchased property, and set about making the visual training aids he alluded to back at Saint Hill. He wrote the scripts for the 26 technical training films, as well as a number of other films for external release intended to enlighten the public on Scientology.

While Hubbard had first announced the need for visual

training at Saint Hill back in 1963, the need to fulfill that vision took on a heightened urgency when he requested videotapes of auditing sessions from the Los Angeles Church. He was appalled at what he saw. The auditors' execution of the Scientology procedures they had learned on their courses was, in his view, horrific. Though in reality they were being taught with materials he had developed and approved. His decades of work providing written texts and recorded lectures for use in the training of auditors had failed to yield the kind of consistently positive results that he deemed necessary if Scientology was going to expand and survive. So, to solve the problem, he scripted the 26 films designed to correct their auditing mistakes and prevent them from ever recurring. He then ordered the failed LA auditors to La Quinta where many of them joined the Sea Org and took part in making the films.

The training films fall into two categories. Ten of the films deal with the correct use of the E-meter, including such things as interpreting the reactions of the E-meter needle—called a "read," distinguishing between a meter read and the movement of the needle caused by inadvertent body motion, the proper set-up for an auditing session, and so forth. The other 16 films teach the communication skills needed for a person to become a successful auditor and, according to the training materials, to be successful in life. These skills include conducting proper communication with the preclear and showing examples of incorrect and correct communication.

Hubbard conscripted a rag-tag crew made up of kitchen staff, groundskeepers, a few of his teenage messengers such as David Miscavige, and loyal holdovers from his days on the *Apollo*. There was the indefatigable sea captain Norman Starkey and, of course, the abysmally bad auditors from the Los Angeles Organization. Not one among them, not even Hubbard, despite his alleged work for Hollywood, had likely ever made a film or witnessed any of the various processes that go into producing one. For all their effort they only managed to produce a handful of amateurish low-quality films. Yet they were so infatuated with their own work that in the case of one particular public film titled *The Problem of Life*, the film's editor wrote a memo to Hubbard in which she expressed their desire to enter it in the Cannes Film Festival, certain it would take top honors.

SEVEN

WELCOME TO GOLD

I T WAS BACK IN THE LATE '70s that the Scientology film production facility, known as Golden Era Productions, or Gold, relocated to the broken-down resort known as Gilman Hot Springs about 60 miles northwest of its headquarters at La Quinta, California. Gilman Hot Springs sits in a desolate bowl of scrub land dotted with dairy farms. Located 90 miles east of Los Angeles in Riverside County, in an area that was part of the euphemistically dubbed "Inland Empire," a name concocted back in the 1880s by land speculators. With summer temperatures topping out in the low 100s, the air would fill with dense swarms of flies driven by the stench of waste lagoons located at the nearby dairy farms.

The Gilman Hot Springs location was also home to the International Management Base. The property was essentially bisected by California State Highway 79, with the Religious Technology Center and International Scientology Management located on the north side of the highway, and Golden Era Productions located on the south side. Over the coming years the property would be transformed into a sparkling oasis of whitewashed buildings with blue tiled roofs surrounded by lush green landscaping, with administrative offices and production spaces connected by a network of paved pathways. The 500-acre property sat in stark contrast to the surrounding blighted hillsides. While the design rationale of architects such as Frank Lloyd Wright called for buildings to be inspired by and to reflect their environment so as to achieve a natural integration with their surroundings, Hubbard's inspiration for the Gold/Int Base was his vague recollection of the lush Scottish countryside. The result came off like an aggressive attempt to overpower the desolate lifeless surroundings, resulting in two clashing environments separated by an Ultra-Barrier spiked fence, ground sensors, security cameras, and high-intensity lighting. While the security fencing kept the staff from leaving, it could not keep out the swarms of flies and the stench of the bovine waste lagoons emanating from the nearby dairy farms—blending the two environments together.

Back in those days, the location of Gold was kept top secret. If an unauthorized Scientologist were to discover its location, they could wind up in serious hot water, facing an interrogation from an Ethics Officer. Public Scientologists viewed Gold with reverence and awe; it was a mythical land commonly referred to as "over the rainbow" where the top managers of Scientology orchestrated all aspects of Church business. And above them was the top tier of all Scientology realms, the Religious Technology Centre or RTC, with its supreme leader David Miscavige, who was now running the entire Scientology universe in the post-Hubbard era. His was the final word on all things Scientology, from lording over international management, to ensuring the scriptures were available and unadulterated, to managing the details of legal matters. Not even the smallest details, such as the guest toiletries at the Church's luxury religious retreat in Clearwater, Florida, escaped his scrutiny and final approval.

Following years of producing unusable films, Miscavige was desperate to get film production rolling. After all, his job description included ensuring everything was in place so that Scientology could be delivered to the public as Hubbard intended—and that included having the 26 Hubbard-scripted Technical Training Films, which formed the core of auditor training. Yet the efforts to produce the training films continued to yield nothing but poor-quality junk.

Unbeknownst to me, shortly after Miscavige ordered the Marketing Unit to relocate to the International Base, he banished the entire Gold film crew to the galley where they would spend their days washing dishes and scrubbing grease out of the fryer, and forbade them to go near their equipment. The crew—who had been operating directly under Miscavige's purview, and of which he was a former cameraman—had earned his ire. It was at that point that he officially issued the order to hire a professional film director.

Soon after, I received an invitation to meet with the Commanding Officer of the Commodore's Messenger Organization Gold, or CO CMO Gold. Ted Horner was an affable, easygoing yet all business veteran Sea Org officer. Ted had invited me to meet with him to discuss having me direct a tech film. The organization Ted headed up was a special branch of the CMO Hubbard originally organized to oversee Golden Era Productions. The CMO first originated out of Hubbard's Messengers on the *Apollo*. The first Messengers were mostly tween and teen girls with cheerleader looks who were ferociously loyal to the Commodore, as Hubbard insisted on being called. The Commodore's Messengers were uniformed in highly-sexualized, tight shorts and knee-high socks—though no one, not even the original Messengers who fled Scientology and spoke out, ever reported one instance of inappropriate sexual behavior between Hubbard and any of his female messengers. Sex was not Hubbard's kink—at least not during his Scientology days. Rather, he preferred to fuck with people's minds. In the beginning, the Messengers served to round up crew members and bring them to Hubbard, or to deliver verbal messages. They were drilled to deliver those messages mimicking the Commodore's exact verbal tone. If the Commodore wanted to yell at someone, a Messenger would deliver the message yelling. While the CMO originated on the Flag Ship *Apollo*, rounding up people, delivering messages, and following the Commodore around with a compact voice recorder, an ashtray, a lighter, and a pack of Kools, the CMO eventually grew into an international organization responsible for the policing and compliance of Hubbard's orders. Their authority was second only to RTC. That Hubbard established a CMO branch specifically for Gold, was an indication of the importance he placed on Gold. Some years after I met with Ted Horner, Miscavige dismantled all top management functions and dissolved CMO GOLD. Ted Horner, caught in Miscavige's reign of terror, fled to Alaska,then settled in Belize.

But at the time of our initial meeting, Ted was in command of CMO Gold. The meeting was held in an office at Scientology's garishly painted "Big Blue" building. I found Ted to be a pleasant individual with a straight forward demeanor, but his body language hinted that he was disclosing very little of the intent behind the meeting—namely the pressure to get the training films produced. He played it cool, but I could practically hear his stomach churning as he laid out set renderings and a script for my review. I discovered later that the sets for that particular film had sat untouched in the studio for the better part of a year and that the crew that was meant to shoot the film had been assigned to kitchen duty until further notice. As I reviewed the material, I couldn't help but feel I was being scrutinized under a 1,000x microscope. It was awkward, to say the least.

Before you can arrive at Gold you must be given a security clearance. Forget that you are the most qualified person they could find to help them solve a problem that if left unsolved could cause Scientology to fail. Forget the fact that you have been a dedicated Scientologist for years and have ascended to the upper levels of the Bridge as well as becoming a trained auditor. If you want to come to Gold, you'll need a security clearance, which includes a thorough background check run by the Church's legal department, a self-written history detailing every person you ever had sex with in excruciating detail, and any connection you or your friends or family may have to the perceived enemies of Scientology, such as government agencies, local authorities, mental health workers or institutions, the media, or anyone who has ever spoken out against Scientology. I awkwardly and embarrassedly answered all their highly personal questions, blaming myself for having been less than one hundred percent moral and upright without ever realizing that, not only were they vetting me, but they were also gathering information they could use to attempt to crush me if I ever spoke out against them. It never occurred to me at the time that the organization to which I had pledged my loyalty might someday hold that information over my head, as I have now witnessed them doing to so many who have left and spoken out.

My clearances were approved, and I was a go—a forgone conclusion as Miscavige had ordered my hiring subsequent to the Dianetics campaign success. The clearances were just a formality. Finally, the big day arrived—an introductory visit to the Base to press some flesh and get some face time with Gold Execs. I was driven to Gold by the head of public relations for Author Services. I had known Susie Watson-Taylor for a few years. We got along well. She came of age during the London music scene of the 1960s, so we had plenty of stories to share of growing up in the midst of a cultural revolution—she in London and me in LA. But on that particular sunny Southern California morning, Susie was in a panic fearing we might be late to our appointment at the Base. The fear was palpable. A quick stop to eat was rushed and cut short. She did her best to disguise her anxiety beneath a veneer of calm British humor. Unbeknown to me at the time, her panic was the standard setting on the emotional thermostat of all Sea Org members. She seemed obliged to maintain a calm and energetic demeanor layered over the fear that circumstances could conspire at any moment to land her in an uncomfortable and time-consuming ethics action simply because a truck jackknifed on the freeway causing us to be late.

Other than Susie's subdued anxiety, the drive was uneventful. We headed east on the 101, and then transitioned onto the 60—that was the first clue that Gold was somewhere inland. By the time we crossed the 15, I was fairly certain we were headed to some desolate corner of Riverside County. I remember thinking to myself how much I hated driving through Riverside, even at twelve-years-old heading out to the Riverside International Raceway to watch the Grand Prix, where, in the years we attended the race, my older brother and I would be certain to get tickets on turn 6 because that's where Steve McQueen always sat. Fondly, I recalled how McQueen would buy beer for the crowd and the time I saw him passed out drunk under the bleachers. It didn't matter because he was such a hero to us—the man who invented cool. As a teenager, my brother pumped gas at a station on the corner of Laurel Avenue and Sunset Boulevard, at the eastern entrance to the Strip. McQueen, who lived in Nichols Canyon, the canyon directly east of Laurel Canyon, regularly stopped for gas at my brother's station, and he'd only let my brother pump gas into his British racing green 1956 D-Type Jag. By the time we caught up with McQueen at the Raceway, he and my brother were on a first name basis, and my brother let everyone know it.

As an adult, I made that drive numerous times on the way to Palm Springs, promising myself to spend as little time as possible in that horrifically blighted, inland environment—a promise I unfortunately did not keep. I felt more than a little nostalgic as we passed the site of the former Raceway. It had been bulldozed to make way for a complex of big box stores. A large chunk of turn 6 was still intact and I wanted to stop and chip off a souvenir, but Susie was on a dead run to get us to the Base.

As we turned onto Gilman Springs Road, the broad valley spread out before us, rimmed by rocky hills that had a jagged, prehistoric silhouette. We pulled up to the security gate on time and headed straight to the *Star of California*—a faux three-masted clipper ship adjacent to an Olympic-sized swimming pool and tropical garden originally constructed as a meeting place for entertaining special guests and as a venue for local events. With its tropical flower beds, clumps of palm trees, and peacocks strutting freely throughout the grounds, the area was meant to replicate a Polynesian paradise in the wastelands of Riverside County. Landlocked in the desert, the *Star of California* was never to escape her mooring and, as I was soon to discover, neither were most of the crew at the Base. On the deck of the "ship," we were greeted by a small contingent of execs and offered a lavish assortment of freshly prepared and beautifully curated gourmet finger foods and beverages—more than we could possibly consume. It all felt like a facade—a pantomime being put on by people who wanted to come off as well-mannered but weren't, and who wanted to appear to be tasteful but were actually lacking taste. Our hosts were going through an awful lot of trouble to make a good impression, not the way people do because they have class, or manners, or adhere to tradition, but because they are buttering you up, making you compliant for the big ask that's sure to come. It's difficult to explain what it's like to believe in something like Scientology and yet detest aspects of its organizational structure, its practices, and its culture. But despite the colorful tropical plants, the soothing sound of the waterfall splashing into the koi pond, the garish peacocks, and the cool, inviting water of the pool, the whole affair was rather tacky. Following initial introductions and refreshments, our tour of the Base got underway.

The Gilman Hot Springs property was once a popular resort established in the 1890s. The unverified story as relayed to me was that the Army Corps of Engineers, while blasting through a nearby mountain, had inadvertently diverted an underground river, depriving the springs of their source of water. By the 1970s the resort went bankrupt and was secretly purchased for cash in 1978 by the Church of Scientology using the alias "Scottish Highland Quietude Club." Though purchased as a secluded base for Hubbard to continue with the film projects he began at La Quinta, he barely set foot on the property, preferring, I assume for security reasons, to live in the nearby town of Hemet, in an apartment the staff referred to as "X," until his security at the Base could be assured.

The resort property also included a nine-hole golf course, which Hubbard used as a backlot for filming. A modest hacienda-style house with a commanding view of the valley below was designated as Hubbard's home, though he never actually lived there. I did hear he once used the house to celebrate Thanksgiving. The house referred to as "Bonnie View," was tended to by three full-time staff, not counting groundskeepers. The interior was NASA cleanroom immaculate. Nothing was out of place. Glasses full of fresh water, sitting on paper doilies, and covered with plastic wrap, were conveniently situated in case the house's intended occupant—currently on vacation from planet Earth after "voluntarily" departing his physical body in 1986—arrived thirsty. In the master bedroom, clothes were laid out. I recognized some of the clothing, having seen Hubbard posing in it in published photos. You would think that if Hubbard were to actually return to Earth there'd be plenty of advance notice to lay out his wardrobe and fill drinking glasses. Walking through the house and listening to the staff describe the setting, I got the feeling that the house is not maintained to accommodate Hubbard's imminent return, but rather, is maintained out of a deep sense of worship. Church doctrine claims that, within Scientology, Hubbard is considered to be just a man and is not worshiped as a god. But that doesn't explain why that house is maintained in such a ritualistic manner. Looking back at this now, the staff remind me of the Cargo Cult—the primitive Melanesian people who perform rituals which they believe will cause a more technologically advanced society to deliver goods that will improve their survival. In the case of Hubbard's house at Gold, the rituals included intense cleaning, the laying out of wardrobe, and filling drinking glasses.

As we continued with our tour, walking through the various film and audio production spaces, I couldn't help but reflect on how the Gold film studio was organized in the same fashion as the original Hollywood Studio system pioneered in the silent era by studio mogul Thomas H. Ince. It was Ince who first organized film production into departments, such as props, sets, wardrobe, and makeup. Everything within Ince's studio system was self-contained: even the writers, directors, and actors were departmentalized and obligated to exclusive studio contracts. The studios also owned and operated movie theaters with names that reflected their own—the Warner, the Paramount, etc. While that system was broken up in an anti-trust suit in 1948, with the studios no longer able to own theaters or maintain exclusive contracts with actors, much of Ince's original methodology remains in use today. Scientology's film studio was an eerie reminder of that early system, as it often called upon its own contracted staff to appear in films, and its theaters were located in its own churches. In Scientology's case, being a non-profit religious entity, none of this was an anti-trust issue, but it was reminiscent, nonetheless.

Coincidentally, the circumstances surrounding Thomas Ince's death have an odd connection to Scientology's own history. Ince's close friend, William Randolph Hearst, had once thrown a birthday party for Ince on his yacht. Charlie Chaplin was one of the guests. Rumor had it that Hearst was convinced Chaplin was having an affair with Marion Davies, Hearst's romantic partner. Hearst, mistaking Ince for Chaplin, who he thought was entering Davies's stateroom, shot him.

Ince was taken off the yacht by a private physician, loaded into an ambulance, and later died at home. There was no autopsy. The official cause of death was listed as a heart attack. Shortly after Ince's death, gossip columnist Louella Parsons, who had attended Ince's birthday party on Hearst's yacht, saw her gossip column become syndicated nationally in all Hearst-owned publications, launching her to national fame. But most inexplicably, Ince's widow received a substantial cash gift from Hearst. She used the money to build the Château Élysée, a 1920s replica of a 17th-century French-Normandy chateau in Hollywood, today the home of Scientology's Celebrity Centre International. The official story still accounts for Ince's death as a heart attack.

No one in Scientology had ever heard of Thomas Ince, yet they had unknowingly fashioned their studio after Ince's prototype, and they had purchased a building intended to cater to their elite Hollywood devotees that was originally built with blood money from Ince's questionable death. It was an odd coincidence but one I relished at the time.

A few days after my initial tour of the Base, with plans in place and a firm go-ahead to direct the film, I drove the ninety miles from my home in LA to Gold to begin my "one-film" assignment. I was assigned an apartment to myself, a short drive away in the nearby town of Hemet, a mostly depressed area of urban sprawl flanked by two Walmart Super Centers. What it lacked in culture, it made up for in big box stores, an unfair trade-off if there ever was one. I would make that ninety-mile drive twice weekly, leaving LA on Monday, and returning Friday evening, and each day I'd drive the 25 minutes each way from the apartment in Hemet to the Base. It was an awful lot of driving. The crew, who mostly lived nearby, eight to an apartment, stuffed themselves into crowded buses for the trip to and from the Base.

Before production could begin on the film, I had to complete a battery of basic film courses. Gold had never experienced what it was actually like to work with a filmmaker who knew how to make films. Everything they knew about filmmaking they had gotten from a textbook or an "advice" written by Hubbard. The result of that training was some of the very worst filmmaking I'd ever seen. Yet Hubbard's "Cine Tech" was so sacred there was no way they were going to let me near their film set without having the benefit of his basic film training, the core of which was "The Cine Basics Course." Although I had been a working professional for twenty years, no matter my prior experience, I was required to complete those courses. I sat there in the course room thinking, "You hired me because I could make films because you couldn't, yet you require me to take your basic film courses, the same ones that failed to successfully train your own people." It only took two weeks to complete the training and I was being paid to study. The courses did inform me as to the crew's level of expertise and how their filmmaking practices and procedures differed from my own—they had different names for certain things as well as some difference in methods, so at least the courses were helpful in that respect. I had learned filmmaking from professors such as the dean of the CalArts film school, Alexander McKendrick—a towering figure in the history of the British Cinema, while the Gold crew learned the cinematic arts from reading advices written by Hubbard, reading books approved by Hubbard, and watching crappy VHS copies of Hubbard approved movies. None of them ever seemed to have aspired to filmmaking because they were in love with the art form, but rather they seemed driven by the need to comply with an order, to make a target or suffer the consequences. Taking their film courses did have a curious and rather significant downside, it would later enable the powers that be to claim credit for my being able to make films at all—to claim that it was they who taught me to make films. It's just one of the ways Scientology hijacks your identity. Especially at Gold. They'll require you to learn something you already know how to do and then take credit for teaching you how to do it—as though without them you are nothing and have no identity.

I felt oddly out of place that first night in the tightly packed course room. Everyone but me was dressed in Sea Org uniforms. The thick smell of body odor mixed with stale smoke filled the room; Sea Org members were often smokers and the odor lingered on their clothes. (To be fair, I didn't quit smoking until December 2011.) The situation wasn't helped by the fact that all Scientologists eschew the use of any type of scented product for fear that such can produce unwanted mental pictures resulting in negative emotions. Shortly after I cracked open the Cine Basics course pack, my attention was drawn to the sudden motion of four men striding into the room in a single-file line heading, without pausing or slowing, from left to right. They were all wearing a peculiar uniform, one I'd never seen—dark blue slacks and a matching stand-up collar, zip-up jacket with subtle gold officer bars. The uniform had an almost monkish look.

I recognized the gentleman in the lead as David Miscavige, who referred to himself as the ecclesiastical leader of the religion. I had not laid eyes on him since he appeared on stage at the Palladium to speak at the announcement of Hubbard's death. I only recognized one of the three men following him. It was Ray Mithoff, who I'd known from my early Scientology days at Celebrity Centre. Unbeknownst to me, I was looking at the Inspector General Network, or IG Network, the pinnacle of Scientology organizational power. Ray Mithoff, now the Inspector General for Tech, responsible for overseeing the application of Scientology auditing technology, was followed by Marc Yager, the Inspector General for Admin, responsible for the application of Hubbard's administrative technology. And finally, there was Mark "Marty" Rathbun, the Inspector General for Ethics. In Scientology, "Ethics" is a body of principles and procedures intended to ensure the long-term survival of organizations as well as individuals who apply "ethics tech." Scientology Ethics is most notable for being wielded like the hammer of a police state to keep adherents in line, as well as for containing a method of managing by statistics and for enumerating the codes of correct conduct along with the penalties for breaking them, known as the Scientology Justice System. Being Inspector General for Ethics made Marty the top cop of Scientology.

The four made a beeline across the front of the course room and then in perfect unison their heads pivoted, their laser-like gazes momentarily fixing on me; then their heads rapidly snapped back to front-facing as they marched out. They were obviously giving me the once-over, the four most powerful individuals in all of Scientology, doing this strange dance that I was not supposed to notice, but looked like something out of a Marx Brothers movie. For all their subtlety, they might as well have run into the room with their hair on fire.

It would be years before I'd fully discover what happened in the run-up to Miscavige ordering that a professional director be found. With the odd appearance of the Inspectors General that night in the course room, I was beginning to get an inkling that something significant must have preceded my arrival. That "something" traces back many years to when Hubbard proclaimed that there is no more important method for communicating than using audio-visual technology. In fact, he had written on the matter proclaiming, "It's an A/V world," again stressing that the very future of Scientology was dependent on its ability to master all methods of audio-visual presentation. For the past few years, Miscavige had been intensely focused on bringing Hubbard's words to fruition, purchasing audio, video, and film equipment, building music recording and mixing facilities and a small sound stage for filming. But when it came to producing the actual media, his vision and his efforts were so hampered by the staff's lack of ability that he ultimately decided to hire outside help. An extensive search had been done to locate a qualified individual, ideally a Scientologist. I knew none of this at the time. I just sat there baffled, not knowing what to make of the attention I'd just been given.

All Scientology organizations are divided into seven divisions delineated in excruciating detail on an organizing board, a large board with colored lines tracing out an organizational chart, filled in with countless labels enumerating post titles and the names of the people who hold the posts. Such an "Org Board" is displayed on a wall adjacent to the administrative offices in every Church of Scientology and was backed up by numerous thick volumes containing the administrative policies issued by Hubbard. The organizing board gives the exact purpose of each division, delineates all its functions, and lists all the posts. It is a stifling hierarchical structure that leaves no room for autonomous decision-making or spontaneous, creative thought or action. Orders flowed down; compliance flowed up. Like cookies stamped out in a baking factory, all of Scientology is governed by a management system that is intended to produce a predictably uniform end product. Of course, no organization can survive without form and structure, but the Hubbard system of organization, used to govern Scientology, favors form and structure over individuality and, all too often, the top-heavy weight of authority only serves to crush whatever (or whomever) lies below.

In a public Church of Scientology, Division 4 is the production division. Its *production* is the delivery of Scientology training and auditing to parishioners. In a non-service organization like Golden Era Productions (non-service = doesn't service the public), Division 4 produces audio-visual products. I thought I'd been hired to direct a film, but unbeknownst to me, directing a film at Gold meant I'd be occupying the second highest position in Division 4, the Cine Division, with the topmost position in each division being the divisional secretary, or Sec. At the time of my arrival, the post of Cine Sec was being held by the eldest of the two daughters Hubbard had with his third wife, Mary Sue. Diana Hubbard was a lovely woman in her thirties with the Hubbard signature red hair, a mellifluous voice, and a proper British accent. Diana had been brought in from an upper level management organization known as Exec Strata, which was headed up by the "Executive Director International" or ED Int—a position L. Ron Hubbard specifically created for the purpose of running Scientology.

Under normal circumstances, a transfer from Exec Strata to Gold would be considered an extreme demotion. In this case, Diana Hubbard had been temporarily assigned as the head of the Cine Division, in order to ensure my transition to the position of director came off smoothly. I recalled seeing Diana around Celebrity Centre back when she was briefly out of the Sea Org and pursuing her music career, but up until then, I did not know her personally. That was about to change when she became my "Senior," introduced me to the "Cine Crew," and oversaw the production of the film I was hired to direct.

It was early evening, and the conference room was packed. One wall was lined with chairs facing a long conference table surrounded by about 30 more chairs. Diana introduced me to the crew explaining that their current director would be working under me as an apprentice. Oddly, I had not been told this, but I didn't pay it much mind. I had no idea the crew I was meeting with, and was about to embark on a film with, had just been released from weeks of kitchen duty prior to my arrival.

A few days later we began shooting. The crew snapped to attention whenever I addressed them, referring to me as "Sir" or "Mr. Brisker"—not an unexpected practice on a film set where the director is a literal dictator. But in the case of this crew, it felt like it was being done with the fear of new recruits at a boot camp who at any moment might be ordered to "drop and give me 20." Years later, Gary "Jackson" Morehead, who was the

Security Chief at the International Base at that time and who had designed its entire security apparatus, explained that he was in charge of making sure the crew showed me the utmost respect and obedience. They were under tremendous pressure to follow my orders without question or face dire consequences. One crew member from my early days at Gold, who escaped in the late '90s, reached out to me after I left.

> "Did you know that almost all of us in the Gold crew back when you arrived were told not to ever 'fraternize' with you, never talk about personal stuff, don't ask personal questions, don't say anything personal or get into any small talk? It was weird."
>
> —Gold shoot crew member

At the time, I just thought they were being oddly compliant and weirdly cooperative. Things calmed down once they discovered I was not difficult to get along with nor easily offended. Once we completed a few films, the restrictions on fraternizing with the new director loosened up a bit.

The first day's shots, the "rushes"—also known as "dailies," being the term for the raw, unedited footage that was rushed through the lab and usually viewed the day after shooting—were seen and approved with a great deal of fanfare. There was a sense of relief, and the buzz was everywhere that the Cine Crew was back in production and getting shots approved by Miscavige. Suddenly, the previous director was unceremoniously removed from post and put in charge of cleaning dumpsters with a toothbrush. Miscavige even created a new job title just for him, "Dumpster in-Charge," or "Dumpster I/C." I had been fed the cover story that the current director would work under me, but in reality, they were just waiting to see if I could pull off the job so they could dump the guy. In my professional experience, if you were ever approached to replace another director you were duty-bound to inform that person you had been approached to replace them. It's considered professional ethics and is mandated in the bylaws of the Directors Guild of America. No such professional code of ethics exists in the Sea Org; instead, they abide by a code that allows for individuals to be summarily removed from their job positions. People deserve to be treated with dignity and respect, even when their job performance calls for their removal. I imagine that if I couldn't have pulled it off, I'd be sent away with a "Thanks for trying," and the crew would once again be banished to the galley.

Over time, I couldn't help but notice that no one on the crew, or any of the other staff I'd met, showed any interest in aspiring to the position of director. It seemed odd that they'd managed to fill every position needed to get a film made except director, even though there were volumes of formally written and issued "LRH Advices" on how to accomplish every aspect of filmmaking, as well as numerous textbooks on directing that he had approved for study, and a list of 200 films that he felt should be studied. In other words, the post of *director* was highly regarded. It was lauded and came with prestige. And if you truly wanted to follow in Hubbard's footsteps, as all Sea Org members aspired to do, what better way than to direct his films? Yet not one staff member pursued the position. In my past experience, there would have been a line of eager replacements standing behind the guy that just got booted out. As the saying goes in the film industry, even Ralph the talking dog wants to be a director. So, one day I asked the script supervisor about this.

The script supervisor's answer explained why staff were reluctant to pursue the position and why it had been so impossible for the Sea Org to produce usable, high-quality films. The cold, hard truth was that they placed such a high cost on failure that no Sea Org member would dare take the risk. The few who tried had failed and been severely punished. Yet being allowed to fail without harsh consequences is key to artistic growth—there will be plenty of that once you find your footing. If you're constantly punished and humiliated for your failures while honestly attempting to do something good, you only learn to be compliant, to paint within the lines, and to obey authority. And that is where artistic expression goes to die.

There it was. If you made a serious mistake on a film, you were threatening the future of every human on Earth and could be reassigned to a reeducation program consisting of harsh physical punishment, forced confessions, social isolation, hard labor, and intense Scientology study known as the "Rehabilitation Project

Force," or "RPF." If you were lucky, you'd only be busted to groundskeeper or transferred to the galley and made to scrub pots. If you were very lucky and the mistake was not too serious, you only received a "Cramming Order," requiring you to restudy the material you messed up on and then pass a test on the E-meter to show you had in fact handled whatever caused you to make the error. That was the mindset. Hubbard wrote extensively describing the environment outside of Scientology as dangerous, full of hate mongers, and "merchants of chaos." According to Hubbard, the world is fraught with enemies out to enslave the population and, because they cannot tolerate anything good, put an end to Scientology. At the same time, Scientology creates an internal environment where its own staff are too fearful to aspire to the post of film director at a facility established by Hubbard to make films. Is that not a dangerous environment? The post of director has since been successfully held by a staff member (apprenticed by me for seven years). But despite that, I'm sure they'd step over the bodies of all those who were slaughtered failing to direct a Scientology film and claim it never was a problem.

Shortly after asking that question of the script supervisor, I experienced a real-life example that supported the script supervisor's answer. An error was discovered in the film I was directing. An erroneous E-meter read had been shot. The script supervisor, the cameraman, and I were summoned to the office of the Senior Case Supervisor International, John Eastment, who took over the post when Ray Mithoff was promoted to Inspector General for Tech. Also in attendance was Hansuli Stahli, (whom I thought of as Hansuli "Stasi" after the East German Secret Police), a notorious Miscavige enforcer with a nearly indecipherable Swiss accent and a humorless personality. Stasi was noted for being sent on missions to bully errant parishioners into submission by subjecting them to lengthy and arduous Security Checks. As John Eastment launched into a torrent of soul-crushing threats aimed at the script supervisor and the cameraman—I was positioned off to the side, as apparently they wanted me to witness the dressing-down without standing in the direct line of the shit spray—Hansuli would smirk in agreement, at one point looking over at me and winking as if to signal "You are not in trouble," while at the same time revealing that this is how they control the staff. The erroneous meter read was a simple mistake that never would have made it past the electrified perimeter of the International Base. It was easily corrected, and it had been discovered by the very people whose job it was to catch such errors; no harm was done. But it was blown up into something that could have destroyed Scientology globally if not caught and the blame for that was laid at the feet of these two terrified staff members. This was my first exposure to the coercive tactics employed by the Church to control staff through fear. I stood there maintaining my composure—trying not to be noticed—while witnessing the blatant emotional terrorism, thinking to myself, "There but for the grace of God go I," and being grateful that my time helping Gold to make films would only last a few months, after which I'd have the space to process and rethink my experience there... or so I thought at the time. John Eastment would himself soon be reassigned to motorpool where he was to spend (according to Miscavige) his next thousand lifetimes covered in grease, washing cars, and performing oil changes. Stasi eventually ended up as a grunt on the film crew where he held the position, at least in my estimation, of "most clumsy dolly grip ever," (*dolly grip* is the designation for the person on a film crew who is responsible for pushing the camera dolly).

I originally accepted the commission to direct the one film thinking I could help my group out of the swamp of producing poor-quality films while ensuring that the studio achieved Hubbard's original intention to produce his instructional films, the lack of which supposedly threatened the forward progress of Scientology. Plus, at the time, I thought the invitation involved a commitment of only a month or so. That month would stretch into decades, and unlike the secular world where you build value over time, in the world of working for Scientology your value diminishes the longer you stick around. Eventually, you will be blamed for things you didn't do, while others will take or be given credit for your successes. You will be humiliated and traumatized. Sometimes, something discreditable you've done in your private life, especially if it had anything to do with sex, will be disclosed triggering traumatic interrogations resulting in being assigned to perform humiliating penance.

Hubbard claimed that Scientology is a cousin to Buddhism. In a poem titled "Hymn of Asia," he presents himself as the second coming of the Buddha. But with its pervasive cycle of interrogation and long list of penalties, Scientology more resembles the Western practice of confession and penance than anything found in any Eastern religion. Buddhism does not believe in sin; does not require confession or atonement; does not demand strict adherence to doctrine; does not even demand that one interact with an organization. Most markedly, Buddhism, while recognizing the psychological importance of the ego, teaches that the sense of self is an illusion; that over-attachment to the ego is a fundamental ignorance that causes human suffering. Buddhism strives to free the individual from the trap of ego, while Scientology promises to pump the ego into a god-like state. Buddhism also does not present itself as the only hope for mankind, but as a path to enlightenment. On the other hand, Scientology belief consists of Cold War-influenced Western thought—a mix of New Age religion, confessional procedure, Freudian psychoanalysis, and a hefty dose of space opera with a sci-fi-inspired narrative to explain how humankind wound up in its current condition. Not much Buddhism going on there.

One would assume that Scientology, with its emphasis on Hubbard's technology for knowing how to learn any subject, would be able to solve the problem of making films. The self-imposed barriers to creating quality artistic products did not arise from a lack of knowledge about the subject or an inability to study it, but from a mindset that placed such crushing penalties on failure that the resulting pressure inevitably sucked all the creative oxygen out of the room.

The body of Scientology knowledge (or Technology, as it is termed) is composed of audio and filmed lectures, textbooks, policy letters covering administrative procedure, technical bulletins covering auditing procedure, LRH advices, and Executive Directives or EDs. Of the latter, Hubbard wrote 500 EDs devoted to all aspects of the performing, recording, and cinematic arts. One particular Cine ED, "Time Expectancy," mandated that a film crew was held to a quota of 16 shots per day minimum and was to complete any given film in 2½ weeks—no matter the length of the film. Gauging a film's progress by counting shots is the equivalent of calculating how many miles you drove on a road trip by counting the number of times you stopped to pee. The actual standard measure of production progress in film is calculated by counting the number of script pages completed. In any event, the 2½ weeks completion target had never been achieved, not even by Hubbard on the few films he managed to complete himself. Generally, they would take months or, in some cases, a year or more, or never be completed at all.

When the film I was commissioned to direct was completed

in under 2½ weeks, the reaction was Earth shattering. It was as though I had led the shoot crew out of the wilderness of abysmal failure and into the promised land of hopeful success. From my perspective, I had done nothing out of the ordinary. I was not trying to set any records. I was quite literally mystified, and the adulation was entirely unexpected. I was beginning to feel like, as the old saying goes, in the land of the blind, the one-eyed man is king.

So much had happened in the past month. I had discovered that in the local Sea Org culture the post of director came with tremendous liability. I got to peek behind the curtain that day in Sr. C/S Int's office and glimpse the emotional terrorism used to control the staff. I had experienced the crushing bureaucracy of endless "coordination meetings" and paperwork required to move your completed work through a gauntlet of micro-managers as it wound its way through the approval process until it finally reached Miscavige's desk. Each of those micro-managers, or in Scientology parlance "approval terminals," was only concerned with one thing: how a "reject" (the term for a rejection) from above might blow back on them. I'd witnessed the condescending attitude of executives who often acted like angry parents when speaking to their "juniors" such as the shoot crew. In one case, with about a week's worth of preparations left to ready a film for production, Ted Horner, that same friendly exec with whom I first interviewed, the CO of CMO Gold, ordered the crew to start shooting immediately the following day stating, "You are a bunch of juvenile delinquents who just get in trouble when you're not busy." No doubt he had been asked by Miscavige why the crew wasn't shooting. Not wanting to give a negative answer, he turned around and ordered them to do so immediately. While that doesn't rise to the level of the physical abuse and forced confinement that would later occur at the Gold base, it does reflect the toxic nature of the culture at Gold. The rank-and-file staff always seemed to be operating under the threat that at any moment they could be punished. Not to mention, ordering your juniors to start shooting a film without first completing the preparations would often result in mistakes being made, triggering severe punishments. It was a never-ending cycle of being forced into production with incomplete preparations and then being punished when the lack of preparation caused a problem.

All things considered, I had been looking forward to completing the film and getting on with life back in LA. But the circumstances surrounding that success would conspire to ensure I wasn't going anywhere.

EIGHT

IN THE LAND OF THE BLIND

Scientology organizations are managed by statistics. All strategic decisions are based on the organization's current statistic as compared to a previous statistic, measured in the short term Thursday to Thursday at exactly 2 PM. The same holds true for the individual, as well as every division and department within the organization, each activity or post having exactly defined statistics. The benchmarks used to statisticize the Cine Division, such as "shots in the can" (shots put onto film or video) completed films, etc., had been abysmally poor since Hubbard stopped directing some 15 years prior. So, imagine what it meant statistically to the organization when that tech film got completed within the time frame mandated by Hubbard. How significant was this? There is a tool in Scientology management technology called "Why Finding." When any significant change occurs, whether for better or worse, Why

Finding technology can be used to tease out the reason "why" something occurred. Miscavige ordered Mike Rinder, one of his top lieutenants, to find the "why" behind the statistical surge caused by the recent film completion.

At the time, Mike held the post of L. Ron Hubbard Personal Public Relations Officer International, or in the vernacular of the acronym-obsessed Sea Org, LRH PPRO INT. I always got along well with Mike. I respected his calm, intelligent approach. I never had a run-in with him and, in fact, always considered him a friend. Except for the one time I pissed him off and, struggling to come up with an appropriate insult, he began to stammer, "You, you, you FCCI!," which stands for "Flag Completed Case Intensive," a designation for public Scientologists receiving auditing at Scientology's "spiritual headquarters," or Flag, in Clearwater, Florida. Sea Org members routinely think of Scientology public as dilettantes who simply pay for expensive auditing while Sea Org members are the ones keeping the show on the road. I'd never heard that term used as an insult before. We both had a good laugh and forgot about whatever it was we sparked over.

We were sitting in his office in the management building that they called "Del Sol," a holdover name from the old resort days, when Mike handed me the results of the "Why Finding." Plain as day, the "why" turned out to be... wait for it... drum roll... ME!

I thought, "This is ridiculous!" I was under the impression that for something to be *the* "why" you had to be able to replicate it over and over—to recreate the success. The purpose of Why Finding, after all, was to reveal the thing that was correctly done so that it could be repeated or to find the thing that was done in error to avoid doing it again. Designating me as the "why" meant I was going to have to continue directing for Gold for an indeterminate period of time, or leave and become *the* reason "why" the organization's statistics returned to their previous abysmal state. For me to consider that I was only there to complete the one film meant that I would be responsible for crashing the organization's statistics when I left. In reality, the actual "why" had been hiring someone who knew what the fuck they were doing— which is an action that could be replicated over and over. By making me the "why," Miscavige had ensured I'd be subjected to intense scrutiny if I chose not to continue directing films for Gold. The Why Finding was never needed in the first place, at least not for finding out what had caused the recent statistical increase, but like a witch doctor stabbing a pin through a voodoo doll, Miscavige used the Why Finding as an administrative spell, cast to ensure that I had to stick around or face uncomfortable consequences.

This was nothing less than a covert form of coercive control. The script supervisor's caution, that staff did not aspire to directing because of the potential for getting in trouble, had taken on a new meaning. In the culture of the Sea Org, you could get in as much trouble for succeeding as you could for failing. Success could place you in the position where your own plans and purposes would have to be cast aside while the pressure to perform would be driven by an incessant demand for increasing statistics. My success on the film had landed me in a unique kind of trouble; now I had a few hundred people expecting—demanding—that I repeat that success for as long as they required, or their lives would revert back to the existence I'd just helped them escape. For better or worse, I genuinely cared about many of the staff on the crew and would prefer not to see them fail.

The next day I found myself staring nervously at the large Org board nailed to the wall just outside the Hubbard Communications Office, or HCO—the division responsible for human resources among other things—located in the bottom floor of the Gold administration building. One of the HCO staff had seen me passing by and ran out to grab me. "Mitch! You've got to see this," he said catching his breath. There it was, just below the Cine Sec at the top of Div 4, "Mitch Brisker - Director (NSO)—'NSO' for 'non-Sea Org.'" The staff member standing next to me beamed and said, "COB personally put your name up there." I was literally frozen in fear. The ultimate organizational handcuffs, I thought. But why didn't I just leave? "Thanks for the offer, but no thanks. I'm afraid I had other plans." The simple answer: I was a Scientologist, fully committed to achieving the gains Scientology promised me and the aims it pursued. My not taking responsibility for having turned around a situation that I had no idea was even a situation, would trigger a conversation that I did not want to have—a conversation involving heavy ethics actions, invasive security checks, and a thorough investigation to uncover my "counter-intention." I would be viewed as unwilling to contribute, something which is severely looked down upon in Scientology. I knew a conversation was coming. No one expected that I would do anything but stick around. All those years ago, when I'd dragged my heroin-addicted ass into Celebrity Centre, a group of caring Scientologists had helped to put me on a path to becoming drug free, which freed me to pursue my goals. Now that same organization was taking that freedom away by dictating what those goals should be. I guess it was time to pay the piper—one thing about karma, it doesn't care if you believe in it or not.

The conversation I had anticipated came in the form of a visit from Greg Wilhere. Greg had been a rock star in the world of Scientology. A frequent guest speaker at local Church events aimed at signing people up for upper-level auditing services at Flag, every active Scientologist at that time knew who Greg was. He'd quarterbacked for Villanova and had movie-star good looks. That he served with Hubbard on the *Apollo* and was one of the first class XII auditors, the highest level of auditor training one could attain, rounded out his credentials. I knew Greg's wife Sandy, who was also a Class XII auditor. She was my solo auditor case supervisor when I was doing upper levels at the Advanced Org of Los Angeles. I also knew their son Darius who was nine-years-old and quite the little terror at the Org when I first met him and, now in his twenties, was to become my protégé for a time. I certainly knew who Greg was when he dropped by to pay me a visit.

Greg wanted me to know how pleased Miscavige was with current film production. He wanted to get my agreement to complete the seven additional training films—the ones that Gold had failed to produce. To reiterate the importance of these films to Scientology's core mission, you could not train to become a Scientology auditor without seeing these films, yet no one taking auditor training courses, nor their instructors, had any idea additional films had been scripted and never produced. They were unaware that any training they had ever done was incomplete for not having all the films, for they contained information that did not exist anywhere else in the body of Hubbard's technical Scientology materials. If I didn't complete the films, who else would? Scientology auditor training materials would remain incomplete and that would be on me. In my Scientology mindset, I had *pulled* in this situation simply by displaying a competence that others had failed to exhibit. At least that's how I guilted myself into it. If the films didn't get done, it would be my fault. It had taken about a month to prep, shoot, and edit the film I'd completed, so seven films should then take about seven months. Or so I calculated. The fee I accepted was far less than what I had been paid for similar work. It was my Church and I thought that was the right thing to do. To sweeten the deal, Greg assured me any Scientology services I needed would be provided at no charge—auditing and training would be 100% free as long as I worked for Gold.

I hadn't accounted for the dam that was about to burst wide open now that Cine was successfully producing. Films were needed to be shown at international Scientology events, ads were needed for television, and infomercials were needed for Dianetics. Exhibitions had been envisioned but never moved forward for lack of creative planning and film content. There were Hubbard's Scientology books, hundreds of articles and essays covering all aspects of Scientology and Dianetics that Hubbard advised should be adapted to film, and more. When the dam exploded, that seven months stretched out to almost thirty years and consumed every aspect of my life. Striking a balance between handling work and managing one's personal life is further complicated when you're dealing with individuals who'd committed their next billion years to the mission of rescuing an entire sector of the universe from a downward spiral they believed would result in the extinction of all consciousness. In those kinds of circumstances, it is awkward to say you have plans for the upcoming weekend—let alone expressing your intention to pursue your personal artistic goals, which did not include completing the tech films.

I agreed to stay and complete the remainder of the films.

On the far eastern end of the Gold property, there was a cluster of five cottages called the Gs after the groundskeepers who'd lived there during the heyday of the Gilman Hot Springs resort. The Gs were being readied as short-term housing for visiting VIPs and the renovations were nearly complete. I was informed one of the units was being made available for my use.

It seemed that with every new day at Gold, I met a new person that I needed to coordinate with about something. A young staff member in her twenties, who went by the nickname KK, had been assigned to oversee my living arrangements. She was posted in the CMO but had no experience hiring outside professionals. She was unaware that, in the case of hiring film professionals, the production company is responsible for covering living expenses when requiring someone to work at distant locations. She proposed that my room and board be taken out of my director's fee. Once Miscavige caught wind of her proposal, the problem instantly vanished, and KK and I went on to have a friendly working relationship. At one point, out of the blue, KK confided in me that she'd had five abortions. At first, I thought that it was irresponsible of her to have gotten herself into that situation. After all, she was a Sea Org member (by this time Miscavige had forbidden Sea Org members to give birth). She knew pregnancies were not allowed and that when a Sea Org member became pregnant, they either terminated the pregnancy or left the Sea Org. And with that thought, I had reflexively stepped into the Scientology mindset of always blaming the victim. I didn't press her for further details. She needed someone to listen, so I just listened.

The Church of Scientology adamantly denies forcing Sea Org staff to terminate pregnancies. If by "forcing" you mean strapping someone to an operating table and performing an abortion against their will, I seriously doubt that ever happened. If it means giving someone a choice between having an abortion or ending their commitment to the Sea Org, being cast out onto the streets pregnant with no income and potentially no place to go, and possibly having to disconnect from anyone in Scientology, potentially including family who are Scientologists, then the person feels she has no other choice but to terminate her pregnancy. What I witnessed with KK, and what I'd see many times during my years working with the Sea Org, were circumstances that served to coerce women into consenting to have abortions.

Many years later I saw the position on staff pregnancies soften, at least at Gold. Sea Org couples who became pregnant and wanted to start a family were allowed to leave after going through an extensive "routing out" procedure during which they were separated from the group, and each other, put through extensive security checking, given a bill for all the auditing and training they had received as staff members, and then unceremoniously ushered out the gate to fend for themselves.

I eventually lost track of KK: like so many other staff at the International Base, one day she was suddenly absent. I heard she'd left the Sea Org and had started a family.

According to Hubbard, achieving spiritual levels above the state of Clear requires telepathic communication between yourself and myriad invisible entities, known as "body thetans," that are stuck to your body. To accomplish that telepathic communication and rid yourself of your body thetans, you'd need to learn to be your own auditor. The second of the remaining films I tackled was titled *The Solo Auditor*. Back in the '60s, if you wanted to progress past the state of Clear you had to travel to Scientology's worldwide headquarters in England and train to become a Class VI auditor—an expensive and time-consuming commitment. The bottleneck created by Scientologists wanting to get to Clear and beyond was a huge liability for Scientology's income which at that time was dependent on moving people up the Bridge. Hubbard's answer was to get people to audit themselves. In Scientology, any problem hampering progress up the Bridge—the auditing and training steps one needed to accomplish to progress in Scientology—was often met with Hubbard releasing the latest breakthrough, often described as an "undercut" to previous practices and procedures. No matter what the public ran into while trying to ascend the Bridge, there was always a solution to the problem, always something new to sell them to solve their problem.

Hubbard's original script for *The Solo Auditor* was idiotically simplistic. In a bare white set, a young man sits at a small folding table, while a male commentator, seen only from the shoulders down, instructed the young man on how to set up and run a solo auditing session. That was it. Without altering any of the Hubbard scripted narration or technical information and inspired by the 1943 film, *A Guy Named Joe*, I re-envisioned the commentator as an invisible female "guardian angel" who telepathically leads the auditor through his paces, turning it into an epic story replete with the guardian angel visiting heaven where she is given her assignment by a female God-like voice. *The Solo Auditor* film was also completed within the 2½- week time frame. The final edit was transcribed into script form and documented as the script written by L. Ron Hubbard. The public seeing the film had no idea that, while Hubbard had written all the dialog, I had completely re-scripted all the visuals. All of the credit for the revised script went to Hubbard—which was fine by me as I was not working for Gold for the screen credit.

With film production now humming along at Gold, Miscavige decided it was time to show off the place in the hopes of boosting staff recruitment at the Gold base. His initial target audience were the attendees at the upcoming week-long celebration on the *Freewinds*, Scientology's floating religious retreat, luxury cruise ship, and home of Scientology's highest spiritual level, OT8. The plan involved producing a 45-minute video showcasing all the wonderful things Gold does. All film production came to a screeching halt and the crew was put onto producing the Gold video. With so little time to get it done, a crisis was manufactured out of thin air. Working in film production prior to coming to Gold, especially working on commercials, I'd had my share of all-nighters and canceled weekends. But this was something different. It was five brutal days of little or no sleep with security staff prodding people to stay awake while the medical staff handed out nutritional potions, such as liquid vitamins and a god-awful tasting mixture of apple cider vinegar, cayenne, and lemon juice. It was the first time I experienced severe sleep deprivation but it wouldn't be the last.

The Gold Recruitment video was shown on the *Freewinds* and recruited exactly zero people.

My commitment to completing the seven films would be interrupted again and again. Miscavige had an endless capacity for putting extreme demands on Gold, resulting in one crisis after another. During the rare times when production flowed smoothly, a crisis would be manufactured. I used to wonder if everyone at Gold needed a crisis to validate the importance of their work. Like an army during peacetime, they needed a battle to feel they were fulfilling their purpose to conquer an enemy, in this case, the reactive mind and the evil forces bent on Scientology's destruction.

And then there were the expensive gifts from Miscavige, always carefully timed to assure that what whatever I'd just gone through was amply compensated for. At least I had most weekends off to rest and relax, unlike the crew who spent weekends studying in a crowded course room, working on renovation projects, or cleaning their workspaces. They were allowed a couple of hours Sunday mornings to take care of laundry and such, then back to work Sunday directly after lunch. I don't know how they did it, I never understood how this could be a tolerable lifestyle. Yet if you asked any of them, they would tell you with a smile that it's exactly what they wanted to be doing. To think otherwise meant you were "PTS to the middle class"—a reductive label given to anyone who was going about life trying to make things better for themselves, their family, and their associates, rather than choosing a life of austerity and self-sacrifice in order to clear the planet. "PTS" stands for potential trouble source. When someone is connected to a "suppressive person," a person who stands in opposition to the aims of Scientology, they are considered PTS. Hubbard surmised that the middle class were largely connected to suppressive persons via the press, television, and their elected officials, and so the middle class was mostly PTS. Hence, most people outside of Scientology were PTS to the middle class. The term is also used to label Scientologists whose commitment to Scientology is in question. Want to send your kids to college rather than pay for their Scientology? You're PTS to the middle class. Want to use your time off to take a much-needed vacation rather than go into the Org to do your next Scientology service? You're PTS to the middle class. The ultimate proof that you were *not* PTS to the middle class? You joined the Sea Org.

Consider the following. You've bound yourself to a religious order for a billion years, and you believe that fulfilling the mission of that religious order is the only hope for the future survival of humankind. All your worldly possessions most likely fit into a banker's box. Everything you interact with in your daily life—your work tools, workspace, living space—is owned by the religious order. You are paid the same pennies-on-the-hour as your peers regardless of the job you perform. You are forbidden any intimacy with the opposite sex unless married, and you are forbidden to pleasure yourself sexually. You are threatened with severe penalties for any infraction. Your identity is defined by your job description, which can be taken away from you if your performance suffers. All your outside communication is monitored by security staff. Anything that threatens your job—your identity—is perceived to be a threat to your immediate survival. That is the lot of your run-of-the-mill Sea Org member. To accept this as normal, you're going to have to suppress an awful lot of impulses to do otherwise.

This often results in bizarre reactions to minor events. For example, I once told Amber O'Sullivan Mellor, my "immediate senior," that I needed to leave half an hour early. Without hesitation, she grabbed the nearest phone and called security telling them I'd physically assaulted her. While nothing came of her accusation, her reaction was deeply troubling. The only explanation I could come up with was that the threat of my absence represented an assault on production which she perceived to be no different than a physical assault directed at her—a strange mental state arising from having no existence or identity beyond one's job.

Maybe it was the sharp contrast of being a public Scientologist and spending 70% of my time on a Sea Org base that afforded me the objectivity to perceive that the Sea Org has a great deal in common with Soviet-style communism. Just as in the Soviet Union, all production in the Sea Org is accomplished in facilities owned by the Church. All members—workers—are paid the same wage, regardless of their position and, except for a select few who comprise the power elite, they all share the same penalties when production suffers. For rank-and-file Sea

Org members, resources, such as time, food, education, and personal movement, are tightly controlled. All communication to and from the workers is monitored by a security force, and workers are obligated to report one another to the security force when they are seen engaging in any kind of forbidden activity. While public Scientologists have a great deal more personal freedom than Sea Org workers, they are discouraged from coming into contact, via the Internet or any other medium, with any material that may expose the organization's bad acts, divulge its confidential secrets, or offer a differing opinion— with steep penalties for violators, including being subjected to expensive thought-reform procedures known as Sec Checks. If one notices a fellow member violating any of the mandated codes of ethical conduct, or suspects they are committing a crime as defined by the Scientology justice system, they are required to submit a written "Knowledge Report." Anyone not filing a report becomes an accessory to the crime. Scientology is not communism. In fact, Hubbard was a vehement anti-communist. He had accused Soviet agents of stealing early Dianetics texts intending to alter its methods to facilitate brainwashing. Yet in terms of the way the organization is run, the similarities to Soviet-style communism are unmistakable.

NINE

LRH Life Exhibition

SOMETIME IN 1992, THE NEXT
crisis arrived. I received an urgent message from Miscavige
asking that I inspect the ongoing progress at the LRH Life
Exhibition which was under construction at street level in the
Scientology management building on Hollywood Boulevard,
located in the old Hollywood Guarantee Building, known
to Scientologists as the HGB. Plagued with shoddy work
and cost overruns, the construction of the exhibition was
hopelessly behind. This was the first of many times I was
asked to drop everything to solve some disaster. Calling it
a *disaster* was putting it mildly, as most of it had to be torn
out and redone. The only component of the exhibition that
had been completed was a life-sized animatronic tableau of
a scene from *Battlefield Earth* featuring the hero and villain
facing off. It looked like something out of a cheap carnival
show—a portent of how awful the film version would turn

out years later, and for which the film's screenwriter, J.D. Shapiro, would write a two-page apology for penning "the suckiest movie ever."

I was put in charge of getting the exhibition back on track and spent much of that year doing nothing else. So much for my seven-month commitment to complete the tech films.

In particular, the display covering Narconon was a catastrophe. The centerpiece of the Narconon display was planned to be a widescreen film showing the scourge of drugs on society followed by a lively tour of the Narconon program; its history, facilities, and successes. To achieve a widescreen effect, an outside firm sold the exhibition planners on the idea of placing three 50-inch projection TVs (state of the art, for the time) next to one another and projecting a single video across the three screens. By the time I was assigned to the project, all they had to show were three expensive television sets and no video. The outside vendor, despite being paid tens of thousands of dollars, could not figure out how to solve the technical challenge of projecting a single video across three screens. They wanted more money. I told Church management to cut their losses, tear the entire thing out, and start over. I proposed hiring a company known for shooting widescreen film presentations for special installations at museums and amusement parks. Their system employed a super-wide screen film format using modified film cameras, with the final result displayed via a custom projector. The deal included two projectors and a maintenance contract. For a fraction of what they'd already wasted on the three-TV idea, the film was produced and installed. It also had the advantage of being shot on film, so it could easily be converted to a digital format as technology advanced.

The opening sequence of the Narconon film called for recreating a drug bust, featuring cops breaking down the door of a suspected drug dealer's house, complete with gun-wielding perps being shot and a fleeing suspect jumping through a plate-glass window. While the Church of Scientology may claim to be the world's leading authority on drug prevention and rehabilitation, it established its International Base in Gilman Hot Springs, adjacent to the methamphetamine capital of Southern California—Hemet. Thus, I didn't have to travel far from the Gold base to find a location that could serve as a drug dealer's house. I settled on a decrepit two-story Carpenter Gothic with peeling paint and dead landscaping with most of a picket fence busted out. The staff member responsible for public relations—whose personal wardrobe, despite her holding a public-facing position at Gold, was always at least twenty years out of date—had the harebrained idea to contact the local Narcotics division of the Hemet Police and ask them to participate in our mock drug bust. Likely, she did this as a way of "Safe Pointing" the local narcs. "Safe Pointing" is a Scientology tactic that calls for developing friendly relations with any type of authority, especially local authority. After all, Scientology runs the Narconon Drug Rehab program, so of course the local police would want to help. Narconon boasts an 80% success rate—80% of those who *complete* the program are drug free a year later. When you consider that most people who enter the program never finish, the claimed 80% is, in reality, a far smaller number. As for outcomes beyond a year? No figures exist. Drug rehab is a dangerous business. It is estimated that approximately 1,300 drug rehab facility related deaths occur a year. Narconon has had its share of those deaths.

The Public Relations Officer's invitation to the local narcotics unit was likely also motivated by money, as she had asked them to volunteer their time free of charge to consult on and participate in the fake bust. Sea Org members responsible for spending money, whether to feed staff, buy film, hire actors, or pay for location services are under intense pressure to spend as little as they can get away with or risk being accused of wasting funds, considered a serious crime in Scientology. Even with film crew members each being paid only $50 a week, the Cine division needed considerable sums of money for production. A committee of division heads, convened weekly to dole out funds, would haggle over their division's weekly budgets. The combined budget for the organization would then wind its way up the chain of command for final approval. Film budgets were usually reduced to the absolute minimum. This false economy often led to disastrous results, such as a lack of toilet facilities when the crew were shooting on location. At Gold, renting motorhomes or portable restrooms—a necessity even on low budget shoots—was considered a waste of parishioners' donations and was only done to prevent a public relations nightmare when hiring professional, non-Scientologist actors.

The crew would end up using facilities at McDonald's or gas stations, or at America's de facto public restroom, Starbucks. Non-Scientologist actors were often forced to change wardrobe in the grip truck. I can't remember how many times I apologized to actors for the lack of facilities. I used the excuse that the motor home had broken down on the way to the location, and we were doing everything we could to get a replacement. All the while, I thought I was helping to improve conditions on Earth and that by my participation I could help Gold rise to the level where the crew would be treated with the respect they deserved.

Saving money by using volunteer cops in place of hired actors was a recipe for disaster. They are not bound by conventional actor/producer rules, and they could be called away for an emergency at any moment, not to mention the potential for having live ammo on the set. But no matter, the PR person had procured on-camera talent for free!

I met with the lead detective, an undercover narc who could've passed for Serpico's stunt double. He had shoulder-

SCIENTOLOGY - THE BIG LIE

length hair and a thick beard, wearing Levi's and a plaid shirt, with a firearm strapped to his hip in a low-slung ballistic nylon holster. He seriously wanted to help, explaining that he was frustrated at having to arrest the same perps over and over and had been convinced Scientology's drug education and rehabilitation programs might reduce recidivism. One very helpful service he was able to provide—explaining how they went about busting a suspected drug house.

On the day of the shoot, "Serpico" arrived with two other members of his narcotics unit, he in his undercover clothing, and the others dressed in full tactical camo gear. They looked at the house and chuckled, "We busted this place a month ago." They popped the trunk of their unmarked Crown Vic and pulled their weapons from padded cases. As the script called for one of the perps to be shot while firing a gun at the cops, a motion picture armorer was hired to handle the weapons, along with a special effects makeup artist to handle the bullet hits. One of the cops was holding a long-barreled shotgun and the other a small machine gun with a silencer. The armorer, concerned there might be firearms on the set that were not under his control, immediately came over to brief the cops that their weapons must be unloaded and that no live ammunition would be allowed anywhere near the set. Violating this would cost the armorer his license to handle weapons in the film industry, not to mention endangering the cast and crew. The armorer was particularly interested in the machine gun; he'd never seen that model. The cop proudly explained that it was a recent addition to the weapons used by Special Forces and was only available to military and law enforcement. Apparently, it takes a while for such advanced firearms to trickle down to the movies. I asked him about the silencer. He explained that drug dealers and meth labs often had guard dogs that you had to "take out" before going in. He aimed low and pretended to make a sound like a silenced round being fired. Turning to his partner he said, "Hey, remember last week we took out that dog and it turned out to be the wrong house?" They both chuckled.

Despite the narc's offer to use a live shotgun round called an "Avon Charge" ("Avon calling") to blow the lock off the front door, the usual procedure law enforcement followed in such operations, the day's filming came off without incident.

From the Church's perspective, the Life Exhibition was a smashing success. It met its deadline and opened with a huge celebration replete with a ribbon cutting and fireworks. At least for a while, it seemed to do well competing with other Hollywood Boulevard attractions. I always thought having an exhibition dedicated to L. Ron Hubbard located on the Hollywood Walk of Fame positioned it with kitschy attractions such as Madame Tussauds Wax Museum and Ripley's Believe It or Not!—just another tourist trap vying for the attention of sightseers in flip-flops and cargo shorts. A few blocks down the street, at the Chinese Theater, you could sign up for a tour of the stars' homes, (including of course, the dead ones), get your photo taken with a celebrity impersonator, or experience the life of Scientology founder L. Ron Hubbard. A stone's throw from the intersection of Hollywood and Vine, next door to a strip club, the Church of Scientology had planted its flagship exhibition as though it were just another tourist trap. Bookending the Hollywood Walk of Fame, with Author Services to the west and the Life Exhibition to the east, did nothing to help the reputation of the religion or its founder. Though it briefly shined in the '90s, it would sink like the proverbial lead balloon by the decade's end.

With the successful completion of a few training films and now the Life Exhibition, I had become Miscavige's trusted hired hand. On the one hand, it seemed I could do no wrong. On the other hand, I was being absorbed into a machine that would be nearly impossible to escape. Working with the Sea Org, I was beginning to experience the same fate as its members, having no identity outside of my job. Like them, I was being reduced to a sum total of the work I did for Scientology. Nothing else mattered or counted; not family, not social life, not personal identity. When you are constantly treated as though your job is your identity, after a while you begin to believe it.

TEN

WALK OUT LIKE YOU OWN THE PLACE

L. RON HUBBARD originally incorporated The Church of Scientology in April 1952 as a for-profit business called the Hubbard Association of Scientologists (HAS). How exactly Scientology became a religion is the subject of debate. In one version, members of the HAS claimed Scientology fulfilled their basic religious need for religious community and spiritual fulfillment and asked Hubbard to formalize Scientology as a religion, which would also allow for the Church to sanction such rituals as weddings and "naming ceremonies"—Scientology's version of a baptism. Another, and more likely account, has Hubbard pursuing the "religious angle" as a device to improve Scientology's business prospects. But whatever the reason, in December 1953, Hubbard incorporated the first Church of Scientology in Camden, New Jersey. Soon after, the first Scientology weddings and baptisms were performed. Within a few years, Scientology's business prospects were improved when the IRS granted tax exemption to its organizations in Washington, D.C. and California. In 1967, Scientology's tax-exempt status was revoked on the grounds that Hubbard and his family had profited from the Washington Church of Scientology, triggering a twenty-six year long battle with the IRS.

By 1991, the battle with the IRS over Scientology's tax-exempt status had turned into an all-out war. To regain its tax exemption, the Church instigated more than 2,500 lawsuits against the IRS and had reportedly hired private investigators to dig up dirt on individual IRS agents. Though barely a footnote in the war against the IRS, Scientology also sponsored a national public-interest group called "Citizens for an Alternative Tax System," or "CATS." CATS was founded by attorney Steven L. Hayes, who happened to be a Scientologist. The group masqueraded as a grassroots movement which proposed having the states collect income tax, along with sales tax, thus putting an end to the IRS. There was nothing grassroots about CATS. The CATS concept of a flat tax was based on an idea originally forwarded by Hubbard and the organization's expenses were paid for by the Church of Scientology. While history remembers the lawsuits Scientology filed against the IRS, its campaign fronted by CATS, to replace the IRS with an alternative tax system, is largely forgotten. Miscavige wanted to produce a series of videos presenting the CATS agenda. I had no idea how the videos would be shown, or to whom. I shot the first one at Steven Hayes' CATS office, located in the headquarters of the Office of Special Affairs, or "OSA" (pronounced Oh-Sa), the branch of Scientology that handles legal affairs and coordinates retaliatory smear campaigns against its critics.

Apparently, Miscavige was not impressed with Hayes' performance and so decided to cast himself as the on-camera talent for the next video—to be shot on an office set, and on location in Washington DC. Miscavige is a challenge to direct. While he was entirely willing to submit to being told what to do, where to stand, look, etc., you had to deliver those instructions without the slightest hesitation or he'd eat you alive. As the director, I oversaw the set, and he respected that. But I was not in charge of his time—wasting a moment of it could be hazardous to your health. I survived the office portion of the shooting intact. I then flew to DC with Kurt Weiland, the Commanding Officer of OSA, a heavy-set Austrian who'd come to his position via stints working for OSA in Germany. Kurt was a well-known personality who had earned some renown blustering his way through speaking engagements at international events. I lost track of the number of drinks he'd consumed on the flight. I'm sure he'd lost track as well. Miscavige flew separately along with his top lieutenant, Marty Rathbun. The video called for shooting Miscavige while he spoke about the need to replace the IRS with a consumption tax, shot with iconic DC locations such as the Supreme Court building, as backdrops.

Finally, it came time to shoot him in front of the IRS building. I had mistakenly assumed the behemoth IRS building would have some form of prominent identifying signage. I couldn't have been more wrong. The square post on the street corner displaying the address, and the words Internal Revenue Service in three-inch type did not offer a usable photo op. The only other signage was a small brass plaque next to the front entrance at the top of a flight of stairs. I had no clue how to compose a shot featuring Miscavige and the signage in any readable form. Having him say, "I'm here at IRS headquarters," would be corny and inconsistent with the other sequences we'd shot. His patience was running out fast. I punted. "OK, here's what I want you to do. Go into the building and when you hear 'action' on the walkie-talkie, walk out the door like you own the place, throw a nonchalant gesture towards the brass plaque, delivering your lines as you walk down the stairs." He enthusiastically agreed and headed off into the building. The idea was to fill the frame with the brass plaque so you could read it, then pull back to reveal Miscavige as he walked out of the building past the sign. Directing the leader of Scientology, the man behind the thousands of lawsuits against the IRS, and who orchestrated numerous investigations into the private lives of IRS agents—to walk into IRS headquarters and then walk out like he owned the place—what could possibly go wrong?

On the first take, the cameraman zoomed back too late, missing Miscavige's entrance. The second take was better, but we needed a third. As he took his position in the building, I could hear a female security guard over the walkie-talkie having a brief exchange with Miscavige. "Action" was called, ending the conversation with the security guard. The third take was perfect, so we went for one more to make sure we had it. As Miscavige got into position, the security guard started pestering him, wanting to know if he had a permit to film on the property. I called "action" and this time as Miscavige made his way down the stairs, he was flanked by four IRS security guards in blue blazers and gray slacks. As Miscavige and Kurt Weiland discussed the situation with the guards—they wanted to confiscate the video—out of the corner of my eye, I noticed Rathbun standing next to the cameraman who ejected the tape and replaced it with a blank cassette. He then handed the original to Rathbun, who slipped it into the pocket of his trench coat, faded into the background and disappeared into a cab. Miscavige finally capitulated and agreed to turn the (blank) tape over to the guards. We were done for the day. We had the shot.

That shot gained a lot of attention. Not only did it appear in the CATS video but was also used in countless other Scientology videos to signify how Miscavige had confronted the IRS head-on in his quest to gain tax exemption. It was not long after we produced that video, that Miscavige walked into that same IRS building and asked to meet with commissioner Fred Goldberg, kicking off his final assault on the IRS. In October 1993, David Miscavige walked onto the massive stage at the former Los Angeles Memorial Sports Arena, and standing amidst an oversize stage design that looked like a cross between one of Hitler's Nuremberg rallies and a daytime game show, before an assembly of 10,000 Scientologists he declared, "The war is over." The Church had regained its tax-exempt status, allowing it to amass a fortune while paying no taxes in the US. And with the First Amendment protections that came with being recognized by the IRS, Scientology became virtually immune to ever being held accountable for its abuses.

Not surprisingly, CATS was unceremoniously jettisoned once tax exemption was granted. The Church had been a staunch proponent in the fight for tax reform right up until the moment they received tax exemption, after which they cared little about who the IRS was screwing over, as long as it wasn't screwing over Scientology. I asked Miscavige about CATS, about what would happen with the struggle to reform the tax system. He explained to me, "You don't keep fighting your enemies after you've beaten them. The IRS is no longer our enemy. We're friends now." There never was any intention to reform the tax system, but only to be as big a nuisance as possible to the IRS.

ELEVEN

ORIENTATION

EVERYBODY IS A WONDERIN' WHAT AND WHERE
THEY ALL CAME FROM
EVERYBODY IS A WORRYIN' 'BOUT WHERE THEY'RE GONNA GO
WHEN THE WHOLE THING'S DONE
BUT NO ONE KNOWS FOR CERTAIN AND SO
IT'S ALL THE SAME TO ME
I THINK I'LL JUST LET THE MYSTERY BE

—IRIS DEMENT, "LET THE MYSTERY BE"

SCIENTOLOGY WOULD HAVE you believe it contains the answers to some of life's most fundamental questions: "Who am I?" "Where do I come from?" "What is death?" "Is there a hereafter?" Scientology also wants you to believe it is a religion, specifically an applied religious philosophy; the "applied" part refers to tools you "apply" to your life. In Scientology there is an answer for everything and tools to solve all of life's problems. Borrowing from the vernacular of the carnival barker, Scientology refers to this sales pitch as the "come-on." If this come-on appeals to someone, and they wish to move forward in Scientology, they will have to spend 50 minutes in a small screening room watching a film I directed titled *Orientation*. After viewing the film, they are required to sign a legally binding release which documents the fact that they've seen the *Orientation* film and that they understand what they're getting themselves into, and cannot later claim otherwise. In addition to signing the *Orientation* waiver acknowledging they understand the religious nature of Scientology, new members are obligated to sign three other enrollment forms in which, among other things, they forfeit their legal right to sue the Church and agree to submit any dispute to the Church's in-house arbitration. No one is allowed to enroll on any form of paid Scientology service without first seeing the *Orientation* film and signing the waivers.

The *Orientation* film is part of what Hubbard referred to as the *Public Scientology Motion Picture Series*, or *PSMPS* films. Hubbard wrote a total of 50 treatments for the *PSMPS* series. Now that the tech films were finally rolling along, Miscavige decided it was time to get to going on the public films, starting with *PSMPS Number One, Orientation*.

Hubbard's purpose for *Orientation* as stated in the film's treatment, was "To help a new person get around the organization and to forestall litigation"—or in plain speak, to neutralize any lawsuit based on claims that the Church made false promises. It achieved the former by giving a tour of a typical Scientology Church. It attempted to achieve the latter by giving a description of Scientology intended to inform the viewer as to the religious nature of Scientology. The new person watches the film and then signs an affidavit confirming they have seen it. If the person ever tries to sue, claiming they'd been deceived and didn't know what they were getting into, the Church could present the affidavit in court and the case would be thrown out. One would think the way to avoid litigation would be to not engage in activities they could be sued for, but in Hubbard's mind the very nature of Scientology's mission—to lift individuals out of the trap that enslaves them—made it a magnet for lawsuits. Deflecting responsibility for Scientology's egregious actions, Hubbard drew the analogy that as all new religious movements throughout history had been attacked, so too was Scientology—it was no different. In fact, he convinced adherents that the attacks themselves were proof that Scientology was a threat to the status quo. The *Orientation* film was intended as a way the Church could protect itself from disgruntled members claiming they'd been lied to by a cult calling itself a religion.

The film was fronted by spokesperson Larry Anderson, a Scientologist and professional magician, with a decent list of TV and film acting credits, who I had directed in numerous Scientology films. When *Orientation* eventually leaked onto the Internet, the public was given an inside look at one piece

SCIENTOLOGY - THE BIG LIE

of Hubbard's strategy for recruiting new people. In the film's narration, Hubbard, referring to himself in the third person, attempts to position himself with the Buddha: "Like Siddhartha Gautama, the Buddha, L. Ron Hubbard was just a man"—an overtly blatant attempt to inflate his position and write his own hagiography. The narration asserts that "science never proved God didn't exist, it simply said there isn't one," while onscreen, in a bizarre visual mashup of deity-based religious belief and Darwinian theory, a transparent man with a long white beard wearing a robe, floats inches above a jungle floor, then gently places a monkey on the ground. With these images, Hubbard attempts to invalidate Darwinism by insinuating that a non-physical force is responsible for life.

Since the Age of Enlightenment fundamentalist religions have opposed science. If a religion requires its adherents to adopt a belief having no basis in rational thought then science, with its foundation of critical thinking, must be opposed. Scientology went one better. Rather than simply opposing science, it attempted to supplant it with its own brand of "scientific" breakthroughs. In the case of Scientology, many of those so-called "breakthroughs" are revealed one layer at a time, as adherents move up the levels on "The Bridge to Total Freedom" which are delineated on the Scientology Chart of Gradation and Awareness where each level is named and described.

Once adherents achieve a certain level of spiritual awareness, they are granted access to the confidential levels where Scientology becomes truly batshit crazy. Here the eligible learn of the Xenu story—the 75 million year old origin myth, wherein an evil overlord, bent on solving over-population across a federation of 765 planets, rounded up the populace, trapped them in blocks of frozen glycol as disembodied entities, then dropped it into volcanoes here on Earth, and then exploded them with hydrogen bombs resulting in those souls becoming stuck to the bodies of every person alive.

The only way you can attain spiritual freedom is by using Scientology to rid yourself of those entities, referred to as body thetans, or BTs. That the volcanoes named in the Xenu incident didn't exist 75 million years ago (a geological fact,) matters not. Science is wrong. The Xenu story is to Scientologists what dinosaurs are to a paleontologist—their prehistoric existence is not in dispute. While the vast majority of Scientologists will never make it far enough to read Hubbard's handwritten and highly confidential account of the Xenu story, the *Orientation* film helps to ensure they are firmly planted on a path where believing is seeing. Oh, and at the same time they'll learn a bit about how a Scientology organization works, and be exposed to its arcane hierarchical structure.

The film's claim that science never disproved the existence of God is shorthand for "Science is wrong." Once the audience believes that premise, they become willing to bypass the age-old method of pursuing knowledge—the exercise of rational thought. But science and religion do not have to be at odds with each other. That they can co-exist is evidenced in Albert Einstein's statement: "What really interests me is whether God had any choice in the creation of the world." Science has never held the goal of disproving God. Hubbard's assertion that science and religion are at odds is simply the narrow end of a wedge intended to separate a new person from critical thinking. The vast majority of Scientologists will never advance far enough to learn the fantastical Xenu story. They will either leave before that point or they won't be able to afford the hundreds of thousands of dollars it costs to gain admission to that level. But for the new mark watching *Orientation*, Hubbard's message is clear: we may have evolved from monkeys, but it was a non-physical force that placed that monkey on Earth (or put it on its evolutionary path).

Hubbard reinforces this idea with his self-stated breakthrough declaring that all life has one thing in common: *Survival!* This one single—idiotically simplistic—concept, is the foundational thought upon which Hubbard built his entire house of cards. He further claimed that the thrust to survive is divisible into eight categories, or "Dynamics." In their simplest form, they are: self, sex-family, groups, all humankind, plants and animals (all non-human life), physical objects, the non-physical spiritual world, and lastly, the concept of infinity, often referred to in Scientology as "The God Dynamic." So while Scientologists don't believe in God per se, they have a placeholder, the 8th dynamic. That diaphanous, white-bearded deity gently placing the monkey on the jungle floor; that's the 8th dynamic.

You won't find that explicitly stated anywhere in Scientology, but it is clearly illustrated in the film—it's just for the new person watching *Orientation*, a bit of visual sleight-of-hand where if you look closely, you'll see how Hubbard co-opts religious symbols to manipulate the viewer.

To support Hubbard's claim that Scientology is a valid religion, the film covers the subject of dualism versus materialism, aligning itself with the long-held religious belief that the universe has a non-material, or spiritual component, a belief held by a majority of people, religious or otherwise. If you believe the non-material idea that a person has a vibe, then you likely don't believe everything is purely physical. With that, Scientology positions itself as the authority on something you probably already believe—that reality comprises more than just the physical, and in that way attempts to insert itself as an authority over what you already probably believe. But the kicker was the ending statement of the film. Gathering his thoughts, the commentator looks fixedly into the camera, and in a dead serious voice says: "If you leave this room after seeing this film, and walk out and never mention Scientology again, you are perfectly free to do so. It would be stupid, but you can do it. You can also dive off a bridge or blow your brains out. That is your choice." The implication was clear: not joining Scientology after seeing *Orientation* was tantamount to killing yourself. The *Orientation* film, intended to protect Scientology from litigation, turned out to be one of the most embarrassing examples of its twisted and tone-deaf recruitment style. Hubbard's reference to Scientology versus suicide was not only an unsuccessful recruitment pitch, in a culture increasingly concerned with reducing harm, it was a vulgar reference.

With the *Orientation* film having leaked onto the Internet, there was an urgent need to produce a revised version without the offensive lines. When the film's star, Larry Anderson left Scientology in 2009, claiming the Church never delivered the spiritual gains it promised, it became clear the film would have to be scrapped and entirely redone. Miscavige asked for a revised script deleting the controversial lines and—to mitigate any possibility of having to reshoot the film again due to an on-camera spokesperson leaving the Church and giving Scientology the finger—the new version was shot with an offscreen narrator, in and of itself an admission that Miscavige was well aware that anyone representing Scientology might leave and blow the whistle. The Larry Anderson fiasco was not a one-off. Eventually a long list of Scientology Training and Public Films would need to be reshot because Scientologists who appeared in them were abused or otherwise mistreated and financially exploited then defected, spoke out and were later declared Suppressive Persons (SPs)—enemies of the Church. The situation got so bad, in fact, that Miscavige eventually forbade Scientology's own film production facilities from ever hiring a Scientologist to appear in a Scientology film for fear they would later leave and speak out—a strange case of reverse bigotry wherein Scientology was biased against its own members.

TWELVE
CULTURAL ATTITUDES

I N   S P I T E   O F   M A N Y
interruptions, I managed to fulfill my original commitment to
complete the seven unproduced training films. Once completed,
the difference in quality between the new and old films was so
striking it became clear that the previously existing films would
have to be redone.

In preparation for remaking the previously produced technical
training films, I was given a four-inch thick binder to study,
containing all of the original Hubbard tech film scripts—highly
confidential documents that were forbidden to ever leave the
property. The scenarios in the scripts ranged from demonstrative
show-and-tell, to elaborate space opera, and complex, character-
driven dramas. As I reviewed the scripts, I noticed the writing,
beyond its purpose to instruct auditors, revealed much about
Hubbard's own attitudes and mores, most of which I attributed
to his provincial upbringing in rural Montana.

MISOGYNY

In his book, *Scientology: A New Slant on Life,* Hubbard expresses his attitude concerning the role of women in society: "A society in which women are taught anything but the management of a family, the care of men, and the creation of the future generation is a society which is on its way out." The central female character in the first film I was commissioned to direct, *Start, Change and Stop,* was an expression of that outmoded sentiment. The title refers to a Scientology process that is part of what are known as "Objective Processes." Unlike Scientology auditing that directs a person's attention inward, objective processes direct the person's attention onto the world around them. In objective processing, the auditor commands the person being audited to move objects, such as a paper clip or the person's own body, from one designated spot to another. Hubbard claims that every individual has some portion of their attention stuck in the past. By directing the person's attention to their immediate environment, their attention is restored to present time. Among his claims, objective processes cure accident-proneness. However, in reality they condition a person to blindly comply with instructions and to obey the auditor, who acts as a proxy for Hubbard and the organization.

The film features a ditzy young housewife who breaks everything she touches, including driving a station wagon through the back wall of a garage. Her husband, out of an abundance of proto-patriarchal attitude, hires a Scientology auditor to come to the house and straighten her out. Her character is written as a clownish, low-IQ caricature of a housewife, clumsy and unaware of her issue—things just seem to break around her. Over the course of her auditing, her accident-proneness is cured, and she is brought into line with Hubbard's vision of the obedient housewife: managing the household, caring for her husband, and creating the future.

RACISM

From his use of the term "Wog" to denote anyone who is not a Scientologist, (originally British slang designating a person of color), to the letters of support he sent the pro-apartheid government in Rhodesia, to the racial slurs that had to be edited out of his lectures to make them marketable, there is abundant evidence that L. Ron Hubbard was a racist. The Hubbard-scripted tech film *How to Set Up a Session and the E-meter* is a fictional account of a Sea Org auditing mission sent to an imaginary African country. When a poorly trained auditor butchers an auditing session with the king's son, the mission is faced with expulsion from the country. Receiving an urgent telex regarding the matter, Hubbard then casting himself in the role of white savior, arranges to travel to Africa and personally handle the situation. In one particular scene, the script calls for an indigenous African woman and two small children to peer through an open window, curious about what's happening inside the "auditing hut." The script describes the two children as "Pickaninnies," a derogatory term for Black children. In keeping with that description, Hubbard called for the woman and children to be eating bananas, reflecting the stereotypical view that black people are like monkeys. Out of concern that any of the African actors we'd hired might see the racially offensive script, and despite the fact that these were Hubbard's written words, I had the scene description revised. While at the same time, being fully aware of the racist nature of Hubbard's words, I compartmentalized my own feelings for the sake of the mission. His racist remarks must, I thought, be inconsequential artifacts left over from an earlier time when you could be racially insensitive and not be an actual bigot. Such are the lies we tell ourselves when in the bubble of a cult.

CRIME AND PUNISHMENT

According to the Scientology justice system, it is a high crime to report or threaten to report a Scientologist to civil authorities. In Scientology, criminal matters are handled internally. The training film *The Session* perfectly illustrates how Scientology fails to report criminal activity to civil authorities. The film is a near-future, sci-fi story where a patrol craft picks up a miner who'd been marooned on a planetoid. Driven half mad from isolation, he is fixated on killing his partner, who he claims left him to die. The officers on board the patrol craft hold an emergency meeting. The ship's doctor wants the guy put in quarantine fearing he has a "space disease." The ship's chaplain, who happens to be a Scientologist, wants to give him an auditing session. During the session, the miner confesses to having drugged and raped his partner's girlfriend; in turn, his partner marooned him to die. Having unburdened himself of his crime, the miner's remorse turns into joy. Through tears of happiness, he proclaims he is going to find the girl he raped and his former partner and get them some Scientology auditing to make sure they are okay. With the crime of rape handled with an auditing session, there's no need to report to the authorities. This idea is so deeply ingrained in Scientology culture—that Scientology alone can reform the criminal—it even appears as a theme in films used to train its practitioners. While Scientology teaches its practitioners that Scientology through the application of auditing has the power to rehabilitate the criminal and heal the victim, in the real world it does the opposite—enabling and protecting criminals while terrorizing victims. Just like the spaceman who drugged and raped his partner's girlfriend, perpetrators, such as life-long Scientologists and convicted rapist Danny Masterson, are protected by the Church from facing the legal consequences of their acts by burying or refuting claims brought to them by the victims, or even worse, blaming the victims themselves for, "pulling in" the abuse.

Ironically, Danny Masterson's first starring role was in a Scientology Technical Training Film titled *The Use of a Doll in Training*, a reference to student Scientology auditors using large dolls in the place of actual humans when practicing the

SCIENTOLOGY - THE BIG LIE

procedures they will later use. The Doll film is based on the idea that after hours at a Scientology Church, the dolls come to life and audit each other. One particular doll, named Cap'n Jack and played by Danny Masterson, was being flirty with a female doll, resulting in him neglecting his "student auditor" and leaving him poorly trained. The poorly trained auditor then gives an auditing session to the Executive Director of the Church, who falls ill as a result of the poor auditing. Cap'n Jack goes on the lam (actually hiding out in the Church's attic, where he's become an alcoholic—addicted to sniffing empty liquor bottles because "Everyone knows dolls don't have stomachs") and the drama unfolds from there. I experienced Danny as an energetic and eager young actor, with an always-on, center-of-attention-grabbing personality that was exhausting to be around. Having gotten to know Danny as a teenager on that film, and subsequently over the years, I can't say I was surprised to learn he'd been charged with multiple counts of forced rape. In my opinion, such behavior was not out of character with the narcissistic, most-important-person-in-the-room personality that I had known him to be over the years. And like the crimes of the marooned spaceman in the film *The Session*, Scientology failed to report Danny to the authorities, even though they were aware he was a rapist and that his crimes against his fellow Scientologists had been documented in their internal ethics reports and in the notes Scientology auditors make during auditing sessions. Scientology's "always blame-the-victim" mentality, and its policy of forbidding its members from reporting, or even threatening to report, their fellow Scientologists to the authorities enabled Danny to continue his crime spree while preventing his victims from seeking justice for almost two decades.

On May 31, 2023, Danny was convicted on two of three counts of forceable rape. The following September he was sentenced to life in prison with the possibility of parole after 30 years.

THIRTEEN

A Scientific Basis for Hate

I GREW UP IN WHAT MIGHT be referred to as a progressive household that stood against bigotry in any form. By the time I encountered Hubbard's extreme bias against homosexuality, I was deep into the Scientology mind-trap with its promise of self-improvement wrapped in an invitation to help build a new and better civilization. I'd become accustomed to rationalizing Hubbard's views on homosexuality as being a product of the 1950's anti-gay sentiment that permeated the culture back when he wrote his seminal work on Dianetics and Scientology. Within the narrow confines of cognitive dissonance, I thought to myself that if he were alive today or were to come back in the future (something Scientologists believe will happen), he would certainly revise his thinking on homosexuals, right? That's how I justified his proclamation that homosexuality was a perversion, that all homosexuals should be dispatched without pity, and that homosexuality could be cured with auditing. It ˄was just something he forgot to revise before he departed his body. But the fact is, he was virulently homophobic and spread that hatred to his followers.

While you could take Hubbard's words as an abstraction, the manner in which they were echoed by my fellow Scientologists, especially Sea Org workers, was very real. In Scientology, the bias against non-heterosexuals was rooted in Hubbard's "scientific" discoveries as described in his writings and lectures on the subject he calls the "emotional tone scale," a numeric scale delineating all the emotional states human beings are capable of exhibiting, extending from "Total Failure" at -40 at the bottom of the scale to "Serenity of Beingness" at +40 on the top of the scale. According to Hubbard, a person's position on the tone scale determines their survival potential in life. The higher one is on the tone scale, the better one survives. As one descends the tone scale, their survival potential lessens. Homosexuals are said to occupy the emotional tone of Covert Hostility at 1.1 on the scale—commonly referred to as "one-one." Scientology auditing is said to raise one's tone level and in doing so "afflictions" like homosexuality naturally fall away. In their fervent criticism of psychiatry, Scientologists are quick to condemn the psychiatric practice of labeling people based on a diagnosis. Yet Scientology's practice of assigning labels based on a person's perceived position on the tone scale is no different than using psychiatric labels such as "psychotic" or "bipolar" simply because you want to stigmatize someone's behavior. I'm not saying whether conditions like psychosis or bipolar exist or not, but in Scientology, just as with psychiatry, labels are often assigned to stigmatize, not to diagnose.

Probably because of my position in the organization, I never got in any trouble for voicing my disagreement with Hubbard's views on homosexuality. When a staff member made a derogatory remark about someone's sexual orientation, I often challenged them to explain why they thought homosexuality was an aberration. Their responses were often humorously illogical: "Because LRH said so," or the tired argument that if everyone were gay the race would cease to procreate and so become extinct. (Whoever thought that never read about the baby factories in Huxley's Brave New World.) But in all seriousness, that argument falls apart by pointing out that if everyone joined the Sea Org, the race would also cease to procreate, as Sea Org members were forbidden to have children. According to their logic, in terms of procreation, there was no difference between being in the Sea Org and being gay, assuming that gays couldn't procreate, which in reality is not the case. One staff member with whom I worked closely for years paraphrased a Hubbard quote that said homosexuals are covertly hostile because they trick us into thinking they are one gender, when they are actually behaving as the opposite gender: "You see a man and you expect him to be into manly things and the opposite turns to be true." In all fairness, she was paraphrasing; I never heard the lecture myself. Regardless of whether Hubbard said this, it was what she believed to be true, and is typical of how Scientologists in general, and Sea Org members specifically, view homosexuality. Ultimately, Hubbard's view of homosexuality is no different than that of other fundamentalist religions—homosexuality is a sin against God, curable by adhering to one's faith. Conversion therapy, as practiced by numerous Christian denominations, relies on prayer as a mechanism for reprogramming an individual's sexual orientation. While in Scientology, as the individual's emotional tone level rises up the scale as a result of receiving auditing, they naturally become heterosexual. Both beliefs are based on the same magical thinking—that through some form of mental activity, homosexuality can be "cured." Not to mention, being based on the bigoted view that homosexuality falls outside the spectrum of normal human behavior and should be cured.

At the core of Scientology is the belief that only through applying Hubbard's technology, in strict accordance with his teachings, can one achieve spiritual awareness, and that the technology must remain pure and never altered. There is no evolving with the times; no adjusting to shifts in cultural norms, no room to grow or evolve. That chiseled-in-stone mentality includes Scientology's basis for its bigotry against the LBGTQI+ community.

FOURTEEN

THE SEDUCTION OF OPPORTUNITY

I N MARCH 1995, I WAS
sitting in a small office at Golden Era Productions reading
Leni Riefenstahl's 672-page eponymous memoir, *Leni
Riefenstahl*. The first time I heard the name Leni Riefenstahl
was during a film history class at California Institute of the
Arts. Riefenstahl made her directorial debut in 1932, starring
in a classic of the German Mountain Myth films, *The Blue
Light*—a genre noted for tales of fearless young mountaineers
shot in spectacular alpine locations under extreme conditions
with narratives centering on supernatural themes. *The New
York Sun* described *The Blue Light* as "one of the most
pictorially beautiful films of the year."

With the success of *The Blue Light*, Riefenstahl was
commissioned by Hitler to make the pre-war films, *Triumph
of the Will* (1935) and *Olympia* (1938), recognized as two of the
most effective and artistically monumental propaganda films

ever made. Initially, I didn't think of Riefenstahl as a Nazi filmmaker, but rather as an artist with an obsessive dedication to achieving her aesthetic goals. Perhaps she was seduced by having unlimited resources with which to point a battery of cameras at an emerging fascist regime, lifting propaganda to new artistic levels. While she claimed to be unaware of the Nazi atrocities, I'd like to think that an artist has a responsibility to know if they're working for a regime intent on slaughtering an entire race of people. Casting doubt on her claim of ignorance, for her second feature film *Lowlands,* completed in 1944, the film's extras were Romani people interned at Marzahn, a nearby concentration camp.

After the war she was arrested as a Mitläufer, a Nazi traveler who is not convinced by the ideology of the group but merely offers no resistance out of a lack of courage or for opportunism— remember those words, *offers no resistance out of a lack of courage or for opportunism.* She was never tried, nor did she ever apologize. Decades later she was quoted as saying, "What do I have to apologize for? My films took the top awards."

But what struck me the most about her autobiography was the following passage:

> Phillip wrote he had found a gifted American author to collaborate on the script. "This American," he enthused, "is a brilliant and famous writer, who has written many screenplays for Columbia in Hollywood. He is also the head of a great international organization that

THE SEDUCTION OF OPPORTUNITY

is spread across the entire globe and has more than a
million members. His name is L. Ron Hubbard, he is
a psychologist and Scientologist."

—Leni Riefenstahl, A Memoir, page 448

Phillip Hudsmith, a 35-year-old British film editor who at
the time was taking Scientology courses at Saint Hill, knew
Hubbard personally, and was obsessed with remaking *The Blue
Light*. He suggested Riefenstahl collaborate with Hubbard on
a modern English language version. Hudsmith introduced the
two and their collaboration ensued.

I immediately tabbed the page, jotted a quick note to
Miscavige, and sent it to his office. An hour or so later, an RTC
courier handed me a thick file folder clipped to a handwritten
cover note from Chairman of the Board Religious Technology
Center. "Dear Mitch, Here's the data on Leni Riefenstahl."
The folder contained a copy of Hubbard's rewritten version of
The Blue Light, as well as correspondence between Hubbard,
Hudsmith, and Riefenstahl. Also included were Hubbard's
extensive notes to Riefenstahl on plot and character development
as well as numerous photocopies of press clippings giving
context and background. I had a keen interest in film history
and Riefenstahl's work was uniquely fascinating to me. There
was something about her working for Hitler while, at the same
time, always maintaining her artistic independence.

In Ray Mueller's three-hour documentary, *The Wonderful,*

Horrible Life of Leni Riefenstahl (1992) she spoke at length about her filmmaking techniques but continued to insist that her association with the Nazis had not compromised her artistic independence. Her situation seemed relevant to my making films for Scientology. Not the part about her working for Hitler, but that her work for Hitler was a case study of an artist creating for the sake of an ideology while fooling themselves into believing their artistic independence was intact.

It was 1960 when Philip Hudsmith suggested to Riefenstahl that Hubbard would be a good candidate to update her script for *The Blue Light*—a mere 15 years since the Nazis were defeated. Even though the memory of Riefenstahl's collaborations with Hitler was beginning to fade, her career as a filmmaker was essentially over. Perhaps an English language remake of *The Blue Light* might be her comeback.

In a lengthy reply to Hudsmith, dated March 14, 1960, Hubbard gushed about his glory days as a Hollywood screenwriter, and gladly accepted the offer to revise Riefenstahl's script, expressing his delight in a tone that suggested he saw the offer as an opportunity to reboot his own screenwriting career. And in that moment, the writer with the cult following and the filmmaker who's work for the Nazis redefined propaganda, saw each other as a way to recapture their past glory:

> "This is a great story in all senses of the word. I feel honored that my box office has not been forgotten and am very happy to be allowed to exercise another and

fond part of my activities. I love scripting and always have and what wonderful stuff this 'Blue Light' has. Further, I have an enthusiasm for out-doing Hollywood. It is a private vendetta. I wince when in California producers recall fondly the box office, for it has always been my opinion that it would have been much greater if they hadn't gutted my scripts. And also, Ed Muhl, the manager of Universal-International, needs a lesson."

Hubbard's response went on for three more pages.

Despite the party line claiming that Hubbard enjoyed success as a Hollywood screenwriter, his contribution barely deserves a footnote. In Hubbard's time, literary giants such as Herman J. Mankiewicz, F. Scott Fitzgerald, Dorothy Parker, William Faulkner, and Raymond Chandler were lured to Hollywood at the prospect of the easy money to be had writing screenplays. As *Citizen Kane* screenwriter Mankiewicz famously remarked to his fellow scribes, "Your only competition are idiots." Among the idiots he was referring to were most certainly the writers who scripted the B-movies and the serials that ran before the main feature. Many of Hubbard's dime novels were used as source material for such serials, the most notable being Columbia Pictures *The Secret of Treasure Island*. In a classic example of the never-ending hyperbole Scientology grinds out when describing Hubbard's various achievements, *lronhubbard.org* claims that *The Secret of Treasure Island* was the most successful serial of all time.

However, people didn't go to the movies to see serials. They went to see the main feature. So, by what measure was it the most successful serial of all time? I would have thought such praise would have been awarded to something like *Buck Rogers*, or at least something that had lodged itself in the culture's collective consciousness, not something no one has ever heard of.

Then there is Hubbard's inexplicable mention of Edward Muhl, the Universal Studios head of production from '53 to '73, many years after Hubbard's largely inconsequential association with the studios came to an end. And what was the nature of the vendetta he referred to? I suspect it was due to the fact that his writing talent was never tapped for anything more significant than as source material for the serials which ran while half the audience was still at the concession stand, in contrast to fellow pulp novelist Raymond Chandler who went on to become one of the most acclaimed American novelists of the 20th century, scripting the classic film *Double Indemnity*, for which he received a Best Screenplay Oscar nomination in 1944.

During their collaboration on *The Blue Light*, Riefenstahl lived in Hubbard's London apartment where she would meet daily with Hudsmith who, hoping to generate interest in the project, began arranging for Riefenstahl to meet with local journalists. At that point her past as a Nazi collaborator caught up with her. The reaction from the press was so negative, the planned shooting of *The Blue Light*, which Riefenstahl believed was imminent, had to be called off.

A few years later, Hubbard traveled to Rhodesia (now Zimbabwe) where he hoped to establish a safe base for Scientology with sights set on founding the first country run on Scientology principles. But not even his pro-apartheid stance had prevented Rhodesia's racist government from deporting him. Years later he wrote to Riefenstahl while she was on location in Africa shooting a book of photography. It can be assumed from her response that he'd sent her a letter requesting a photo of a South African village. In a letter dated August 11, 1979, she replied with the following:

> "Dear Ron,
> I was very much surprised and pleased to hear from you after such a long time.
>
> I regret to say, that I cannot provide photos of a South African village, because I have never been in that part of the continent. I spent my time mostly in the Sudan or in East Africa.
>
> However, I can send you a photo of a Nuba village, if you want. In this case I have to know, whether in colour or in black and white, and which size.
>
> I hope you are doing well. I should be glad to meet you again!
>
> With kind regards,
> Leni Riefenstahl"

Her letter was addressed to Hubbard c/o Saint Hill Manor, in England, but in 1979 Hubbard was at his Southern California desert compound in La Quinta working on the technical training films. Most notably around that time, he was writing the script for the film *How to Set up a Session and the E-meter* and was likely turning to Riefenstahl for location research pertaining to the film's setting: a fictional African nation.

Hubbard's rewrite of *The Blue Light* was never produced. In the '70s and '80s he wrote a handful of feature-length film scripts, none of which were ever made.

Riefenstahl continued her artistic career behind the camera, publishing a few notable books of photography but was never to make another film. Hitler's favorite film-maker remained a pariah of the German cinema until she finally passed away in 2003 at the ripe old age of 101. Upon her death, she was referred to as both a feminist icon and a fascist filmmaker.

Reflecting back on the odd meeting of the minds between the Nazi propagandist and the founder of an abusive cult, I wonder: was I always so quick to look past her Nazi association in order to appreciate her art because it was so aesthetically magnificent, or was it because doing so helped me to justify my working for Scientology? I may never know the answer.

FIFTEEN

NORTON AIR FORCE BASE

Aᴄᴄᴏʀᴅɪɴɢ ᴛᴏ
Scientology management technology, if a specific group, such as an auditing unit or a film crew routinely produced at a high rate, it was eligible to receive increased funding, more staff, and maybe even a new building. An area that did not produce, received minimal or no funding. By the late '90s, film production at Gold had increased to the degree that Miscavige was eager to construct a large film studio, enabling Gold to expand the scale and quantity of its film production. In the meantime, having outgrown Gold's tiny shooting space, known as the "Gym," that was literally no larger than a basketball court, and had gotten that name when Gold planners, wanting to maintain secrecy concerning the actual plan to build a film studio, falsified a request for building permits claiming they were building a gym. Having outgrown that "gym" we needed to rent a larger studio until an adequately sized facility could be constructed

on the Gold property. We had rented studios in the LA area when absolutely necessary, but that was a rare occurrence. When it came to the "bean counters" at Gold (as Scientology liked to refer to its finance people, adopting whatever slang was available to avoid making any direct reference to money), the idea of renting was as anathema as garlic to a vampire. I was looking forward to the possibility that I might be working in a rented stage closer to home while the new studio was built; what transpired was a different story altogether.

In his crusade to rebuild the military, President Bill Clinton looked to cutting out waste and focusing on the kinds of wars it would face in Bosnia, Kosovo, and Afghanistan. Norton AFB and March AFB, two of the military bases under review for the chopping block, were a mere 15 minutes apart, and 40 minutes from Gold. Over the years, most of the day-to-day operations in the area were handled out of March, so the Clinton military planners determined that Norton should be shut down, and its functions and personnel moved to March. It happened that Norton was home to the Air Force Audiovisual Service, which included a large sound stage. It also happened that Norton had been built on ancestral territory once owned by the San Manuel Indians. With the closure of the Air Force Base, the land reverted to a consortia of local governments including San Bernardino county, with part of the land being returned to the San Manuel tribe—the part of it where the sound stage was located. I have no idea how someone at Gold ever found out that a local Native American tribe were the new owners of an Air Force-built film studio and were only too happy to rent it out for a fraction of the cost of an equivalently sized stage rental in the LA area, but they found out and a deal was struck.

With their long-braided hair flowing down from 10-gallon Stetsons, snake-skin boots, and shiny turquoise rodeo buckles, it was obvious that our new landlords didn't need the rent money—their casinos provided plenty of that. Shortly after we took possession of the studio at Norton, a small contingent of the Tribe's leaders arrived in their blacked-out Suburbans to graciously invite us to their casino for a banquet and fun. I recall one of them excitedly explaining how he envisioned turning the sound stage into a tourist attraction with a rooftop restaurant and cocktail bar. Back at Gold I lobbied for permission to take my Sea Org crew for a visit to the Indian casino. I argued it would be an insult to turn down their generous invitation. No one agreed.

The studio at Norton was built to Cold War specs. With its mammoth two-foot-thick concrete stage doors, the building was designed to withstand a nuclear blast and soundproofed so that you could hear a pin drop as a fighter jet took off on the adjacent runway. If you overlooked the clusters of black widows and scorpions in the restrooms, and the wasted time driving back and forth from Gold, it was not a bad place to film. At least it was quiet and spacious.

Film production at Norton ran smoothly enough until we

shot a film titled *TRs In Life*—"TR" being short for "Training Routine." The TRs are exercises or drills used in Scientology to teach a person to communicate effectively so they can control people and situations—at least that's the claim. In reality, they force a kind of rigid communication style and push the magical thinking that through thought alone one can control their environment and other people. Structurally, TRs are composed of repetitive actions, or a total absence of action, while fixating on a person or an object and thereby produce a kind of trance state that can be experienced as euphoria by the person doing the drill. There are what are known as "Professional TRs," a ridiculously high standard of supposed communication skills that are a requirement of professional auditors. The passing standard for professional TRs—students must receive a "pass" from a supervisor before they can progress—includes having the student sit across from another student, staring at them until they can do this with no discomfort for two hours. In all, there are nine TRs, each teaching what Hubbard defined as the skills one needed in order to succeed as a Scientology auditor or in life. Then there are the more permissive TRs, sometimes referred to as public TRs, comprising the communication skills one needed to succeed in everyday life. The public TRs are not different from the professional TRs. They are merely a watered-down version. Because so many of our interpersonal problems stem from social conflicts resulting from communication difficulties, the idea of improving your life by improving your ability to communicate is a strong selling point for Scientology. The passing standard for public TRs is deliberately low, making it easy for the new student to have a "win." The Scientology course teaching public TRs, *The Success Though Communications Course,* or *Comm Course* for short, is probably the most attended course in all of Scientology and has probably introduced more people to Scientology than any other Scientology offering.

The technical training films are only available to students enrolled on Scientology training courses, except two films Hubbard designated for the general public—the target audience being non-Scientologists. One of those two "public films" was titled *TRs In Life,* in which, through a series of vignettes featuring supposedly real-life situations, the audience is shown how an exact violation of each one of the nine Hubbard-defined communication skills leads to disastrous results. The film concludes with all the main characters miraculously transported to a Scientology Chapel where they receive a lecture on the proper use of TRs.

The film was shot entirely on location except for the end sequence, which was shot at Norton. As usual, the day's schedule started early in the morning. Due to various disruptions, we were still going after sundown. During the execution of the grand finale shot, the computer-controlled camera crane kept having technical problems. As a result, and in violation of labor laws for filming, twenty professional actors, many of whom were Scientologists, were kept on the set until sunrise. It was a bloodbath. The crew member responsible for running the set insisted the shot had to be completed that night as the film was on a tight deadline to be shown at an upcoming international event. The film had been included in the event planning approved by Miscavige. The weight of that approval caused the crew to push to get it done that night, resulting in the mistreatment of the actors, some of whom were not Scientologists, and a major PR nightmare for Gold. Miscavige sent out a dispatch reprimanding the crew and proclaiming he never ordered the film to be completed for the event. In a literal sense, he never gave such an order. He did however *approve* the plan that it be shown at the event and that approval had the same authority as an explicit order to get it done now. It was a distinction without a difference and a management tactic he, and execs below him, employed as a way to deflect blame away from themselves. The road to failure at Gold was paved with the bodies of those who had been given an impossible order and then punished for failing to complete it.

As a result of our failure to get the film done on time, everyone involved in the shoot was hauled into Ethics and subjected to brutal, weeks-long security checks, during which time the crew was required to sleep outdoors in tents. During the day, they were subjected to hours of strenuous marching led by a veteran Sea Org officer, brought to the Base by Miscavige specifically to run the crew through military-style bootcamp drills. I was sitting on a bench outside the HCO offices, taking a break from my metered interrogation, when the crew marched by, their drill master sounding off, "Hut, hut, hut," their eyes fixed forward. One of the gaffers on the crew, a young man who couldn't have been more than eighteen years old, turned his head to look at me. A few years later he was called out by Miscavige in front of the entire Base in the most humiliating way. His life ruined, he had no hope for any kind of a future, so he hopped the fence with $500 to his name. Not long after I ceased all interaction with Scientology, he phoned telling me he recalled the day he saw me sitting on that bench outside of HCO and thinking that if I, an outsider who had been hired as a skilled professional, wasn't safe from Scientology's oppressive justice system at Gold, then no one was. Practically in tears, he relayed how he'd waited twenty years to tell me that it was working with me that gave him the courage to leave and the confidence to start—what turned out to be—a very successful career. At least I have the satisfaction of knowing I did that.

This was the first time I was treated to Scientology's version of being pilloried in the town square. It would not be the last.

SIXTEEN

DIANETICS: SEPARATE BUT EQUAL

I
N THE MID-2000S
I wrote and directed—for the third time—a four-hour instructional video titled *How to Use Dianetics*. Around that same time, there was an intense interest in growing Scientology's Black membership with new Churches planned to open in Harlem and Inglewood, predominantly Black neighborhoods. Pointing out that the media produced by the Church was overwhelmingly white, Miscavige wanted an identical version of the video produced featuring Black actors specifically aimed at the Black community. Like something out of Jim Crow America with its infamous segregated drinking fountains, he wanted a "separate but equal" Black version of the video. Conforming to Scientology's obsession with abbreviations, the African American Dianetics film became known as AF-AM. In spite of feeling uncomfortable at the prospect of directing a Black-centric version, I went along

with it. For me, the biggest challenge in creating the AF-AM version was defining a visual approach that accurately reflected Black American culture. As no ethnic culture in America is monolithic, the design of the film would center on the video's target demographic—upwardly mobile, urban Blacks.

The approach to production design at Gold followed Hubbard's cookie-cutter mentality as dictated by the Cine EDs (Executive Directives) he'd written on the subject—a woefully incomplete compendium of snippets stitched together from various texts on color, costumes, lighting, and set design, supplemented by notable textbooks interpreted through the distorted lens of Hubbard's definition of art, a definition which in and of itself is one of the best examples of Hubbard's circular, reductionist thinking. As Hubbard defined it, "Art is a word which summarizes the quality of communication." While telling you nothing about art, that definition established Hubbard as the ultimate arbiter of taste among his acolytes. The impulse to create art originates in the human mind. Hubbard claimed to have a greater understanding of the mind than anyone in history, so with his writings on art, he sought to establish himself as a preeminent thought leader in the field of art. Yet, despite his spreading that wisdom around, directing much of it at his top echelon creators, the Art Department at Gold produced mediocre work at best.

By providing specific examples taken from paintings, architecture, and other films, I was able to wrangle them into executing acceptable designs. I honestly believed that with enough patience I could help the Art Department to evolve to the point where they could contribute original ideas and not just follow instructions. In the case of the AF-AM video, I insisted we hire an outside production designer who understood Black culture in America. Pointing out the educational value of having an established feature film production designer work with the Art Department, the expensive hire was approved—a talented Black production designer who had substantial credits on well-reviewed, popular films. I loathed the prospect of shooting the same film over again, not just because I'd already done it, but because the fact that it was being reshot with a primarily Black cast made it obvious Scientology was pandering to Black Americans. In spite of that, and in light of the film having a top level production designer, in the final analysis, the AF-AM version was superior to the original version, and with that I had the blessing to continue hiring outside production designers to work on Gold films—which had been a hard won objective. I thought I'd finally solved the problem of being limited to working with an art department hampered by the constraints of Hubbard's reductionist thinking on art.

Shortly after the film was completed, a key member of the Art Department went missing. Demanding to know what happened to her, I was informed she had "blown"—the Scientology term for leaving without authorization. Soon after,

I was told that the production designer I hired to help with the AF-AM video was no longer qualified to work for the Church. Years later I found out she'd escaped Gold to be with that production designer, had gotten pregnant, and moved back to her home country. While visiting friends who'd worked with her during her time in the Sea Org, I noticed a photo on their refrigerator. It was the girl from the Art Department standing next to her young son, both of them smiling for the camera. I was happy to see she'd found a fulfilling life outside of the Sea Org.

By the time the AF-AM video was completed, it had become obvious that having a separate but equal version of the Dianetics video only served to illustrate how out of step the Church of Scientology was with contemporary. The Black version of the *How to Use Dianetics* video was never released. Internally, it was a complete disaster, a waste of time and money. Had the general public ever become aware of the two versions, one for whites and another for Blacks, they would have clearly seen Scientology's racist attitude.

SEVENTEEN

FLYING MONKEYS

THE FLYING MONKEYS (MORE accurately winged monkeys) that first appeared in the 1900 children's novel, *The Wonderful Wizard of Oz,* are described as jungle monkeys with bird-like feathered wings. They are natively playful, intelligent, and speak English. But when under the control of the Wicked Witch of the West, they enact pure evil and are bent on destroying Dorothy, her friends, and her little dog.

In the vernacular of pop psychology, a "flying monkey" is an agent who acts on behalf of an abusive person. Scientology has its share of loyal followers who are often called upon to act as flying monkeys for David Miscavige. Sometimes they are sent out in the guise of the "Squirrel Busters" to torment defectors accused of practicing Scientology outside the authority of the Church—"Squirrel" being the Scientology term for such individuals. Sometimes groups of flying monkeys are sent to torment defectors who have spoken out against the Church, often ambushing their prey in public, hurtling abusive remarks while videotaping the person's reaction in an attempt to push them over the edge so they can capture an unflattering moment to use to embarrass the target in the media.

I was once invited to accompany a group of Squirrel Busters traveling to Texas to antagonize Marty Rathbun, the number two ranking executive who had defected and set up his own brand of Scientology while blogging about the abuses he had witnessed and experienced. There was no love lost between Rathbun and me—not because he'd left the Sea Org to become Scientology's enemy number one, but because of all the years of grief, torment, and verbal abuse he had directed my way, earning him the top slot on my list of "biggest assholes who ever lived." Marty would make the rounds at Gold, playing the tough guy, letting you know he had his sights on you and that you had better watch out. He'd do things like suddenly appear in my office, then slip into a chair facing my desk, scoop up my Palm Pilot (state of the art before smartphones) and scroll through the contacts, declaring; "I should confiscate everyone's address books [referring to public Scientologists such as myself, who had high-level contacts within the Church], cross-reference them, see who knows who and then put you all on the Meter." He'd then toss the Palm Pilot onto the desk and walk out. While those sorts of visits were annoying and intrusive, they were far from the worst Marty was capable of—nothing like being the unfortunate recipient of a special auditing procedure called the "Truth Rundown," delivered personally by Marty. On the "Truth Rundown," specifically designed for Sea Org members and occasionally given to public, the auditor would locate a negative thought about some aspect of Scientology or one of its leaders.

In my case, I was being asked about what negative thoughts I'd had concerning Miscavige. Considering the abuses I'd seen him mete out, I had plenty. Through a lengthy and tortuous verbal procedure, the auditor would work the person over until they convinced themselves they had imagined whatever caused them to have that negative thought in the first place. Long before pop psychology adopted the term "gaslighting," Scientology had become skilled at gaslighting Scientologists into doubting their own reality to the point where they'd become delusional. The Truth Rundown was perhaps the most weaponized form of gaslighting ever invented. Even the title of the rundown itself—which insinuates it has something to do with getting at the truth—was intended to deny a person's reality.

During the Truth Rundown, you are asked to look at your own conclusions about something or someone, then asked what evil thing you did right before coming to that conclusion. By incessantly getting you to connect the evil you believed you saw in others—such as personally witnessing Miscavige terrorize staff members—with things that you might have done, you will, after many hours over the course of weeks and sometimes months, come to believe that you were delusional when you came to that conclusion. You know what you saw. I absolutely saw Miscavige abuse staff. But maybe it only looked like abuse because I was looking through a distorted lens.

Far worse than being treated to the Truth Rundown by Marty, was being Security Checked at the hands of his 14-year-old female protégé. While she was under his guidance, he subjected her to extreme verbal sexual abuse while administering the Security Check to me.

The purpose of a Security Check in Scientology is to get a person to admit to having committed transgressions against the mores of the group. These transgressions are defined as "Overt Acts," meaning something the person has done which harmed their own survival or the survival of another person or a group. As a result of having committed an overt, the person now has a "Withhold," meaning something they are withholding for fear they will get in trouble, or out of fear of harming their reputation. In some cases, the overt acts are classified as some level of criminality, as described in the book *An Introduction to Scientology Ethics*, which details the misdemeanors, crimes, and high crimes as defined by the Scientology Justice system.

Anything disclosed in a Security Check is actionable, meaning the person will be held accountable and consequences will be doled out. Generally, those consequences involve being assigned a "lower condition." A person thus assigned has to perform a series of prescribed steps involving identity-destroying self-examination; acts of contrition; the making of amends through performing extra work or making financial donations; delivering an effective blow to the enemies one has been pretending to be part of despite personal danger; and finally presenting their transgressions in writing to their fellow group members along with what the person has done to make up the damage. Then, only when a majority of fellow members sign the person's petition for re-entry to the group, are they allowed to move out of lower conditions. If the Puritans had the lower conditions, they would have had no need for scarlet letters or pillories. When it came to keeping a flock docile, contrite, and well behaved, Hubbard had developed far more powerful tools for public shaming than the Puritans ever imagined.

I don't even recall why Marty hauled me into the Sec Check. Like a vampire in need of human blood, Marty needed to feast daily on the fear he could extract from others, and somehow, I ended up on the menu. Miscavige was in Clearwater, tangled up in some legal matter or another, so Marty was free to roam the Base with impunity, bullying and mind-fucking anyone he wished. Hubbard developed a particularly devious technique called "Murder Routine" employed in Scientology Sec Checking. Murder Routine calls for asking the person if they committed an overt so outrageous that they will counter by saying the thing they actually did. For example, say the person stole a paper clip from the org but refuses to tell the auditor, despite the needle reactions on the E-meter, that supposedly indicate the person is lying. The sec checker then asks the person for an outrageous overt such as, "Did you murder someone?" The person then counters with, "Well no! All I did was steal a paper clip." If the person doesn't cough up the overt, the severity of the exaggerated accusations become more extreme.

That was the case with the sec check I received from Marty's 14-year-old protégé. I was sitting across the auditing table from LD (her initials), holding the cans so that she could see them as required to ensure I wasn't moving them around trying to artificially influence the Meter, braced for what I thought would be a garden-variety, extremely invasive interrogation on the E-meter. Per the Sec Checking procedure, LD asked, "Has a withhold been missed?" Meaning, did someone nearly find out about something you did that you did not want them to know about, or did you suspect that they might know? This is the entry point to chasing down the overt. LD was distracted and occasionally fiddled with her right ear. That's when I noticed she was wearing an earpiece. Then I heard it. At about the same volume and ferocity as a buzzing fly, as when you hear sound bleeding out of someone's earbuds, I heard Marty's voice screaming into her earpiece.

I couldn't make out the exact words, but it didn't matter, because LD was repeating them—outrageously exaggerated questions of a highly explicit and obscene sexual nature. I'm not going to repeat them. Whatever you might imagine Marty screamed into her earpiece, magnify that by ten times and you still won't be close e.g., "Did you put your___in the___of a ___?" And on, and on, and on. Questions only the sick mind of a deranged psychopath like Marty Rathbun could come up with, and all of it being repeated by a frightened child. Years later, after Marty escaped from the Base for the last time, LD came to see me in my office in the Cine Castle. She was in her early twenties and was still in RTC. She actually apologized for her part in that Sec Check. I later heard LD left the Sea Org. I'd be surprised if she's still in Scientology.

The overriding reason for my refusing to join the Squirrel Busters in their mission to torment Rathbun (or anyone else) had nothing to do with his having become an enemy of the Church, or with the grief he'd personally caused me. Rather, in my view, public spectacles, such as those the "Squirrel Busters" engaged in, only added to the Church's reputation as a corrupt entity that shamelessly, and very publicly, harassed its critics.

There were a few times, however, when I was persuaded to play the non-combative role of a Miscavige flying monkey, such as the time I was ordered to reach out to actor Jason Beghe to try and dissuade him from attacking Scientology.

I originally met Jason in 1998, soon after he became a Scientologist. He visited the set of a film we were shooting at a rented stage in LA. He had been suggested for an upcoming part in a Scientology film. After getting to know him, I appreciated his intensity and respected his artistic abilities. We subsequently worked together on a number of projects for the Church, and we became good friends. On one of those projects Jason portrayed a marooned space miner in the training film *The Session* which years later had to be reshot after he made his spectacular exit from Scientology in 2008.

Jason had been invited to my upcoming birthday party. He had RSVP'd and personally expressed his intention to attend. Surprisingly, he was a no-show. At that time I was receiving auditing from an RTC auditor, meeting with her for sessions in LA when I was home on weekends. She also happened to be Jason Beghe's auditor. The next time I saw her she asked how the party went. I happened to mention that Jason did not show up. She gave me one of those "Oh no!" expressions, then said "What I'm about to tell you is strictly confidential and cannot be repeated to anyone." Such a statement from an RTC staff member is not to be taken lightly. She went on to explain that the day before my party, while exiting the freeway, Jason flipped his convertible and was in the hospital, being kept in a medically induced coma due to the severity of his injuries. She assured me he was being well cared for by a team of auditors provided by RTC, in addition to receiving top medical care.

Always wanting to limit the spread of bad news, especially anything tragic happening to a valued Scientologist such as Jason, I was sworn to secrecy.

A few days later I received a frantic call from my former assistant, Lisa Allen, the Commanding Officer of Gold at that time. Jason was urgently needed to come to the base to record narration for a video. Unable to contact him, she was asking for my help. After seeing her spend considerable time spinning her wheels trying to reach him, I felt I had to explain the situation, emphasizing I'd been sworn to secrecy by an RTC staff member.

About six weeks later, Jason was fully recovered and arrived at the Gold Base for a scheduled shoot. Upon walking into the studio, the entire crew gathered around him and started to applaud, telling him how happy they were that he'd survived his injuries. Apparently, once I'd confided in Lisa, everyone on the Base knew. I was beyond embarrassed. Apparently, at Gold a secret was something you told one person at a time.

Beyond the embarrassment of having my confidence betrayed in such a public way, the incident served to prove that in Scientology, and especially in the Sea Org, it is not possible to have friends since a primary role of a friend is someone you can confide in. Further evidence occurred when staff members with whom I'd become close and with whom I confided personal details, later escaped and shared those details with members of the ex-Scientology community. It can be disheartening when you confide in someone only to find those details on the Internet.

A few years later, Jason called "bullshit" on Scientology and made headlines with his dramatic, tell-all YouTube interview. I never thought I'd speak to him again until the day Tommy Davis handed me a recording device and said, "The Boss wants you to call Jason." Tommy, the handsome young son of Oscar nominated actress Anne Archer, had risen up the ranks in the Sea Org to become, for a time, an international spokesperson for the Church and one of Miscavige's trusted flying monkeys. I knew Tommy years back when he was posted as a designated celebrity wrangler at Celebrity Centre. Tommy eventually became a sort of de facto chief of staff for Tom Cruise, while his then-wife Jessica acted as Katie Holmes' handler. I had once cast Tommy in a Scientology music video playing the role of a man standing on a majestic mountain top, staring off into the sunrise, absurdly symbolizing a person achieving a higher state of existence. During the course of filming, I had unloaded Tommy, white-knuckled and shivering, from a helicopter onto a precarious mountain peak. You could say we knew each other. Soon after Jason Beghe's infamous interview hit YouTube, on a bright and sunny day at Gold, Tommy approached me with the request to call Jason. "He's gonna do the Matt Lauer [Today] show and the Boss wants you to talk him out of it," Tommy explained. He says you're friends and he'll listen to you." He handed me a little recording device attached to a wire with a suction cup. "Here," he said, "attach this to your phone. The Boss wants the call recorded." Apparently they'd tried everything to reach Jason in an effort to dissuade him from being interviewed by Matt Lauer on the *Today Show*. I hadn't spoken with Jason in a while; considering he was now playing the role of noisy apostate, I was certain I was one of the last people he wanted to hear from. If I were able to reach Jason, I wanted our conversation to be private. After all, we were friends and I felt I had a right, even an obligation, to have a private conversation with him. So, I attached the mic to my phone, but never turned on the recorder. Plus, when it came to recording phone conversations, California is a two-party state, meaning it's illegal to record a conversation without the consent of the party being recorded. I knew this from shooting hidden camera videos for anti-psychiatry documentaries. (We always shot those in Texas where it was legal to record someone without their consent.) So, wanting to keep the conversation private and not wanting to break the law, I disregarded the recorder.

Jason answered on the second ring. "Hello Jason. It's Mitch Brisker."

To my astonishment he replied, "Hello, sir."

What! Why had he called me sir? I thought maybe he was caught off guard and reflexively used the "sir" term out of respect for my having directed him in numerous Church films. I opened with, "I hear you're going to do an interview with Matt Lauer." Jason began screaming into the phone about what a piece of shit Matt Lauer is, how they'd called him and wanted him on the show, saying he wasn't sure if he was going to do it.

It's not that I didn't care that Jason was attacking the Church. It's just that, at the time, I never believed Scientology would live or die based on the claims of ex-members. In my true-believer mindset, I thought they should be utterly ignored, as all the attention they were given only amplified their message. Plus, I liked Jason, and had valued our friendship. I explained to him that if he continued being so visible as a Church attacker, his name would forever be inseparable from his attacks on the Church. In press articles that had nothing to do with his departure from Scientology, he was already being referred to as Jason (ex-Scientologist) Beghe. I expressed my opinion that while his YouTube interview quickly earned 500,000 views, the YouTube numbers did not represent new fans but, like gawkers slowing down to see a bloody car accident, the YouTube audience would just as soon see him drown in his own puke than succeed as an actor. He continued to complain that his young son was now forbidden to play with the son of a mutual friend of ours. "They can't play together because you're an SP, Jason. You took the course. You know the Policy," I explained.

"If I'm an SP, then declare me," he demanded.

"I'm not the Church," I replied. "I don't declare people.

If you want to be declared, you'll have to ask them to declare you."

His voice softened and he said, "Mitch, why do you want to waste your talent working for Scientology?"

Somehow Jason had momentarily pierced the cognitive dissonance barrier that allowed me to speak with him and think that I'm right. I had no answer because there wasn't an answer.

Later that day, I handed the recorder back to Tommy, claiming it had failed to record. Soon after that call, Jason phoned me two or three more times just to express his reasons for leaving. For years to come, I would ask myself that same question, why was I wasting my talent working for Scientology? Jason never did the Matt Lauer interview, and I never spoke with him again. His departure from Scientology, and subsequently speaking out, didn't hurt his career. Someday I hope I get a chance to thank him for asking that question and to apologize for being a Scientology operative.

I originally met Paul Haggis at Celebrity Centre in the mid '90s, when he hosted a performance of a Scientologist-founded improv group called Interplay that had just relocated to LA from New York. Back when I was directing ads for the Dianetics campaign, Paul was asked by his good friend at the time, Scientology marketing executive Bill Dendiu, to write and direct a Dianetics commercial. Bill was an interesting character. He was so manic and fast-talking that

I'd taken him for a closet coke-head. Bill called me into his office one day, his voice and his body language signaling he had bad news. Apparently he felt that by asking his friend Paul Haggis to write and direct a Dianetics commercial he was somehow encroaching on my territory. Bill asked me to act as the ad's producer, which I was happy to do as I liked Paul and respected his talents. Beyond that, I only knew Paul as a fellow Scientologist and only interacted with him at parties or Scientology functions. I wouldn't say we were friends—we didn't exactly hang out together—but we were friendly enough for Paul to include my name on the recipient list of his Scientology resignation email letter. In the letter, addressed to Scientology spokesperson Tommy Davis, Haggis declared he could no longer remain silent about Scientology's extreme anti-gay stance and so was resigning from the church. Two of Paul's daughters were gay and had themselves been discriminated against by the religion they were raised in. In response to the letter, Tommy Davis requested a meeting with Paul at his west Los Angeles office

Never one to show up for a fight without plenty of backup, Tommy decided to bring Miscavige attack dog Dave Bloomberg, the exec who had disgraced himself with his laughable attempt to launch Scientology's Internet presence. Also joining us was a Scientology pro writer who seemed to always be trying to get back onto Miscavige's good side by racking up hours participating in those infamous squirrel-buster ambush parties, and me, just because I was someone they felt Paul respected. The four of us donned our flying monkey suits and headed out to Paul's production offices in West LA for the agreed-upon meeting.

If I were to make a bullet point list of the major items that ultimately drove me away from Scientology, accompanying the flying monkeys to meet with Paul Haggis that day would be high on the list. Paul was gracious and respectful. It was clear he wanted to confront Tommy, say his piece, hear what Tommy had to say, and be done with it. I sat there silently throughout the meeting, watching my fellow flying monkeys fumble through their self-righteous efforts to dislodge Paul from his heartfelt beliefs and to convince him that Scientology was in fact a gay-tolerant organization—that any actions to the contrary were done by unauthorized personnel voicing their personal opinions, not those of the Church. This was in reference to a staff member at the San Diego Church of Scientology who had voiced public support for California's Proposition 8 banning same-sex marriage, and had appeared to do so on behalf of Scientology. Paul demanded that the Church make an official statement concerning its stance on gay rights. Tommy ducked and dodged, claiming the Church could not comment on political issues. But in fact, since its inception, Scientology has clung to its founder's words on homosexuality, of which the following is but one example:

Such people should be taken from the society as rapidly as possible and uniformly institutionalized; for here is the level of the contagion of immorality, and the destruction of ethics; here is the fodder which secret police organizations use for their filthy operations.

—L. Ron Hubbard, *Science of Survival*

I sat there in silence, embarrassed that my presence was a tacit endorsement of the lie that Scientology was anything less than vehemently anti-gay. In sharp contrast, in 2023 Pope Francis declared that laws criminalizing homosexuality are "unjust," saying God loves all his children just as they are, and called on Catholic bishops who support the laws to welcome LGBTQIA+ people into the church. And yet Scientology's attitude on homosexuality remains in the dark ages, while its leader declares it to be, "The coolest religion on Earth."

Also on the day's agenda, Paul wanted his guests to answer up to the reports of Miscavige's physical abuse of staff at the International Base—specifically the press reports covering Miscavige smacking people who he'd imprisoned in the "Hole," a building kept to house executives deemed to have erred in some way. Tommy and Dave were all deny-deny-deny, claiming that Miscavige wasn't capable of such behavior. Paul, who was working on a piece about Martin Luther King at the time, made the point that even great leaders, such as Martin Luther King, made mistakes. Dave bolted to his feet, stabbing a finger at Paul and yelling, "How dare you compare a great man like David Miscavige to Martin Luther King." You can't make this up.

This theme, that Miscavige is incomparable to mere mortals such as Martin Luther King, would be repeated over and over for all the years I remained in Scientology. A writer who'd been hired to pen a flattering book on Miscavige reported the following interaction. In a one on one conversation, he'd told Miscavige that at some point they were going to have to talk about the times he felt he'd made an error in judgment or had a lapse of faith, or experienced self doubt. Such anecdotes are what make all great leaders relatable and believable—in essence, make them human. From Gandhi to Mandela, from Mother Teresa to JFK, all of them have spoken of their self-doubt and mistakes. It's one of the things they are admired for. Following the meeting, two of Miscavige's top aides took the writer aside and told him "You have to understand, your dealing with a man who is perfect. He has never made a mistake." It was at that point, the writer explained to me, he knew that book would never be written.

While Scientology executive Dave Bloomberg may have worked hard that day at convincing Paul Haggis that the Church was gay friendly, in private, his words told an entirely different story.

Back in 2006, two films were in hot contention to win the best picture Oscar—*Brokeback Mountain* and *Crash*. When *Crash,* directed and produced by Paul Haggis, got the nod over the heavily favored *Brokeback Mountain,* the Academy received sharp criticism with film critics and industry journalists complaining that the *Brokeback Mountain* Oscar snub was motivated by homophobia. They claimed *Brokeback Mountain* was the obviously superior film. Even Paul Haggis himself later stated that *Brokeback Mountain* was a better film than *Crash.* But whatever side of that argument you may fall on, the Church of Scientology's dirty tricks department wasted no time in exploiting the controversy for their own ends.

A series of *hate* interviews impugning Paul Haggis were produced and deployed on a website intended to assassinate Paul's character. One of the interviews featured none other than Scientology spokesperson Dave Bloomberg, who energetically accused Paul of being part of a homophobic conspiracy to steal the Oscar from *Brokeback Mountain.* The cinematographer who shot the interview happened to be Rachael Hastings, a talented young Sea Org member who I'd worked with and been friends with for years. Rachael, who would later come out as gay, escape the Sea Org to pursue her filmmaking career and become an outspoken critic of Scientology, told me that she sat dumbfounded listening to Dave Bloomberg blathering on in his virtue signaling role as a defender of *Brokeback Mountain.* When the camera was cut, Rachael asked Dave,

"Have you ever even watched *Brokeback Mountain?*" To which he replied, "Why would I watch that fucking fag movie."

Nothing came of the meeting. Paul continued to speak out against the Church and Tommy Davis continued to insist the Church was gay-friendly. Shortly after the meeting that day I had a personal conversation with David Miscavige, wherein he positioned Paul Haggis's public resignation from Scientology as Paul grandstanding in front of his gay daughters from whom he was estranged due to having been a negligent father. That was very odd as I'd seen both of his daughters at his production company when we met at his office that day. He was very obviously engaged with them and supportive of their careers.

On November 10, 2017, Paul was sued by a former publicist who accused him of sexually assaulting her back in 2013. Paul claimed the suit was part of a retaliatory operation executed by Scientology seeking to discredit him. He was not able to show evidence of the claim, but I can tell you in no uncertain terms, having seen firsthand the lengths to which Scientology will go to destroy their critics, personally I have no doubt that Scientology was behind the suit. In fact, the moment I heard about it, that was my first thought.

Narcissistic sociopaths are noted for engaging flying monkeys to execute smear campaigns against anyone attempting to expose their true nature. It was an unending source of amazement to me how Scientology could suddenly turn against former members, sometimes for doing nothing more than exercising their First Amendment right to leave a religion. A staff member departs without permission (blows) and suddenly the news is out—they had a history of incest, or embezzled funds, or were secretly gay, and on and on. High-ranking Scientology executives and celebrities who left or spoke out publicly were shamed on social media and in the press. Often information acquired in auditing sessions under the guise of confessional privilege is used in the smear campaigns, the church always claiming that such individuals had not left but were dismissed for their crimes against Scientology.

Buried on page 40 of L. Ron Hubbard's sacred text covering Scientology's draconian justice system, *An Introduction to Scientology Ethics*, Hubbard stresses that people leave organizations, marriages, etc., due to their own destructive acts. But the most important statement, perhaps in the entire book, is tossed off as an afterthought: "And certainly one can treat people so badly that they have no choice but to leave." Guaranteed, you will never, EVER, hear that statement repeated anywhere, at any time, by any Scientologist—even though anyone who ever spent any amount of time in Scientology and left, did so because at some point they experienced a return of critical thinking, or they had been treated so badly, or had witnessed the bad treatment of others, or were threatened with emotional harm (being cut off from family and friends), or financial harm (losing employment), that they finally reached a breaking point. Yet when people do leave Scientology, even if they've been held prisoner, put on a steady diet of rice and beans, and made to suffer daily bouts of verbal and physical abuse, Scientologists believe that, for those people to have left, they must have committed crimes against the Church.

I had managed to make myself unavailable whenever called upon to act as a flying monkey in any of the in-person attacks— the exception being the meeting with Paul Haggis, which was civil, and not like any of the encounters I'd seen reported where the flying monkeys would ambush an unsuspecting, whistle-blowing apostate in a parking lot, at the airport, or on a sidewalk, demanding to know "What are your crimes?" I did however contribute an occasional statement to the rumor-mongering hate machine Miscavige aimed at outspoken ex-Church members, such as the time I referred to my old friend Jeff Hawkins as a "small-time marketer who was way in over his head." I hope my previous statements about Jeff have set the record straight.

Flying monkeys are not only called upon to smear and punish at the behest of a sociopath; sometimes they are called on to shore up a flood of negative PR concerning the Church and to whitewash its sinking reputation. In 1998, the former *St. Petersburg Times* (now known as the Tampa Bay Times) correspondents Thom Tobin and Joe Childs did a feature profile on David Miscavige. Tobin was invited to tour the International Base and I was provided as someone with whom Miscavige had worked for many years and could speak to his leadership qualities. I spent a good hour or so giving various anecdotes illustrating Miscavige's leadership. The bubble I was kept in was that effective. I believed every word I said. It eventually dawned on me just how badly Miscavige needed associates such as myself—well-paid, loyal, and isolated from the dark side of his iron-fisted rule—that he could trot out as needed to give a positive interview.

In June of 2009, the year after the worldwide Anonymous protests, the same paper published a three-part exposé on Scientology titled, "The Truth Rundown," again written by Thom Tobin and Joe Childs. In an attempt to hold Scientology accountable for its misdeeds, the article exploded with the power of a nuclear bomb. On the day it was published, Miscavige was ensconced at Flag, Scientology's "spiritual" headquarters in Clearwater, Florida. The voice on the phone call I received was perfectly clear: "Drop everything and pack a bag." I was going to Clearwater to be offered up as part of the response team. The car they'd sent arrived before I finished packing.

It was a typical June day in Clearwater, patches of deep blue sky, billowing clouds, intermittent showers, and the occasional burst of Tampa Bay's signature lightning. Pulling up to the Fort Harrison Hotel, Scientology's premium accommodations located in downtown Clearwater, is much the same as pulling up to any luxury hotel. If you didn't know this was a destination for Scientologists from around the world traveling to receive spiritual counseling and training, you wouldn't be able to guess simply by pulling up to the curb. Upon arrival, a smartly uniformed bellhop takes your bags and politely guides you to the front desk where, unlike any other hotel, you will be asked to fill out an extensive questionnaire as part of a Routing form (in Scientology all physical objects, including human beings, that need to go from one designated point to another are considered "particles to be routed" and are put on a Routing form). A significant departure from the sort of information you are required to give when checking into a non-Scientology-operated hotel, at the For Harrison, you will be asked if you currently have a heart condition or have ever attempted suicide, either of which will disqualify you from staying at the hotel. The hostess at the front desk handed me a routing form, which had already been filled in with my basic information—name, address, phone number, local contact. Then, flipping it to the last page, she pointed to the signature line and said, "Please sign here," indicating that I was not required to fill in any other info. After all, as I was very well known in the Scientology community and was there at the behest of Scientology's ultimate leader, they could be fairly certain I wasn't some schmo with a bad heart who'd traveled to Flag to take a dive off the roof.

My bags were taken and I was shown to one of the luxury

suites with a living room spacious enough for a grand piano to be tucked into a corner without feeling like it encroached on the space. Miscavige had been on his way to the yearly celebration of the maiden voyage of Scientology's cruise ship *Freewinds*. There he would, as he always had, preside over a week's worth of events, mesmerizing the wealthiest Scientology donors with tales of the latest achievements in Scientology, plans for international expansion, and giving the inside skinny on the next big thing they'd be forking over their dough for. When the "Truth Rundown" article hit the newsstands, effectively taking a shit on Miscavige's ice cream, Miscavige diverted his flight to the Caribbean to stop in Clearwater and organize an emergency response to the scathing series of articles.

I ambled through the suite, noting the incredible view of Clearwater Bay, when Miscavige entered the room. He motioned for me to take a seat and then sat down on the sofa opposite me. He looked like he hadn't shaved in a couple of days and seemed smaller than his usual 5'1," as though the pressure from the onslaught of bad news had somehow reduced him further in size. Usually, when something this bad happened, he would explode in anger. As isolated as I had been, I'd seen the outbursts. But instead, he was reserved—or maybe just out of breath from all the screaming he must have been doing. He insisted the newspaper had timed the release of the article to coincide with the upcoming Maiden Voyage event. And why not? News is about timing and what better time to publish such a scathing exposé on Scientology than when one of its most important international events is about to be held? Miscavige complained endlessly about being "fucked over" by Mike (Rinder) and Marty (Rathbun) whom he held largely responsible for the *Tampa Bay Times* article. When scorned, there was no end to the shit-dipped stories Miscavige could conjure up about his former lieutenants and longtime friends-turned-apostate-whistleblowers. By the time Mike and Marty had defected, had publicly voiced their disaffection, and had given witness to Miscavige's brutal treatment of Sea Org staff, Miscavige took to accusing them of having had a (fictitious) homosexual relationship. After all, being gay was the worst possible crime in Scientology. In a slightly manic voice, he relayed how Marty's mother was insane and had been electroshocked when he was in her womb. To emphasize how Marty had taken advantage of his goodwill, Miscavige recounted the first time he had escaped from the Base and was tracked down in New Orleans. Miscavige, out of his generous and caring heart, showed up with home-plate tickets to a major league ball game, reeling Marty back in with a 24-hour bromance, after which Marty agreed to return and do a stint in the woodworking shop at Flag while he recuperated from the exhaustion and other vague medical maladies that surely must have been the cause of his abrupt departure. Miscavige boasted that he paid all of Marty's medical bills and chiropractic bills, arranged for special diets, and then sent him to the ship for a year of auditing, training, and R&R, and now Marty had really "fucked him over." Room service announced itself with a polite rap on the door. They had arrived with a serving cart loaded with Kobe beef sliders and an ample assortment of juices, soft drinks, and specialty coffee to fuel our strategy session.

The next day Miscavige continued on to the Freewinds, leaving me in Clearwater along with a handful of others he hoped would be allowed to give a response to the *Tampa Bay Times*. Meanwhile, Scientologists en masse hit the streets, buying copies of the newspaper and stealing as many as they could get their hands on, putting money in the newspaper vending machines and then emptying the contents. I spent an uneventful weekend at the Fort Harrison, then flew back to LA.

On May 3, 2016, Ron Miscavige published *Ruthless: Scientology, My Son David Miscavige, and Me*, a tell-all memoir recounting the story of David Miscavige's life and his rise to power as the leader of Scientology. It was less than flattering. I'd known Ron Miscavige since I was first at the Gold Base. He was a bandleader and trumpet player with the Golden Era Musicians, and, like all the Gold musicians, was expected to compose music for films and live events. That's how I had interacted with him, as a music composer. Ron was talented enough as a trumpet player to have made a living at it, but in my opinion, he was ill-suited to compose music for film.

Nothing against Ron, the problem actually lay with the Sea Org's practice of assigning people to jobs they were not suited for, didn't have the talent for, and generally sucked at. I was sympathetic toward Ron, not the sympathy usually reserved for the unfortunate, but the kind you feel when you see someone suffering the injustice of being forced into a circumstance for which they were not prepared. Ron was simply not qualified to compose music for film. He was required to address his own son as "Sir"—and if you didn't know he was Dave's father, you never would have guessed it from the way Dave treated him. As Ron tells it, when he discovered his Kindle's Internet connection not only provided a way to download books but, via the Kindle Web Browser, also provided a keyhole through which he could peer into the World Wide Web, a landscape rife with the fruit of truth forbidden to Scientologists, what he saw moved him to set his sights on escaping the International Base along with his wife Becky. Some time after his successful escape, Ron discovered that two private investigators had been hired by the Church to surveil him 24/7 for the previous 18 months at a cost of $10,000 a week. When one of the PIs mistakenly thought Ron was having a heart attack, he contacted his handlers. Upon hearing the news of his father's potential demise, David ordered the PI's to stand down. He is quoted as saying, "If he dies, he dies." That unfortunate bit of news made its way to Ron who, upon hearing it, decided he needed to write a book.

The release of the book was preceded by an interview with Ron Miscavige on ABC's *20/20*, broadcast on April 29, 2016. Once again, the Church, and specifically Miscavige, were under fire from the media. And once again the alarm bells sounded and I was called upon to dust off my flying monkey wings. Miscavige was hopping mad about the book and the upcoming interview. His plan: round up the usual suspects and interview us on video testifying to what an inept criminal his own father was, and claim that his book was a pack of lies from the mouth of an abusive parent and alleged rapist. To cap it off, he intended to send the execs at ABC News truly impressive gift baskets... of fresh baked goods. Yep, you read that correctly—baked goods! What better proof that you care about your staff, or that Ron Miscavige's book should not be taken seriously, or that you are a good and noble movement, than to have your own five-star Italian pastry chef—who bakes fresh bread daily for the crew and provides them with custom birthday cakes—send the *20/20* producers a basket of freshly baked bread and pastries. Miscavige ordered Gold staff member and Sea Org pastry chef, Pianuccio Tissi—the Italian master baker who had created the wedding cake for Tom Cruise and Katie Holmes, to put together a scrumptious basket of baked goods, certain that the goodies would sway the journalists into softening their report on the Church. He actually thought he could win them over with a variety of mini-loaves of delicious, fresh baked bread—carrot cake, gingerbread, poppy seed with lemon icing—all of it decoratively labeled, individually wrapped and thoughtfully presented. I have it on good authority that, upon receipt of the baskets, the producers laughed out loud and posed with the gift baskets the way DEA agents might pose with a cache of captured bricks of cocaine.

Pressed into service, I spent the next few days directing videos intended to extoll the greatness of L. Ron Hubbard, spotlight the humanitarian leadership of David Miscavige, and expose the base criminality of Ron Miscavige. It was all bullshit. By this time, I'd gone full Leni Riefenstahl in her guise as a "Mitläufer, a Nazi traveler." No longer convinced by the ideology of Scientology, I lacked the courage to leave (fearing reprisals and financial uncertainty) while taking advantage of the opportunity to earn a buck. As for my on-camera interview (not really an interview, as I'd written all my own questions and answers), I had given my personal testimony as to why it was okay for Sea Org members to be paid so little, actually pennies an hour, arguing that if you take into account all the elements provided for their overall lifestyle, they are actually supported above the U.S. standard of living—at least at Gold, where the housing is better than most other Sea Org bases, the food is decent, medical care is provided (though restricted and only available for emergencies), and extended educational opportunities are available (as long as they align to your current job). More importantly, what I didn't include in my interview was any mention of quality of life, which is a different matter altogether. While Sea Org members at Gold may have an acceptable and defensible standard of living, they have an abysmal quality of life. To highlight the difference, imagine you are super wealthy, yet are dying of a painful, incurable disease. You would have a very high standard of living but an intolerable quality of life. While being in the Sea Org is not the same as having a painful incurable disease, for many members it is painful, and with a billion-year commitment, it can sometimes seem incurable. Long hours with no or little time off. Soul crushing consequences for not upholding the near impossible demand to produce, and on and on. So, while a case can be made for the standard of living afforded the staff at Gold, their quality of life is so abysmal that it literally defeats any mention that they have basic creature comforts. What good is a state of the art commercial kitchen if you never know when it's going to be ordered to provide only rice and beans for an indeterminant period of time? What good are high quality cotton sheets when you can only visit them when you have permission to sleep? What good is the promise of time off or of a production bonus if those promises are never or rarely fulfilled?

Four days of non-stop shooting and editing, and only one short video clip of Monique Yingling (Scientology tax attorney and Miscavige personal lawyer) made it onto the

20/20 segment, while the remaining hours of interviews produced were repurposed for an Internet hate site dedicated to slandering Ron Miscavige. Fortunately, that was my last gig as a flying monkey.

EIGHTEEN

A Sociopath by Any Other Name

Dᴀᴠɪᴅ Mɪꜱᴄᴀᴠɪɢᴇ ɪꜱ
commonly referred to in simplistic terms. Scientologists
who only experience him through the distorted lens of the
Scientology bubble, praise him as the man who spearheaded a
new era of expansion—an era which saw a dramatic increase in
Scientology's real estate holdings and cash assets, while at the
same time, membership in the Church shrank to all-time lows.
In their delusional view, they describe him as a generous and
charming leader with boundless energy for solving immense
tactical problems. By contrast, his sharpest critics, many
of whom testify to having been physically assaulted and
emotionally terrorized, refer to Miscavige as a brutal dictator,
a tyrannical bully, a malignant narcissist, and a ruthless
sociopath. In the almost three decades I worked with him,
directly under him or around him, I witnessed him exhibit all
these traits, from generous and charming to raging maniac—but

always, the default position was vicious, emotional terrorist. It is important to keep in mind that all of those behavior traits exist along the spectrum of the most severely afflicted and dangerous psychopaths. It is difficult to fathom how an individual could, on the one hand, order the construction of a state-of-the-art commercial kitchen to provide high-quality meals for the crew at the International Base, and on the other hand imprison a hundred or so of his top managers in an office space fitted with window bars, no mattresses, and 24/7 security guards. At times, in accordance with a Hubbard-mandated disciplinary action, that state-of-the-art kitchen would serve the crew nothing but beans and rice three times a day, sometimes for weeks on end. Miscavige's swings between generosity and punishment were unpredictable and could happen in an instant. That constant push-pull cycle of acceptance, followed by rejection, lies at the root of every abusive relationship. It is a tactic used by sociopaths, psychopaths, and narcissists to create dependency in their victims. However, while it may account for Miscavige's mood swings—benevolent one minute, savage the next—it does not give a complete picture of *why* he acts and behaves the way he does.

Miscavige's benevolence and brutality are deeply ingrained in Scientology's DNA and amplified by his sociopathic personality. Hubbard issued extensive orders concerning the care of the crew, while at the same time detailing elaborate systems of punishment, many of which called for sleep deprivation, food deprivation, and strenuous physical labor, carried out in isolation away from public view. The result is a highly dysfunctional group, dependent on its leader for direction and identity.

The glue—the big lie—binding it all together is the shared belief in a mission to save the eternal future of all humankind. Whether Miscavige truly believes in that mission and is convinced that each of us has the potential to exist, lifetime after lifetime, retaining the total memory of our past, with no loss of our abilities and experiences just because we "dropped the body," or is merely committed to that belief system as the surest way to maintain his power as a cult leader, is a question that may never be answered.

At the core of that belief system is an intransigent certainty that humankind is on a downward spiral, falling away from our original, godlike state, and that this lifetime is our absolute last chance to do anything about it, to reverse the spiral and lift ourselves out of what Hubbard referred to as "the mud" that is existence on planet Earth, and thereby achieve total spiritual freedom. Underpinning this is the belief that Hubbard will return to Earth to resume his work. In light of all that, Scientologists believe that Scientology must continue to move forward at any cost. So if Miscavige punches you in the face, puts you on rice and beans for a month, locks you up in an ant-infested prison that was once your office, or forces you to sit on scalding hot cement while he ridicules you in front of your fellow staff members—it's because in his mind you did something to interfere with the mission—even though that mission may have devolved into nothing more than Miscavige maintaining his power as a cult leader.

The time I spent working with Miscavige convinced me that it is the strength of his beliefs, in conflict with the impossibility of ever achieving the so-called aims of Scientology, that drives his behavior towards others, and causes his moods to swing from magnanimous to malevolent. Those beliefs appear to have him wound so tightly that anything which threatens to stand in the way of achieving the goals of Scientology will be met with severe consequences. Or perhaps it's just the sadism associated with the so-called dark triad of personality disorders: a cluster of three negative personality traits—Machiavellianism, narcissism, and psychopathy—which all display emotional coldness, duplicity, and aggressiveness.

I've heard some Scientology defectors claim that Miscavige is solely driven by money and power, that he knows Scientology is a fraud. In my experience, that is not the case. Based on my own personal observation and the many one-on-one conversations I had with him over the course of many years, Miscavige is a true believer being slowly driven mad as the predicted date of Hubbard's return slips further and further into the past, and by his having witnessed Hubbard's mental and physical disintegration at the end of his life.

When I first met Miscavige, despite his sociopathic

tendencies, he seemed genuinely to care about people. He would often pull me aside for no other reason than to have a personal conversation. In one such conversation back in the early '90s, with no one else present, he described how he was struggling to restructure the prices for Scientology services in order to make them more affordable, specifically referring to wanting a "cashier at Vons" (a grocery store chain in California) to be able to afford to go Clear. As for following through on that concern and lowering the cost of Scientology, after his dramatic departure from Scientology, actor Jason Beghe, summed it up like this: "At those prices you couldn't clear Beverly Hills, let alone the entire planet."

Before Miscavige implemented the donation-driven Ideal Org program that transformed Scientology churches into opulent edifices, he would often say to me that he thought staff members working at Class V orgs (Scientology organizations that deliver auditing up to the state of Clear) should be paid enough that working at such an organization would represent a viable career option; he thought there should be BMWs in the staff parking lots. I have no idea if he sincerely believed what he said, or just said it to make himself look good at the moment, or wanted to convince me I was working for a righteous cause, but I believed it at the time and genuinely thought he intended to shepherd Scientology to a higher place.

On top of this was the pressure of the many attempts to name him personally as a defendant in legal actions. As the

Captain of the Sea Organization, David Miscavige is its highest-ranking member. Every Scientologist knows that Miscavige is in charge of the Sea Org and Chairman of the Board of the Religious Technology Center, the ultimate guy in charge. If you want to sue Scientology, you need to name him as a defendant. But the Sea Org doesn't have a board of directors; it isn't even a legal entity. When anyone points to the fact that he's the Captain of the Sea Org, he denies it, fearing his position as captain puts him in legal jeopardy, such as with the case of the Lisa McPherson wrongful death suit.

Texas native Lisa McPherson had been a Scientologist since the age of 18. In 1995 she moved to Clearwater, Florida to be closer to Scientology's spiritual headquarters. She'd achieved the level of Clear and seemed to be doing well in life. On November 18, 1995, McPherson was involved in a minor car accident. Shortly after she was seen by paramedics, she began to disrobe, so the paramedics decided to take her to the hospital. McPherson remarked that she had taken off her clothes in hopes of obtaining counseling. Hospital staff agreed that she was physically unharmed but recommended keeping her overnight for observation. Lisa refused to be observed by psychiatrists and checked herself out of the hospital. With the assistance of local staff from The Citizens Commission on Human Rights (a Scientology sponsored organization), she was taken to the Fort Harrison Hotel and put under the care of Church staff.

She died on December 5, 1995, after being taken to a hospital where she was seen by a doctor who was a Scientologist who pronounced her dead. For the last seventeen days of her life she was described as incoherent and sometimes violent. Her nails were cut so she would not scratch herself or the staff, and she supposedly bruised her fists and feet while hitting the wall. Scientology was indicted on two felony charges, "abuse and/or neglect of a disabled adult" and "practicing medicine without a license." The charges against Scientology were dropped after the state's medical examiner was effectively pressured to change the cause of death from "undetermined" to an "accident" on June 13, 2000. Lisa McPherson's estate filed a civil wrongful death suit against the Church of Scientology. The Church settled the lawsuit, and all terms are confidential. Concerned with fear that he'd be named as a defendant, Miscavige became ever more troubled about being identified as the Captain of the Sea Org.

I would often run into him on his way to a meeting or a meal or to review an edit for an upcoming event. On one occasion, what began as small talk escalated to him becoming incensed over recent threats attempting to name him as the "Captain of the Sea Org." He began manically spewing about how they're trying to get him by proving he's the Captain of the Sea Org. But what if he were not the only captain in the Sea Org? "You know what I'm gonna do? I'm gonna make every one of you fuckers a Captain!" He began stabbing a finger at passing staff.

"You're a Captain! You're a Captain! You're a Captain!" Then he pointed at me, shouting, "You're a Captain!" Impossible, since I wasn't even a member of the Sea Org. There was only one person in the entire Sea Organization whose rank entitled him to be called Captain of the Sea Org—and that was David Miscavige. Even as time rolled on, and he traded in his Navy-inspired Sea Org uniforms for a closet full of luxury brand casual clothes, sharp leather jackets, tailored jeans and torso-hugging knit tops, insanely expensive hand-tailored suits, and custom-made shoes, shirts and ties, and, eventually, bespoke platinum cufflinks adorned with a diamond-encrusted Scientology logo, he was still the Captain of the Sea Org.

Perhaps the most bizarre event I ever personally witnessed in all my years working with Miscavige occurred at Gold during a meeting in the International Management PR conference room. It was just Miscavige, a pro writer I worked with, and I. We were having a casual, relaxed meeting. Out of the blue, Miscavige starts talking about the Lisa McPherson case which had been settled years prior. Reaching into a bankers box, he pulled out a folder and placed autopsy photos of Lisa McPherson's naked cadaver on the conference table. Keep in mind that whatever he had with him in the conference room would have been put there that day or recently, so why was he still dragging the McPherson file around? He proceeded to explain how the coroner had said she was dehydrated. "Look at those thighs. She's thunder thighs. Does she look dehydrated?" I could never understand why Miscavige would still be privately defending his innocence after the case had been settled.

According to accounts of some who've known him throughout the years, Miscavige has likely been a sociopath his entire life. Add to that his unyielding belief in the tenets of L. Ron Hubbard, and the fear that if he fails at his mission to keep Scientology working, all human consciousness will be extinguished for eternity, and you begin to get a picture of the pressure that sometimes pushes Miscavige over the edge. He also feels the pressure to deliver on promises made to Scientology's richest donors that their gifts pay for new churches, social betterment programs, the fight to end psychiatry, expensive Super Bowl ads, a broadcast facility, and on and on. Those donors cannot, under any circumstances, be disappointed.

The term "plate" is high on the list of clichés used in the everyday vernacular of Scientologists—"I'd love to help you, but I have too much on my *plate*." Soon after arriving at Gold in 1990 and successfully completing the first film Gold produced in over a decade, I was visited by one of Miscavige's top lieutenants and thanked for getting the Cine Division "off COB's plate." His "thanks" also served to put me on notice that stepping away would push the whole mess right back onto his plate. I had not previously known it was on anybody's plate, let alone a problem for Miscavige. When I first met with CO CMO Gold—the head of the management unit that oversees Gold—

about taking on a technical training film, he never mentioned taking anything off COB's plate.

With the Cine Division now off his plate, Miscavige's time was freed up to engage in other projects, such as battling the IRS for tax exemption. The Cine Division had been a constant source of distraction, consuming Miscavige's time, and pumping the brakes on Scientology expansion. Having been responsible for getting that impediment out of the way, I was subsequently treated with VIP status, literally untouchable as long as I kept agreeing to take on the assignments that were asked of me. There were perks, like being included in that part of Miscavige's inner circle which gathered in the 30-seat, state-of-the-art rushes theater after hours to watch newly released feature films, courtesy of Tom Cruise or John Travolta, while at the same time I was kept in a bubble isolated from internal disciplinary matters. I was only included in the good stuff, so I thought it was all pretty good. I would occasionally notice the sudden appearance of an executive washing dishes, trimming trees, or performing some other humiliating task, referred to as being "busted," (more accurately stated, the person was being broken), but I thought they probably deserved it and that it had nothing to do with Miscavige. That would all change on one hot summer evening.

Under normal circumstances, Gold staff would get thirty minutes for mealtimes, not counting travel time to and from their work location. If you worked on the other side of the base, mealtime could be cut down to a few minutes. There was no leaving a few minutes early to arrive on time. If you wanted to publicly humiliate someone in front of as many staff as possible—as Miscavige was fond of doing—you'd pick a spot near the courtyard where the mealtime foot traffic converged just outside the dining room. I was headed for dinner when I rounded the corner to see Miscavige standing over three executives, screaming at the top of his lungs. There were two men and a woman sitting on the blistering hot cement pathway being publicly humiliated, their tears mixed with dripping sweat. It was too late to change course—I'd already been spotted. He glared straight at me and then, pointing down at the three execs, began screaming in my direction, "That's why you don't have a Dianetics campaign. THAT'S WHY YOU DON'T HAVE A DIANETICS CAMPAIGN." He continued screaming variations of that statement over and over as staff filed by, noticing but pretending not to. We made eye contact as I slowed to a stop and gave a half-hearted nod, then continued on. He'd let his mask slip. I had finally witnessed the brutality he directed at staff members. At that moment, every violent act I'd ever heard him accused of could no longer be dismissed as rumor, I was seeing the evidence of it right before my eyes. Anyone who could subject people to that kind of emotional and physical terror was surely capable of inflicting the kind of physical violence so many had reported. It was at this moment that I realized how much I'd been shielded from the abuse. I walked away thinking, "You motherfucker. You just triangulated me into your vicious drama. Using my position to amplify your cruel rage." That moment utterly changed how I viewed Miscavige, Scientology, and Gold. It was the narrow end of a wedge that eventually dislodged my beliefs.

Truth be told, the real blame for not having a Dianetics campaign lies squarely with Miscavige himself. He physically abused Jeff Hawkins, the person most responsible for the success of *Dianetics* book sales in the '80s. In fact, it was Jeff Hawkins who was reportedly among the first to be physically beaten by Miscavige. Miscavige had dismantled the Marketing Unit in LA, then reassembled it at Gold and issued a string of orders regarding the types of TV spots that he wanted produced. Where Jeff Hawkins had created a marketing campaign intended to connect with book buyers, Miscavige was only concerned with having a campaign he could showcase at international events. The campaigns he demanded weren't designed to perform well with the general public; they were designed to look good and be appreciated by Scientologists. Often, they were based on ideas that would only appeal to Scientologists, rather than the general public. For example, back in the late '90s when direct-to-consumer TV ads for antidepressants were flooding the airwaves, they all followed the same pattern: talk about a mental illness, talk about the benefits of a medication, end with a long list of side effects. Miscavige decided that antidepressants were a direct competitor to Dianetics therapy. I imagined him watching his favorite sporting event on television, seeing one of those ads, and thinking the target market must be the same as for Dianetics: people suffering from depression and/or anxiety—after all, Hubbard claimed the reactive mind was the source of all depression and anxiety, and that it could be gotten rid of with Dianetics. He ordered the marketing unit to produce a series of Dianetics ads mimicking the antidepressant ads but ending with a list of positive side effects, such as more happiness, greater self-esteem, etc. Imagine for a moment a person who is experiencing extreme mental anguish holding a copy of *Dianetics* in one hand and a bottle of antidepressants in the other, trying to decide whether to take medication prescribed by their doctor or search for a solution in the nearly 700-page, very dense, obtuse, and impenetrable Dianetics book. These two things are clearly not in competition with one another. When played to loyal Scientologists at an international event, the ads garnered minutes-long applause. When presented on television to the general public, the ads failed.

The abuse I witnessed that day, when Miscavige forced those three marketing executives to sit on the scalding pathway, was repeated over and over throughout the years. Most of the abuses I witnessed were verbal—but while you may walk away from verbal abuse without immediate physical damage, such abuse can have long-lasting effects on your physical and mental health. When Miscavige wanted to verbally obliterate someone and I was present, he'd direct me to sit on his side of the conference table and be a witness to his anger; apparently being humiliated in front of a non-Sea Org member made it all the more traumatic for his victims. This happened most often with staff from OSA, though it was not limited to OSA staff. No staff were off limits to Miscavige's savagery.

Around 2002, Miscavige came up with what could be characterized as his "Final Solution." Up until that point, he had been satisfied with punching, kicking, slapping, and berating subordinates for failing to perform. But when the entirety of Scientology's upper management had fallen out of favor or, more accurately, had stood in the way of his relentless drive to consolidate power, the final solution kicked in and a hundred or so top executives were held prisoner in their offices—two double-wide trailers that had served as temporary quarters. Beginning in 2004, Miscavige had turned the trailers into a prison, posting 24-hour security guards. He dubbed the makeshift prison "The SP Hole," ("SP" for suppressive person, someone who is perceived as committing destructive acts against Scientology or Scientologists), or simply, "The Hole." Thinking back on my first night in the course room those many years ago, I never would have imagined that the three men who followed Miscavige through the course room that night would eventually be imprisoned by him in the notorious Hole. Marty Rathbun would escape the Hole to become the first high-level church leader to defect and speak out against the abuses of the man he had enthusiastically followed through the course room that night.

Every staff member at Gold knew about the Hole; after all, it was my employer, Golden Era Productions, that provided the security for the make-shift prison. By the Spring of 2010—partly due to media pressure and partly out of fear of an FBI raid—Miscavige ordered a lessening of the harsh restrictions under which the prisoners were being kept. When not locked in the Hole, they were allowed to eat in the dining room and sleep in their apartments, or were forced to study Scientology doctrine for hours on end.

There were usually about eight professionals working at the Base at any given time; a few in audio, a couple of writers, and two or three other directors, all shielded from the abuses occurring just outside our view. For years we ate in a separate building called the "Tavern" decorated with a faux Knights of the Round Table motif. We had longer meal breaks, and weren't required to attend staff meetings or "musters" (assemblies done about four times a day to coordinate production and ensure everyone was accounted for and none had hopped the fence). Not long after Miscavige established the Hole in 2004, he ordered that the pros were to eat in the main dining room with the crew. Looking back at this now, it's obvious that having the pros eat with the crew was just another aspect of Miscavige's totalitarian mind-set—an attempt to absorb us into his machine.

After Miscavige lessened the Hole's restrictions, each day

as we left the dining room heading back to work we would see a hundred or so staff being marched in single file, flanked by Gold security guards. Many of them I had worked with. Browbeaten and downcast, they looked uncomfortable and embarrassed to be force-marched past us. It was obvious they were being disciplined, but I had no idea until the HBO documentary *Going Clear* was released that I was witnessing the Sea Org members who were being held prisoner in the Hole. The other pros and I never spoke about the daily march of the prisoners. Possibly we'd grown accustomed to witnessing the strict discipline the Sea Org imposed on its members, thinking that's what they signed up for. More likely, as most of us were not only working for the Church but were also Scientologists, we wanted to steer clear of appearing to hold any contrary views. Even if we had known the extent of the physical abuse and emotional terror inflicted upon the prisoners daily, I doubt we would have believed it.

I knew most of the security guards at Gold. For the most part, I thought they were decent people. When I eventually discovered the truth about what went on in the Hole, I was astonished that the security guards had so readily participated. There is possibly no greater testament to the extreme degree of thought control and behavior modification that exists within Scientology than that dark episode when David Miscavige set up his own personal Gulag at the International Base and hundreds of staff either participated or turned a blind eye. The guards did what they were expected to do to ensure that the ultimate mission of Scientology was not harmed. Many of the prisoners did what they had to do to survive, fighting to get back into Miscavige's good graces so that they could rejoin the battle to free men's souls. If you interviewed any of the security guards, they would unflinchingly tell you how the Church of Scientology is on the forefront of organizations working to ensure that the UN Declaration of Human Rights becomes a reality. They would not be lying. They truly believed this, even as they marched their human-rights-deprived brethren to their 15-minute meal of cold leftovers.

Scientology eventually issued a statement claiming that the Hole never existed. Eventually it was shut down and its detainees reassigned to menial jobs. Not one, at least none of those I knew personally, went back to their prior positions. Most were assigned to converting mountains of analog material accumulated over decades,—audiotapes, videotapes, photos in all formats, and hard-copy documents—into digital formats that could be retrieved via a database search query. In other words, they were put onto an assembly line to perform mind-numbing tasks. Accepting their fate like dutiful soldiers, they went at their new jobs with a smile—or at least appeared to. Others were assigned to the sets shop, constructing sets for Gold films. When I originally met Greg Wilhere, he was Deputy Inspector General RTC, a superstar known to Scientologists throughout the world. The last time I saw him he was toiling away at a computer terminal working on the digitizing project. Some, like Heber Jentzsch, were less fortunate. By the time Heber was let out of the Hole, he was a physically broken man who required considerable assistance to get around. But his spirit was never broken. The last time I saw him was in 2019. Despite his physical disabilities, he greeted me with no less enthusiasm than he'd shown when we first met at Celebrity Centre back in 1973.

No one deserved the human rights abuses they suffered as a result of being held captive in the Hole, but at least there was one bright spot. The reassignment of the detainees meant there were individuals I'd worked with in the past that I'd never have to work with again in any capacity. At the top of that list was Lisa Allen.

A few months after I arrived at Gold, Greg Wilhere stopped by my office to see how things were going. I literally didn't have a moment to glance up at him as I pounded away on the computer preparing the daily proposal I was required to submit for Miscavige's approval of the previous day's filming. It was a crushing amount of work to be done in less than an hour. Taking notice, Greg said, "You need an assistant."

The next day he brought Lisa Allen around to my office and introduced her as my new assistant. Lisa, who had just been busted out of CMO Int as the HCO Chief, a post responsible for keeping staff in line, was a gangly Australian with a red dye job, an effusively spunky personality, and the exaggerated feminine walk of a drag queen. She immediately set about organizing my office, my time, anything she could get her hands on that could pass as helpful. She snatched up an empty office next to mine and set about establishing her fiefdom as the Director's Assistant. She swapped out my 16-button phone—the one with all the bells and whistles that was reserved for top execs—for the piece of crap phone she'd found in the empty office next to mine. When I complained she replied, "You don't need it. I'll be making all your calls." Unbeknownst to me, Lisa was on a personal quest to regain the status and privilege she'd lost when she was dismissed from CMO Int. The post of Director's Assistant, a title that had not previously existed in the Sea Org, was a plum position and a perfect launching pad for any self-respecting, glad-handing, ladder-climbing, back-stabbing opportunist. Lisa was all that and a bit of a pit viper. She stuck to me like a pit bull chasing a meat truck, photo-bombing my wedding and the birth of both my kids. She proved harder to get rid of than herpes or old luggage. More than anyone else, Lisa made it impossible for me to separate my personal life from my work life. She was good at administrative work, and ran a tight ship. But even when pretending to have my best interests at heart, I could sense it was transactional—always about what benefited her. Most important for her was the halo effect of being the assistant to the person who was getting L. Ron Hubbard's technical training films completed on a regular basis, and she played that card for all it was worth. Daily proposals, such as the one I was preparing when Greg Wilhere stopped by, were usually

SCIENTOLOGY - THE BIG LIE

returned from Miscavige, graded with a "VWD!" "VVWD!!!"
or a "VVVWD!!!!." ("VWD" stood for "Very Well Done.")
In the world of Scientology staff, your completed work was
graded from "Flunk," to "Done," to "Very Well Done." To
get a "VWD" was a very big deal. To denote spectacular
work, Miscavige would add "Vs" and exclamation points. At
that time my work often received extra "Vs" and exclamation
points. When the responses were read out at musters and staff
meetings, the crew would whoop and cheer, everyone sharing
in the win. Nothing could send their spirits soaring like a
spectacular approval on a "rushes submission"—the proposal
seeking approval to use the previous day's shooting—and with
every approval, Lisa would bask in the glow.

It was not long before Miscavige promoted Lisa to
Commanding Officer of Gold. She'd pulled it off, having fallen
from grace in CMO Int, then bounced back as CO Gold and
one of Miscavige's pets.

Like all executives in Miscavige's direct orbit, Lisa eventually
fell out of favor and was assigned to the Hole where she and a
few of Miscavige's other pets had become the unofficial "Lords
of the Flies" charged with the task of obtaining false confessions
from their fellow detainees. According to escapees, Lisa was
one of the primary participants organizing the beatings and
humiliation doled out to individuals who were specifically
targeted by Miscavige to receive special treatment.

Not long after the Hole was shut down, when I noticed the

lot where it stood had been landscaped over and replaced with lush green grass and flower beds—its demise was no doubt hastened by the *Going Clear* documentary—I ran into Lisa. She made a beeline towards me and with her effusively spunky manner, gave a hearty "Hello. I'm now the seamstress in the laundry room. Let me know if you need any mending." I gave her a half-crooked smile and walked on, satisfied that we'd never have to work together again.

Before moving on, I want to make myself perfectly clear as to my view on whether Miscavige is a true believer or knows he's running a con, my answer is—does it really matter? What matters is not why he does what he does, but that he does it at all. He is a danger to public safety and needs to be stopped.

NINETEEN

AN INDUSTRY OF DEATH

A CCORDING TO
Scientology lore, prior to publishing *Dianetics: The Modern Science of Mental Health*, Hubbard offered his new science of the mind to various medical and psychological bodies, including the American Psychiatric Association and the American Medical Association. As the story goes—and as supported by existing documents that are of suspicious origin—his offer was resoundingly rejected. That rejection is often cited as the cause of L. Ron Hubbard going on the offensive against the mental health establishment.

The Hubbard scripted film, *The Story of Book One*, intended for general public consumption, contains a dramatization of Hubbard's offer and subsequent rejection. As Hubbard tells it, the rejection letters were read in the company of his close friends, John W. Campbell—editor of *Astounding Science Fiction* magazine and a towering figure of the "Golden Age of Science Fiction" that occurred from the mid '30s through the early '60s—and Dr. Joseph Winter, an early proponent of Dianetics who later became the medical director of the first Hubbard Dianetics Foundation. Per the film's narrative, upon receiving the rejection, Campbell and Winter implored Hubbard to write a textbook on the subject which would be published as *Dianetics: The Modern Science of Mental Health*. I accepted that story at face value; I had no reason to doubt Hubbard's claim that he'd offered to give the work away for free and was turned down.

As time passed, and as I became more and more exposed to Hubbard's manipulative tactics, I began to doubt whether he had actually offered Dianetics or just made the whole thing up as a marketing ploy concocted to position Dianetics as mental therapy for the everyday person—the therapy *they* don't want you to know about. In reality, those institutions likely would never have responded with a rejection letter at all. But the most compelling evidence to me suggesting that the account was fictitious was a line in the APA reject letter: "If Dianetics amounts to anything, we'll hear about it." Why would the APA letter propose that someday Dianetics might amount to something? By forging the letters, Hubbard was able to simultaneously signal his fake altruism while gaining a key marketing angle that he would repeat many times in the future—that Dianetics, and later Scientology, is a threat to the status quo.

Whatever prompted Hubbard's bitterness towards

psychiatry, it was given a considerable boost on January 4, 1963, when a group of United States Marshals, FDA agents, and Washington, D.C. police officers raided the Founding Church of Scientology. In their sweep through church buildings, law enforcement agents seized more than 100 E-meters and over 200 separate pieces of literature containing approximately 20,000 pages of text. In conjunction with this raid, the FDA charged the Founding Church with multiple violations and sought the condemnation and destruction of the E-meters and their associated literature. The church was accused of making false claims that the devices effectively treated some 70 percent of all physical and mental illness. The FDA also charged that the devices did not bear adequate directions for treating the conditions for which they were recommended.

Whether one or both of these events—the reject or the raid—ignited Scientology's war against the "Psychs," that war would play a central role in the beliefs and activities of every Scientologist, for in Scientology, psychiatry is identified as the most significant barrier standing in the way of its ultimate goal—"planetary clearing." In fact, Hubbard declared, the psychs had been responsible for the decline of civilization for trillions of years.

Within the Scientology universe, there is no shortage of beliefs in conspiracies driven by prolific foes intent on keeping humankind enslaved. It was the Marcab Confederacy, which

Hubbard described as "Consisting of various planets united into a very vast civilization which has come forward up through the last 200,000 years, formed out of the fragments of earlier civilizations. In the last 10,000 years they have gone on with a sort of decadent kicked-in-the-head civilization that contains automobiles, business suits, fedora hats, telephones, spaceships—a civilization which looks almost like an exact duplicate but is worse off than the current US civilization." Hubbard claimed the Marcabs are one of the most powerful galactic civilizations still active. In a lecture titled *Auditing Comm Cycles* given to students on the Saint Hill Special Briefing Course on August 6, 1963, Hubbard stated "It was the Marcabs who invented income taxes as a punishment."

Then there are the conspiracies involving a handful of families—the Rockefeller family being prominent among them—that Hubbard claims form a secret cabal that controls all banking on Earth. Then there's SMERSH, comically named after an actual Russian counter-intelligence operation—originally coined by Bolshevik Party chief Vladimir I. Lenin, implemented during the reign of Joseph Stalin and later featured as a nemesis in Ian Fleming's early James Bond novels. According to Hubbard, all the world's governments had been taken over by SMERSH, and they are controlling the world through psychiatry. Hubbard proposed to defeat the alleged SMERSH infiltration by smuggling Sea Org members into Switzerland, taking over the World Federation of Mental Health in Geneva, and then discrediting psychiatry by using the organization to promote eugenics and mass euthanasia to the United Nations. The plan was abandoned after the Swiss Federal Office of Public Health caught wind of it. And last but not least, there's psychiatry itself—seen by Scientology as a monolithic organization, funded by governments and Big Pharma, with plans to rule the world and enslave mankind.

The first modern skirmish in Scientology's war on psychiatry dates back to the Alaska Mental Health Enabling Act of 1956—back when Alaska was still a territory. Prior to that time, Alaskans deemed mentally ill were considered criminals and imprisoned. Many of the "inmates" were Indigenous Alaskans whose "crime" might have been deafness, dementia, or simply the inability to speak English. Once found guilty of insanity, they were sent far from friends and family and maintained at considerable expense, in a private hospital in Oregon owned by Henry Waldo Coe, a banker, politician, and close personal friend of President Theodore Roosevelt. Allegations of mistreatment and corruption at the hospital led to the passage of the 1956 law. With the passage of the bill, a trust was set up to treat the mentally ill, using funds raised from the management of a million acres of public land.

But some were more concerned with exploiting the land for commercial and recreational purposes than with funding mental health reform. With Communist paranoia rampant in America—from the Commie plot to fluoridate our drinking water to the Red scare takeover of Hollywood or the Soviet sleeper agents supposedly living next door— there was no shortage of conspiracy theories driven by far-right groups and extremist religious fanatics claiming that the Alaska Mental Health Enabling Act was a Communist plot to subvert the United States. Re-branding the bill "Siberia USA," the rumors put forth by these groups took hold and began to spread. Seizing on an opportunity to expand its attacks on psychiatry, Scientology jumped on the anti-Siberia USA bandwagon. In 1978, the trust that funded the bill was closed down, effectively ending the Alaska bill. Scientology wasted no time taking credit for the defeat, claiming: "The country has LRH and Scientology to thank for destroying this master plan that came within hours of becoming law." But the tragic fact was, thanks to the support of the Church of Scientology, Native Alaskans and other underrepresented classes would continue to be falsely jailed for being found "insane" and exploited for financial gain by corrupt officials. Fortunately, in 1985, the Alaska Supreme Court ruled that abolishing the trust had been illegal and reinstated the organization. It was allotted half a million acres that hadn't been given to commercial interests and awarded $200 million as compensation for lost income. To this day, Scientology continues to claim

AN INDUSTRY OF DEATH

it defeated "Siberia USA" when, in fact, the bill had been illegally suspended then later reinstated.

In 1969, in collaboration with Hungarian psychiatrist Thomas Szasz, the Church of Scientology established the Citizens Commission on Human Rights (CCHR). Szasz was author of a 1960 book called *The Myth of Mental Illness*. A rabid critic of psychiatry, Szasz spent his career arguing that mental illness was nothing more than a means of ostracizing outliers, and that treating it amounted to a kind of abuse. Under the banner of Szasz's credentials, CCHR was able to brand itself as a "Mental Health Watchdog," its stated mission to "eradicate abuses committed under the guise of mental health," but its actual mission is the total obliteration of the mental health industry. This is most evident at CCHR's permanent exhibition located on the ground floor of its Hollywood headquarters, titled, "Psychiatry: An Industry of Death," a punch-to-the-gut walk down the history of psychiatry's greatest hits, concluding with a pitch for donations.

The Church purchased the new CCHR headquarters at 6616 Sunset Blvd in Los Angeles with plans to include the museum on the first floor. The plan was to create a self-guided tour centered around a series of documentaries covering the history of psychiatry. The physical museum was to be designed and constructed in LA while the documentaries were being produced at Gold—all of it under Miscavige's supervision. The development of the Industry of Death Museum was not

251

SCIENTOLOGY - THE BIG LIE

my main focus, nor my concern, at least not until I received another request from Miscavige to take it over, as it was barreling towards a cliff. It was a disaster on steroids, making the Life Exhibition fiasco look like a walk in the park. Little progress had been made on the documentaries despite their having been worked on for over a year. The physical exhibition in LA looked like a middle-school science fair project.

I assumed we had a reasonable time frame to get the museum back on track, completed, and ready for a grand opening. After all, the museum's opening had yet to be announced to the public—no need to panic. The first order of business was figuring out how to design a museum— something I'd never done. I organized two teams: one for the documentaries, consisting of two other directors and a pair of writers, and another team for the design and construction of the exhibition, which consisted of a set designer, a construction crew, and technicians to deploy the audio-video elements, as well as a couple of IT guys to handle automation and video feeds. I compiled books on the history of psychiatry and set up meetings with noted museum designers who had worked on such projects as LA's Museum of Tolerance, the Holocaust Museum in DC, and the British Museum. I studied everything I could get my hands on concerning what goes into a successful museum—how long people are willing to stand before you offer them a perch to lean against, how long they are willing to perch before you need to give them a bench to sit on, then a chair, and so on—all of which had been thoroughly documented. Then there were the challenges of cramming a world-class museum into the first floor of a three-story office building, including audio systems—a technical challenge as it would need to accommodate guided tours for VIPs as well as self-guided tours for the general public.

In June of 2005, during his famously combative interview with Matt Lauer, Tom Cruise stated, "You don't know the history of psychiatry. I do." Of course, Tom was referring to information provided by the Church of Scientology via the Citizens Commissions on Human Rights. The following October at the yearly celebration of the International Association of Scientologists, Mike Rinder, then head of OSA, took the stage to give his usual briefing on the Church's fight against psychiatric abuse, consisting of the typical red meat eagerly devoured by the audience. He included the number of psychiatrists put in prison for Medicare fraud, sexual abuse, elder abuse, etc.; the number of corrupt psychiatric facilities shut down; the number of anti-psychiatry protests worldwide; and on and on, culminating with a hyper-energetic, video-game-like sequence of computer animation featuring white-coated, goateed psychs being shot out of cannons, eaten by fire-breathing dragons and then spit out onto a conveyer belt of prison cells, and similar cartoon punishments. At the end of the presentation, Mike spoke about the new CCHR headquarters being readied for the grand opening and revealed plans for the museum. Two blocks of Sunset Boulevard were to be shut down, and thousands would be attending the grand opening and tour of the new CCHR International Headquarters and the Industry of Death Museum. Mike signed off his speech with, "See you there on December 17th." Time froze as I did the calculation—I had roughly seven weeks to get the museum ready for its grand opening. I thought I was going to pass out.

On June 23, 2005, barely six months prior to the opening of the Industry of Death Museum, Tom Cruise sat down with Matt Lauer on the Today show. Responding to Lauer questioning Tom's negative stance on antidepressants, Cruise responded, "Now Matt, Matt, Matt, you don't know the history of psychiatry, I do." With the Industry of Death Museum, Miscavige was going to cram that history down the throats of as many people as he could, and his plan for doing so had just landed in my lap with no time to get it done. If you want to close down two blocks of Sunset Boulevard on a Saturday night—which the planning for the grand opening of the museum called for—you need to apply for a permit at least a year in advance. Miscavige had a permit and therefore knew there was a date set for the opening and never bothered to tell me. I found out about it with all the other suckers attending the IAS celebration. And what about Mike Rinder? The Industry of Death Museum had been his project, and he'd disappeared as soon as I was assigned to it. Little did I know that Mike was absent because he was being confined in the notorious Hole.

This was a typical Miscavige manufactured crisis. As he often did, he would assign a project to a team who might or might not be qualified, and provide them with fewer resources than were needed to get the job done, and withhold the deadline date until there was no time left to get it done. If there is a capable executive overseeing the project—such as Mike Rinder, who was overseeing the museum—be sure you banish them to the Hole or otherwise prevent them from moving the project forward. What you're left with is a whole bunch of people to blame, with Miscavige screaming, "Do I have to do everything myself?"

That was the state of things when the museum project dropped in my lap, and the consequences of failing to get it done were too gruesome even to consider.

The next dispatch I received from Miscavige assured me I'd be provided with whatever resources I needed to complete the museum on time and that he would personally assist me every step along the way. In a dispatch a couple of days later, he informed me he needed to be in Florida and was busy writing speeches for the upcoming New Year's event. To help me with the crushing amount of scripting that needed to be accomplished in record time, he was assigning Gail Armstrong, one of his speech writers, to work with me. I'd known Gail for years. She joined the Sea Org at 22, straight out of journalism school, thinking she'd found a way to make a difference in the world. She had worked as an editor of the Scientology-published *Freedom* magazine—featuring articles impugning those who speak out against Scientology—eventually making it to the International Base as a speechwriter. It was a relief having someone to help with scriptwriting. Two days later, I received another dispatch from Miscavige, "Sorry. I need Gail to help me with speeches. Much love, Dave." There it was. Even though I had two other scriptwriters, one of them a holdover from the team that never got the scripts done to begin with, I was very much on my own.

Whether you believe psychiatry is harmful or offers help to people in crisis, the fact remains that CCHR, in pursuing its stated mission to reform (destroy) the field of mental health, engages in the same greed-driven fundraising tactics as the abusive cult from which it emerged. The Industry of Death Museum is essentially a bloody sideshow meant to scare people into donating for a cause. Of course, I didn't believe that when I supervised the museum's creation; I thought I was involved in a noble cause. But from where I now stand, outside the bubble, it's clear the Industry of Death Museum is nothing but propaganda disguised as a movement for social good. When I created it, I relied only on information that confirmed my own distorted beliefs. Call it confirmation bias or just another instance of the seduction of opportunity—

I was committed to creating a world-class museum showcasing the evils of psychiatry. In the film *Lawrence of Arabia*, Mr. Dryden (Claude Rains) admonishes Lawrence (Peter O'Toole): "A man who tells lies, merely hides the truth. But a man who tells half-lies has forgotten where he put it." In creating the museum for CCHR, I did both. I told lies, and I forgot where I put the truth.

The tour starts with visitors being let into a padded cell, a small screening room with a few narrow uncomfortable benches. Embedded in the wall is a video monitor behind safety wire. The lights dim, a video begins to play, and a manic-sounding narrator tells how psychiatry has invaded every aspect of the viewer's life. Looking at it now (having recently reviewed the online version), the video reminds me of the over-the-top theatrics of a 1950s horror film trailer like *Invasion of the Body Snatchers*, its commie-scare subtext having been replaced by the psych boogeyman and his overlord, Big Pharma.

Exiting the padded cell, the tour takes visitors from the Bethlem Royal Hospital, the torturous insane asylum that became known as Bedlam, established in 13th century London, with its ice baths, patients tied to chairs suspended by ropes then spun 100 times a minute for up to an hour, or chained, naked, to walls. The public were allowed to wander the facility for a fee—an entertaining outing for the whole family when the circus was out of town. In the 1700s, the more "humane" straitjacket was invented. No disputing the facts. Psychiatry's barbaric past is well documented, a past which, in some sense, can be compared to the state of all medical treatments before the advent of anesthesia or antibiotics. In the rearview mirror, the history of all branches of medicine looks pretty scary.

Moving into the 20th century, there were exhibits showing the development of the lobotomy, which erroneously claimed that the psychosurgical procedure was inspired by railroad construction foreman Phineas Gage, who survived having a steel rod blown through his skull. No evidence exists that his injury inspired any type of psychosurgery, but it made a great story. In truth, the Phineas Gage incident resulted in the successful inquiry into better ways to remove tumors from the brain. But the myth that Phineas Gage's injury inspired the lobotomy remains, to this day, one of Scientology's favorite psych-bashing tropes: like Siberia USA, it is based on a fictitious interpretation of an actual event.

The display featuring the inspiration for electroconvulsive therapy was, however, based on historical fact. ECT had been inspired by Italian neurologist Ugo Cerletti, who witnessed pigs being given electric shocks to the head to make them convulse and drop to the ground, making it easier to slit their throats. It was believed that convulsions were a treatment for various mental disorders such as schizophrenia, so Cerletti adopted the slaughterhouse technique for human use.

Next, there was a display covering the mid-century behaviorist B. F. Skinner, who famously said, "Give me a child, and I'll shape him into anything." Visitors learned about a form of aversion therapy straight out of *A Clockwork Orange*, which claimed that "sexual deviants"—some of whom were just teens—were shown pornographic images while attached to a device that measured the circumference of their sexual organ. If it detected an increase, an electric shock was administered.

By the time visitors got through the last display, they had been subjected to a litany of hyperbolic horror stories. Some, such as Phineas Gage's brain injury, referenced actual historical or scientific facts that had been distorted to suit a false narrative. Some of the threads, such as psychiatry's connection to the 9/11 attacks, were entirely fabricated with no basis in fact or reality. Among the claims: psychiatry was responsible for racism, the Holocaust, countless suicides due to the side effects of psychoactive medication, mass shootings, and the September 11 attacks. One of the advantages of having a devil is that you can blame them for anything.

Every department in Gold's Cine Division was assigned to get the museum completed in time for the grand opening. The schedule was grueling. For seven weeks I'd work till about 4 AM and then be back to work at 10 AM (though many of the staff I was working with told me we were on a country club schedule compared to some days). One particular display was intended to be a rogue's gallery, framed portraits of psychiatry's greatest offenders. It has about the same impact as looking at a stranger's high school yearbook. I thought a chart showing the history of psychiatry would be more effective. The only problem was the history of psychiatry is not like the history of baseball; you can't simply show it a decade at a time. You need something more like an evidence board. So I laid out a 3-by-8-foot piece of white butcher paper across the floor of an unused space near the editing bays and began sketching out the design for the definitive two-dimensional graphic display of the history of psychiatry. I was on my knees, working it over, when Jenny Linson dropped in.

I first met Jenny when she was a little girl. Her mother Lil, ex-wife of film producer and Jenny's father Art Linson, had been a close friend prior to her joining the Sea Org. Jenny was reputed to be one of Miscavige's more vicious attack dogs. Together they formed a two-person hit squad that Miscavige sent out to do his bidding. I was so used to seeing them together—and having fallen into the toxic Sea Org culture of giving people pejorative nicknames—I thought of them as "Zip and Pip" in honor of the inseparable pin-headed twins from Tod Browning's 1932 cult classic *Freaks*. I'd always gotten along with Jenny. That I'd never had a run-in with her was likely due to my being on Miscavige's good side—and that, because of my friendship with her mom, I was a family friend of a sorts. Jenny had been harassing me daily for the past couple of weeks, her single message, "You know COB is counting on you to get this done," and always ending her harassment with, "You're it!" Apparently, she thought her job description included badgering people.

That particular night when Jenny entered the room, as I knelt on the floor diagramming the history of psychiatry, I could no longer take it. She must have said five times in a row, "COB-is-counting-on-you-to-get-this-done. You're it!" I thought about rationally explaining to her that she was not being helpful and that her badgering only served to ramp up the stress. Instead, I opted to address her in what I believed was the only language she'd understand. I stood up and turned to face her. Then, in a calm, steady voice, I said, "Jenny, I have hardly slept in weeks. I'm so stressed out that I constantly feel like I'm going to puke. If you say that to me one more time, if I hear you say, 'You're it' one more time, I am going to shove your head through a wall." She turned and walked out without responding.

Miscavige had been back at the Base for a week or so when he paid me a visit. With a smile that seemed intended to throw me off balance, giving no clue as to his mood, he said, "I hear you had a run-in with Jenny." Thinking things were about to get uncomfortable, I responded, "Yeah, I probably shouldn't have told her I was going to shove her head through a wall." Miscavige gave a sardonic chuckle, then replied, "I don't care if you do." He seemed dead serious.

The field of mental health has had its share of successes and failures. Some in need of treatment are fortunate to respond positively to psychiatric medication—I personally know several people who claim to owe their lives to their meds, and I believe them. Some are fortunate enough to find a mental health practitioner with the skills and compassion to lead them out of a dark place and onto higher ground. Solutions do exist, but are not always as accessible as having a broken limb set. The Church of Scientology points at psychiatry's failures and says, "Give us your money, and we'll fix the problem." But they never do. The Citizens Commission on Human Rights can blast its message as loudly and as often as they wish, but it only serves to dissuade people from seeking help. In my view, the Industry of Death Museum was, at best, a wasted opportunity to inform the public that real help exists and that there are alternatives to such controversial practices as ECT and anti-psychotic drugs. At worst, by demonizing the entire field of mental health, it dissuades people from getting the help they need.

The final documentary in the museum was dedicated to delineating the history of CCHR and to extolling its many victories, including a thunderously self-serving account of Scientology's so-called defeat of the Alaska Mental Health Enabling Act, the defeat that never happened. On February 14, 1992, David Miscavige appeared on Ted Koppel's *Nightline*, claiming that Scientology's defeat of the "Siberia USA" bill was the cause of the psychiatric industry's attempts to destroy Scientology. According to Miscavige:

I don't know if you're aware that there was a plan in 1955 in this country, Ted, to repeat what was done in Russia. There was going to be a Siberia, USA., set up on a million acres in Alaska to send mental patients. They were going to lessen the commitment laws. You could basically get into an argument with somebody and be sent up there. This sounds very odd. Nobody's ever heard about it. That's in no small part thanks to the Church of Scientology. I must say, though, that when that bill was killed in Congress [sic], the war was on with psychiatry where they declared war on us, and I want you to understand something.... It was a major, major, major flap for the psychiatrists when it got voted down, because then the slogan around the country began, 'Siberia USA,' and it was really the first time that psychiatry had been denigrated publicly, that they weren't the science that they had been promoting themselves to be. And they took it upon themselves then to start dealing with anybody who would oppose them."

—David Miscavige, *Nightline*, 1992

Miscavige had a vested interest in maintaining the myth that Scientology's defeat of the Alaska bill had so infuriated the psychiatric industry that, in turn, it was the cause of legal and media attacks on the Church—that it was the stick that poked the devil in the eye. In order to survive, a cult needs a god—a central authority—and a devil. In Scientology's case, it has Hubbard as god, and psychiatry as the devil.

CCHR staff believe they are dedicated to eradicating abuses in the mental health industry, without ever realizing

SCIENTOLOGY - THE BIG LIE

that they are pawns in Scientology's game. The game is played to fool the public into thinking Scientology's formidable foe, the psychiatric industry—and not the blowback from its own abuses—is the cause of the legal and media attacks that are sinking its reputation.

A few days before the grand opening, Miscavige requested a tour of the completed museum. The last of the 18 exhibits, dedicated to CCHR, was designed to be a breath of fresh air compared to the claustrophobic horror show you had to slog through to finally arrive at the grand finale. You would think Miscavige would hold the soldiers on the front lines of Scientology's war on psychiatry in high esteem, or at least give them their due. But instead, at the end of the tour, surveying the space, Miscavige paused, looked around and slowly took it all in. Then he turned and said, specifically referring to the CCHR staff, "I hope these motherfuckers appreciate what we handed them on a silver platter," high praise for the foot soldiers.

The grand opening came off without a hitch. Miscavige freed Mike Rinder from the Hole just long enough to act as the main speaker. Dignitaries, celebrities, and garden-variety Scientologists eager to hurl a metaphorical beer bottle at the psychs, watched as a parade of mental health reformers, appointed and elected officials, and academics thanked CCHR for its tireless public service.

Despite the technical complexity of the museum, once the

doors were open to the public, tours flowed through without a hitch. Visitors were provided with museum-grade wireless headphones plugged into a personal receiver while group tours and VIPs heard the audio via surround-sound systems. All the audio and video files were fed to the displays via a fiber network from a central server. The various objects that made up the displays were of extremely high quality; much of it had been produced by the Gold sets crew and scenic artists, some of whom had been trained by some of the best motion picture studio painters in the business. One of the benefits of being on Miscavige's good side was being able to get requests instantly approved. I happened to mention to him one day that none of the Gold scenic artists knew how to paint. Instant approval was given to bring in professional set painters to apprentice the sets crew. One of the CCHR exhibits had a faux brick wall that I had asked to be painted so as to appear moist and mildewed, as though from a leaking pipe. When the building inspector did the final walk-through, he noted that the water leak would have to be repaired before the museum could open. We had to explain that it was a painting effect—the Gold set painter's work was that convincing.

In the months to come, a local nursing school would require its students to attend the museum as part of its curriculum on mental health treatment. Audio production classes from the nearby Los Angeles Recording School were sent to the museum to study examples of high-quality playback installations—a requirement of their curriculum. Hundreds of visitors were subjected to a horror show of trauma-inducing videos, featuring psychiatric patients being electroshocked and lobotomized, patients sent into uncontrollable seizures caused by insulin poured into a tube inserted through their nose and into their stomach, and glassy-eyed and motionless orphaned children on powerful antipsychotics strapped to beds in Soviet mental hospitals. And on and on. If you slow down at traffic accidents hoping to see a dismembered body, the Industry of Death Museum is for you.

Not long after the museum opened, Jenny Linson handed me a gift bag. Inside the bag was a custom T-shirt, designed and printed just for me. Across the chest, in bright putrid yellow, was a representation of a puddle of vomit, emblazoned with the word "IT."

TWENTY

IDEAL ORGS: LOOKS GOOD ON PAPER

R EGARDLESS OF
variations in architectural design or square footage, religious
sites within a given faith all share common elements: a Torah, a
depiction of the Crucifixion, a marker indicating the direction
of Mecca, a statue of the Buddha. Yet despite the variations
from one site to the next, when you set foot in any of them, you
sense an unmistakable atmosphere shared across all the interior
spaces of each particular religion. By 2003, in the nearly 50
years since the founding of the first Church of Scientology,
the most significant visual cues common to all Scientology
Churches were a receptionist behind a counter, a framed photo
and bronze bust of L. Ron Hubbard, and one or more staff
sitting at desks signing people up and taking their money for
the paid services being delivered in the various rooms beyond.
The atmosphere felt more retail than religious.

Built in the late '90s, Wikipedia describes the Cine Castle

at Gold as "in the style of a Scottish castle," which would be accurate if Scottish castles were covered in sprayed-on stucco and had their turrets and arched entrances underlaid with styrofoam. But in any case, on paper, the Cine Castle's sound stage met the requirements of any sound stage in Hollywood.

The oversized hallways of the 74,000-square-foot in-house film studio are roomy enough to accommodate a small car. Sometimes the hallways were filled with tables on which hundreds of pages of Hubbard-authored text were laid out for review. I don't recall the exact date, but it was sometime in 2002. A section of the Castle's long hallway was lined with easels, each supporting a board displaying mounted photos of existing Scientology Class V organizations.

L. Ron Hubbard was obsessed with hierarchical organization. He sold many of his "basic principles" of Scientology as existing on some form of scale—a graduated range of values with the least desirable trait at the bottom, and the most desirable at the top.

Hubbard's Emotional Tone Scale is a good example. Using scales, he could claim his discoveries had the precision of engineering—a claim he made without ever presenting any research to back it up. But the big daddy of all Scientology scales is known as "The Grade Chart." Emblazoned across the top of the Grade Chart are the words, "The Bridge to Total Freedom." From this is derived the nickname "The Bridge."

The Grade Chart delineates the precise (paid) steps one must take in order to ascend Scientology's levels of "spiritual awareness." One side of the Grade Chart lays out the training steps. The other side, the auditing steps. Two Scientologists meeting for the first time will inevitably ask each other two questions; "Where are you on the Bridge?" and "Where are you 'on lines?,'" ("On lines" being the name of the organization where one does their Scientology services).

The organizations that sell Scientology services—retail Scientology—are organized according to the levels of the Grade Chart they sell. At the bottom are Scientology Missions, beginner organizations offering basic Dianetics and Scientology services to Scientology members and to the general public.

Next there's Class V organizations, which offer Grade Chart services up to Clear and auditor training up to Class V. Beyond that, there are the Saint Hill's, known as Class VI organizations because they train Class VI auditors. Then there are the advanced organizations offering the confidential OT levels. Lastly there is Flag, which Scientology brands as its spiritual headquarters— meaning they have more cash registers and credit card machines than any other type of Scientology organization, enabling them to complete the transactions to purchase their "Flag only" goods. And ultimately there's Scientology's "floating Cathedral," the cruise ship Freewinds, which offers Scientology's most coveted level—operating thetan level 8, or OT 8.

But the bread-and-butter organizations are the Class V orgs, each named after the city where it is located, such as the San Francisco Org, Miami Org, or London Org. I was there in the hallway at the Castle that day because Miscavige wanted to give me a personal tour of the photos, pointing out with disgust the pitiful state of our Churches: storefronts in strip malls, walk-ups over appliance repair shops, and the like. He grunted in disgust that there was no way Tom Cruise could bring his powerful associates to any of these Orgs. They were an utter embarrassment.

What I was seeing was the first step in a massive project to upgrade all Churches of Scientology, transforming them into what Miscavige referred to as "Ideal Orgs." That the program first took shape in the Cine Castle at Gold is a fitting testament to the program's ultimate outcome, which for the most part resulted in glittering showplaces intended to forward the narrative that Scientology is expanding. That narrative was either a deliberate fiction, intended to safeguard the Church's tax-exempt status while giving rise to the greatest fundraising campaign in the history of the Church, or it was Miscavige's honest belief that he'd found a magic lamp, and all that was needed was to release the genie and the new Ideal Orgs would fill with crowds of people clamoring for Scientology. What better place to refine the myriad details needed to plan a network of eye-catching architectural interiors than a movie studio?

Since the launch of the first Ideal Org in 2003, the Church of Scientology has opened a total of 64 Ideal Orgs (as of 2023).

In numerous online blogs, detractors have speculated that the entire project was just a scheme to convert Scientology funds into real estate holdings, driven by the requirements of its tax-exempt status to spend money for the public good.

On the other hand, maybe Miscavige truly believed that a new generation of Churches that even Tom Cruise would be proud to show off to his cohorts, was the answer to expanding Scientology's flagging membership. But beyond swapping out the existing Org buildings, housed in crappy structures located in sketchy neighborhoods, what would it take to make an Ideal Org ideal? In other words, what would it take to sell the idea to the Scientologists who would be called upon to donate the funds to pay for the buildings—sometimes going deep into debt, liquidating retirement and college funds, even losing their homes? To answer that question, Miscavige did what he always does when implementing a plan to get the public to buy more and do more—explain how a book, or a building, or a method of instructing Scientology, or a Scientology auditing procedure, did not align with what the founder intended, and that he has now single-handedly solved the problem, and everyone needs to pony up.

To purchase new buildings to replace the existing Churches, as well as to open new Churches, we had to nail down every detail that needed to be incorporated into those new Churches. Miscavige handed me some Hubbard references to study. According to Hubbard policy, the Public Division, or Div 6, should occupy one-third of a Class V Org. Hubbard advised putting Scientology posters on the walls and having promotional literature available in Div 6, but that was about it. At that time, an average Div 6 in a Class V Org usually occupied one or two small rooms in a remote part of the building and was difficult to locate even if you had a floor plan. Miscavige also gave me a reference where Hubbard stated, "They will know us by our MEST," (an acronym for Mass, Energy, Space, and Time,) implying that the public will know Scientology by the quality of its buildings—the physical space and its contents.

The importance of Div 6, the Public Division, cannot be overstated. Div 6 consists of three separate departments; Div 6A which is responsible for getting new people into Scientology, Div 6B which is responsible for running introductory courses, and 6C, which is responsible for getting existing Scientologists to open new Scientology activities. In essence, Division 6 was the lifeblood of any Scientology public organization, for this is where the con begins.

For years Miscavige had struggled with how best to broadly answer the question, "What is Scientology?" A book of that title had been published and fizzled out. Films of that title had been discussed, written, and then abandoned, all intended to answer that question. It was no small matter then, when Miscavige sent me a dispatch, boldly claiming to have finally figured out the answer. He wrote, "Tell them to go to the Org." He believed that if the Orgs were of a high enough quality and contained the perfect amount of accessible information, the public would look around and say, "Oh, so this is Scientology. Cool." That was the spark that ignited the Ideal Org Program. Most importantly of all, the driving force behind this effort was the pressure to comply with the requirements of Scientology's tax-exempt status to spend money for the benefit of the public.

So that was the assignment. The Orgs were too small and embarrassingly unimpressive. The Public Division needed to occupy a third of the Org, but no one knew exactly what that meant, because no one knew exactly what should go into that space. A third of what? A few posters and some literature wouldn't cut it, not in an audiovisual age. Furthermore, the Church was sitting on a huge pile of cash that it needed to spend for the "public good" or risk losing its tax-exempt status. To pull this off, Miscavige needed to convince Scientologists that he'd found a magic formula so powerful that it guaranteed the expansion of Scientology. He proclaimed that every Org was deficient for not containing the ideal Public Division as laid out in Hubbard policy. With that problem solved, Scientology Churches would be so busy they'd barely be able to keep up with the flow of new people coming through the doors. But what should the interior of an Ideal Church of Scientology look like? What should it contain? To sell it to the public, Miscavige would have to figure out how to connect it back to Hubbard policy—to be able to take to the stage at an international event and tell the public that, within the technology of Scientology, he had uncovered Hubbard's exact intention for Div 6 and for the first time in the history of Scientology, it was being implemented—or some bullshit like that. The story of how he connected the design of Div 6 back to Hubbard begins with the production of the technical training films.

When I first began tackling the training films back in 1990, the art department was run by a dour woman in her thirties who incessantly commented that I was destined to join the Sea Org. In my observation, Sea Org members who tended to make a big deal out of my not being in the Sea Org were usually the first ones to hop the fence and disappear, which is exactly what happened with her. In keeping with the tradition at Gold of telling demeaning stories about any fellow Sea Org member who escaped, she had supposedly "hopped the fence" (a local euphemism for escaping,) to rejoin an ex-husband, (whom she'd known when she was a helicopter mechanic in the Army), gave up Scientology, and returned to her former practice of witchcraft. I wasn't disappointed to see her go. She had only limited experience designing sets for a small-town community college, and when it came to designing sets for film, we agreed on nothing. Everything was a problem. Everything was an argument. Her 22-year-old assistant, a slender Swede in his early twenties, who I thought was immensely talented, was immediately promoted to art director. I took him on as a mentee; even going so far as hiring noted British production designer of *Star Wars* fame, Alan Roderick-Jones—who I'd worked with on TV ads—to help my new art director design our little sci-fi extravaganza, the technical training film *Why TRs*, featuring *Isaac Hayes*.

By the time we'd completed most of the tech films, we'd figured out what the interior of a Scientology Church should be comprised of. At least that's what Miscavige was claiming in a dispatch in which he pointed out that, in the course of designing the films, many of which were set in fictional Churches, we'd figured out what exactly a Scientology space should look like.

Subsequently, the problem of working out the design of Division 6 fell on my new apprentice and me. It was a far bigger problem than anyone was aware of, because without knowing the exact specs of Division 6, no new buildings could be purchased or renovated.

Miscavige often and loudly voiced his mistrust of Scientology staff members. His paranoid resentment of staff rested on his belief that any staff member who tried to explain Scientology to new public would fail at it miserably. While Scientology's early success was in no small part due to the talents of lecturers who would give weekly talks introducing Scientology to new people, Miscavige wanted the existence of the Public Scientology Lecturer stamped out, pulverized, and assigned to the waste bin of Scientology history. What he wanted was a foolproof way that new people could come in and find out about Scientology without the liability of speaking with a staff member who would surely mess up the "comm cycle," (Scientology-speak for back and forth communication). In his own words, Miscavige wanted a means to introduce new people to Scientology that was "push button," as simple as, "Just add water." Referencing the displays done for the Industry of Death Museum, he described a video-based, self-guided tour comprised of an array of video displays, each covering an aspect of Scientology, its founder, and its various "social betterment" programs. The plan was to build the complete interior of an Ideal Org Division 6 in the studio. That way, we'd know for certain what the target size for the new Ideal Orgs would be. The studio was cleared out and for the next 18 months I did nothing but work on the concept and design of the ideal Div 6. No filming was permitted in the studio. All shooting was done on location by another director I'd bought on to help.

After countless iterations we settled on the final design—or I should say we finally proposed a design which Miscavige approved. With that, we built an entire working prototype, laying out every element that should be included in an Ideal Division 6: the public displays, public film rooms, conference rooms, lounges, a café, and on and on, right down to the bathrooms. The final concept occupied 20,000 square feet. The magic number had been cracked. The target size for all new Churches was 60,000 square feet, allowing Div 6 to occupy a third of that space.

The Ideal Org program was organized on a massive scale. To accommodate a project of that size, Miscavige hired the internationally renowned architectural firm Gensler Associates, a global design, and planning firm with fifty-three locations across Asia, Europe, Australia, the Middle East, and the Americas. The architectural work for the Ideal Orgs was handled out of Gensler's Santa Monica offices. At the height of the program, Gensler had a dedicated team of seventy architects, designers, and support staff, headed by principal architect Irwin Miller, the head of Gensler's Santa Monica, California office. Interestingly, nowhere in Gensler's promotional literature, either online or in print, does Gensler or Miller ever mention their work for Scientology. Yet within the Church, Miller became a darling of the Scientology Ideal Org fundraising crowd, a welcome guest at fundraising events, and a VIP invitee to international events.

Gensler would be responsible for adapting our prototype public division displays design to the interior design of each Ideal Org. That meant presenting our designs to Gensler's San Francisco office and its creative team known for their work on Niketown and the Apple Store. The presentation lasted most of the day. When it was done, I could finally step away from building the prototype Ideal Div 6 that would be incorporated into every Ideal Class V Org. Everything in an Ideal Org was deemed "Ideal:" ideal bookstore; ideal café; ideal course room; and so on. Miscavige seemed to have a fetish with the word "ideal" as though repeating a word made it more true.

Next came the fundraising stage. The first of the new Ideal

Orgs was planned for Tampa. Miscavige sent two of his most formidable representatives, my old friend Jenny Linson and Angie Blankenship. Together they obeyed their order to make the local Scientologists responsible for funding their new Ideal Org. Miscavige used funds under his direct control to purchase the building and then make the local Scientologists responsible for raising the funds to repay the mother Church, sometimes charging the parishioners two to three times the actual cost of the purchases, all the while the parishioners thought they were purchasing the building, not just outfitting it. And that was how it went, building after Ideal Org building.

If you're wondering why I cover this subject in such detail, consider this. While the Ideal Org program has been described by detractors as a land grab, a way of increasing the Church's assets while fulfilling its obligation to exist, at least in part, for the public good, I believe it actually began as a legitimate program that David Miscavige truly believed would boom Scientology.

When the crowds of Scientology-hungry public never showed up, and when the Church failed to recruit enough staff to properly run the new Ideal Orgs, what was left looked exactly like what the critics described, a land grab. I say this because every bit of the time and effort we spent perfecting the Ideal Division 6 and the Ideal Orgs overall, as well as the time spent on seeing that the final results were properly exported, was entirely done with the firm belief that it was going to be a smashing success.

Miscavige continues to chase that illusion, raising more and more money to buy and renovate new buildings and with each completed project, announcing Scientology's expansion. Like Sarah Lockwood Winchester, heiress to the gun fortune—who according to legend kept carpenters busy building her mansion, supposedly haunted by those who had been killed by the company's guns and thinking the sound of hammering kept the ghosts away—Miscavige seems to think the incessant drive to open new buildings will somehow fulfill his self-proclaimed prophecy that Scientology is expanding, while keeping the IRS boogeyman away.

TWENTY-ONE

THE INTERNET BREAKS SCIENTOLOGY

We have come to the conclusion that Scientology is
not only an abusive cult, but that it aids and abets
a general climate of Western media self-censorship.
If the west [sic] can not defend its cultural values of
free speech and press freedoms against a criminal
cult like Scientology, it can hardly lecture China and
other state abusers of these same values.

> —Julian Assange,
> Wikileaks Press Release,
> April 7, 2008

I N   H I S   S H O R T   S T O R Y,
Burning Chrome, science-fiction novelist William Gibson
coined the term "cyberspace." He later popularized the concept
in his highly acclaimed 1984 debut novel, *Neuromancer*. Gibson
envisioned cyberspace as a vast computer network controlled
by global corporations that had superseded world governments.
The story centers on a group of mercenary criminals who secretly
work to free an artificial intelligence. With *Neuromancer*,

Gibson presaged the Internet, and his vision of cyberspace was a war zone where freedom fighters would struggle against evil corporations. As the Internet grew to supplant all previously existing forms of communication, and became the central engine of commerce, it represented a substantial threat to free speech and privacy. In response, in Gibson's novel, and later in real life, a new type of activism arose.

The Church of Scientology has never understood the Internet, and never saw it coming. In 1991, the newsgroup alt. religion.scientology sprang up, partly as a joke and partly to discuss the pros and cons of Scientology, but the Church didn't notice. Not until 1995 when Scientology's most confidential "scriptures," the OT materials, were posted on the newsgroup did Scientology take action. Lawyers representing Scientology contacted various newsgroup participants, posting warnings demanding that they cease the unauthorized distribution of OT materials. The lawyers described the documents as "copyrighted, trademarked, unpublished trade secrets," and proclaimed the distribution of the materials to be in violation of copyright and trademark law. But the actions of the Scientology lawyers only served to bring additional attention to the matter and launched Scientology's reputation as a self-interested corporation bent on censoring the Internet.

In the early 1990s, Scientology sought to counter, its substantial negative online presence by creating positive content. It launched a campaign designed to assist Scientologists in creating their own websites on which they could share the benefits of Scientology. This initial gambit proved to be an embarrassing disaster. All Scientologists were encouraged to participate. They were given CD-ROM discs containing a program designed to walk them through the process of setting up a "personalized" website. The websites were basically variations of the same template. You could change fonts and colors, and that was about it. Only a few hundred of these sites ever appeared on the web, and all of them were so similar there was no chance anyone would think they were authentic. Even worse, the CD-ROM installed filters on the unsuspecting Scientologist's computers, intended to block the Scientologists from encountering material the Church deemed offensive. The conclusion, echoed broadly on the Internet, was that Scientologists were mindless robots who do not think or act for themselves. I received a copy of the CD-ROM, and after exploring its contents, I can attest to how utterly lame it was.

As the fiasco of the cookie-cutter websites drifted into the past, for all intents and purposes it appeared as though Scientology was doing its best to ignore the Internet. At least there were no significant public efforts to engage. That would suddenly change in 2004 when Miscavige decided to honor Tom Cruise by awarding him the Scientology Medal of Valor, specifically designed for Cruise, to be presented at the International Association of Scientologists event held yearly at Scientology headquarters in the UK. A hallmark of the

IAS event was the medals, worn Olympic style, presented to Scientologists in recognition of spectacular achievement in support of Scientology's "social betterment" programs, such as bringing down psychiatry or spearheading literacy and morals campaigns. Whenever these awards were handed out, the recipient would be introduced with a short video featuring their accomplishments. At that time these medal winners' videos, as well as the overall event were produced at Gold. I rarely contributed content to the events as I was busy working on films, but I did take notice of Tom's video as it progressed in editing. The video featured highlights from Tom's career and his various successes promoting Scientology. But the capper was an interview with Tom wearing a black turtleneck, proclaiming what Scientology meant to him. My first impression was how closely he seemed to mirror Miscavige's signature intensity. In the years I worked for Scientology, I had many interactions with Cruise—the Tom Cruise we know from the red carpet, being gracious to his fans, not the overbearing Tom Cruise who was interviewed by Matt Lauer or Peter Overton. Having been introduced to Tom as a key member of Miscavige's inner circle, "This is the guy who makes our films," it was not at all surprising that my interactions with him were positive. I always found Tom's public persona to be upbeat, respectful, and intensely focused. But the intensity he showed in IAS video was different from anything I'd ever seen. He had become a fervent believer. His tone and delivery, as well as the statements he made, were perfectly suited for the Scientology audience for which they were intended.

On January 14, 2008, that interview showed up on YouTube overlaid with music from *Mission: Impossible.* Someone had stolen a DVD of the IAS event and leaked it to the Internet. In the wild, playing to a broad, non-Scientology audience, Tom's statements, rather than being those of an ardent follower, came off as the rantings of a manic, fire-breathing zealot. The Church responded by claiming the video had been pirated and edited from a three-hour presentation. Under threat of litigation, YouTube took it down, but by that time the video had propagated onto other sites such as gawker.com, which deemed it newsworthy and refused to take it down. To the internet's new brand of free speech activists, Scientology's efforts to have the Cruise interview expunged from public view was nothing less than a blatant attempt to censor the internet. This did not sit well with the denizens of the anonymous imageboards.

Anonymous imageboards such as 4chan.org were established in the early 2000s for the purpose of sharing images related to a wide variety of topics—from anime and manga to video games, weapons, literature, history, politics, and sports, among others. Anyone can simply go onto one of these sites and post anonymously; no registration is required. It was from these imageboards that the collective of Internet vigilantes, calling itself Anonymous, sprang into existence, gaining international attention when it declared war on Scientology.

In response to Scientology's efforts to take down the Cruise video, Anonymous organized a series of distributed denial of service attacks (DDoS) against Scientology servers. Such attacks bombard servers with more requests than they can handle, effectively shutting them down. On January 21, 2008 Anonymous uploaded a video to YouTube declaring its intention to erase Scientology from the Internet and ultimately dismantle it.

This was not Anonymous's first campaign against what it considered to be corporate threats. Sony had sued a hacker by the name of George Hotz, accusing him of stealing a software key that would allow anyone to access PlayStation games for free. Hotz claimed he was fighting for the consumer's right to do whatever they wanted with something they'd already paid for. In support of Hotz, Anonymous fired off a battery of DDoS attacks aimed at Sony store servers. In the ensuing cyber battle, thousands of Sony user identities, including credit card numbers, were stolen. Anonymous claimed the theft was not their doing and blamed it on a cybercriminal taking advantage of the situation. Remaining true to their manifesto, Anonymous didn't show up to protest at Sony corporate offices or retail stores. Like Russian hackers taking down a power grid, they waged war in cyberspace, not in the real world. With their war on Scientology, all that would change.

On January 28, 2008, a second video appeared on YouTube entitled *Call to Action*. Its stated purpose was to organize protests outside Churches of Scientology to take place on February 10, 2008. How exactly did this group, known for launching its attacks from the shadowy corners of the Internet, suddenly leap out of cyberspace to transform into a bunch of placard-carrying, Guy Fawkes mask-wearing protesters meeting on street corners in front of Churches of Scientology? Was Anonymous the real-world equivalent of William Gibson's AI, breaking its cyber chains and leaping into action IRL (in real life)? Did they actually revise their manifesto to include taking their grievances to the streets—a move antithetical to the very notion of waging war on the Internet? Or did a small group of hackers intending to cause as much trouble for Scientology as they possibly could without ever leaving the glow of their computer screens, accidentally discover that their latest prey came preloaded with thousands of individuals— ex-Scientologists, Scientology haters, human rights activists, and college students who thought it was cool to don a Guy Fawkes mask and possibly get laid—who were just waiting for an invitation to attend global protests? After all, the original *Message to Scientology* video had been produced and uploaded by a lone individual, one of 4chan's original Anons, a hacker by the name of Greg Housh—or at least that's what Housh claims.

In fact, all of the initial shots Anonymous fired at Scientology could have been accomplished by no more than a handful of people working in concert to take over botnets controlling tens of thousands of PCs in order to launch DDoS attacks, send black faxes, make prank calls and order large quantities of pizzas to be delivered to Scientology organizations. That small group posting on 4chan, claiming to be a movement but resembling more a kid playing with a book of matches in a dry forest, ignited a global protest movement without ever leaving their basements, and Operation "Chanology"—a portmanteau of 4chan and Scientology—was born.

Amongst many imageboard users, Operation Chanology was often suggested as a joke, just another target for the Internet Hate Machine to toy with. For more than eight months, the admins over at 420chan had been regularly removing any thread that suggested Scientology as a target; calling it the dumbest idea they had ever come up with. An internal power struggle broke out amongst the old guard imageboard users—those with actual hacking credentials—and the new users—mostly wannabe hackers—who became active with Operation Chanology. As their numbers swelled, the newcomers outnumbered the original group. What had been a joke, became a serious movement as the newcomers genuinely saw Scientology as evil and something to crusade against.

Once the press got wind of Operation Chanology, their message was broadly repeated, and a bandwagon effect took over. Suddenly, protesting against Scientology became a cool thing to do. Anonymous focused the anti-Scientology movement like a magnifying glass focuses sunlight; and for a while, the Church of Scientology was caught in the smoldering beam. Thousands of individuals harboring anti-Scientology sentiments began participating in Chanology's online dialog. All that was needed was for a Pied Piper to come along and lead them into the streets.

That Pied Piper came in the form of Mark Bunker, a regional broadcast journalist who had single-handedly taken on the cause of reporting Scientology's abuses—eventually getting himself elected to the Clearwater City Council in the hometown of Scientology's spiritual headquarters, the Flag Land Base. Bunker was a one-man militia with what appeared to be a seemingly boundless personal vendetta to bring down Scientology. It was Bunker, rechristened "Wise Beard Man" by the Anons, who first began posting the idea that Anonymous should engage in legal street protests, as opposed to DDoS attacks and other illegal activities, to avoid having the movement curtailed by law enforcement. On 4chan and other imageboards, most outside requests for Anonymous to engage in someone's personal vendetta received the curt response, "Anonymous is not your personal army." But, apparently in Bunker's case, they made an exception. On February 10, 2008, approximately 7,000 people protested against the Church of Scientology in at least 100 cities worldwide. Many more protests would follow over the next few years.

At the International Base, alarm bells sounded. A war room was set up. Miscavige wanted a plan. How was the Church going to retaliate against this new global threat? I was conscripted into the ad hoc dream team that would lead the counterattack. Miscavige brought the full might of the Church's media production and legal resources to bear. Private investigators were aimed in the direction of Anonymous protesters. Security at all Churches was beefed up. OSA went on high alert. Daily threat assessments were calculated, and strategy briefings held. Information about the protesters began to flow in from the PIs, some of it highly inflammatory, such as a report that one supposed Anonymous "leader" in Los Angeles was employed as a production manager in the porn industry. With a few buckets of dirt in hand, we began making anti-Anonymous videos.

Per Hubbard's written policy, the operating slogan in such matters is "Always attack. Never defend." Always attack the attackers. None of the videos we made actually addressed any of the issues leading to the attacks. Scientology never responds in that way, believing that doing so would be defending, not attacking. Scientology's online reputation was that of a corrupt entity, so it reacted exactly as you'd expect a corrupt entity to react, flooding the Internet with slick anti-Anonymous videos that looked creepily like something out of the Matrix—not my best work or proudest moment. Scientology operatives kept a sharp eye on the protesters, sometimes mingling in the crowd. If they saw anything that looked suspicious, they'd bring it to the attention of law enforcement (with whom Scientology has a suspiciously cozy relationship). Sometimes the Scientology PIs would just make something up, giving the cops an excuse to question the protesters, forcing them to reveal their identity. In the case of the "porn production manager" and supposed Los Angeles Anonymous ringleader, he'd posted a photo of a firearm on his blog—having nothing to do with Anonymous or Scientology. OSA pointed this out to the police claiming the guy was a threat and had him arrested. He later died by suicide in an unrelated incident.

Beyond the cyber attacks, for which a few individuals were tried and received prison terms, there were real threats of physical harm in the real world. Of course, Anonymous being anonymous, the source of the threats could never be traced back to members of the Anonymous movement.

A small Scientology mission in Glendale, California, was targeted with an anthrax scare, triggering a substantial response from police and fire. I was living in Glendale at the time, when I received a call from my next-door neighbor, a member of the famed LAPD anti-terrorism unit that had thwarted the planned al Qaeda attack on Los Angeles International Airport, after which they set their sights on the Twin Towers in Manhattan. Knowing that I was a Scientologist, he phoned about the anthrax scare and asked if I needed any help. RTC executive Warren McShane, Deputy Inspector General for External Affairs, contacted me to let me know a security detail would be keeping an eye on my home for a few days. The anthrax scare turned out to be a prank; harmless white powder in an unmarked envelope.

In early March following the initial protests, Miscavige called an emergency meeting to discuss how to counter the presence of Anonymous protesters at the yearly event, held in Clearwater, Florida, celebrating Hubbard's birthday on March 13. In attendance were two of Miscavige's personal attorneys, the OSA external security chief, a pro writer, some miscellaneous RTC legal staff and Laurisse "Lou" Stuckenbrock Miscavige's omnipresent assistant and rumored paramour. The first topic of discussion was how to mitigate the visual presence of the protesters along the route the public would take as they made their way into the auditorium. We had the advantage of knowing the protesters would have to secure a permit and that they'd be limited to protesting in the area allowed by the permit. We knew protesters would be standing on a long narrow sidewalk in front of a stark and sinister-looking chain-link fence. I thought the chain-link fence, acting as a backdrop, would enhance the menacing quality of the protesters. I proposed wrapping the fence with a long continuous banner decorated in bright colors with balloons, streamers and "Happy Birthday, Ron" in four-foot-tall lettering. Forcing the protesters to stand in front of that backdrop made them look foolish and gave the impression that they were interrupting a festive event which could then be characterized as bigotry aimed at a religion. My proposal was adopted.

In addition to my birthday decoration idea, Miscavige

suggested a more direct approach for interrupting the protesters.

As it turned out, the anthrax hoax aimed at the Glendale, California Scientology Mission had been part of a coordinated effort by the Church's dirty tricks department to make Anonymous appear to be a terrorist organization. Miscavige intended to have private investigators track down local protesters, many of whom he was certain were young people still living with their parents and send PIs to their homes to rat them out. He was convinced that when mom and dad found out that "little Johnny" was in cahoots with terrorists, they'd be grounded. In fact, it was far more likely that parents of protesters, especially in Clearwater, would share their offspring's dislike of Scientology. Having a PI show up at the door to inform them their son or daughter was exercising their First Amendment right to protest would probably be met with a door slamming in their face—after which they'd give "little Johnny" a pat on the back and maybe a bump in allowance. Having joined the Sea Org at age sixteen without ever having children of his own, David Miscavige was utterly clueless regarding family dynamics. Nonetheless he ordered his plan be put into action.

The birthday event was held the first Saturday after March 13. Approximately 200 protesters showed up at the Clearwater venue to have their photos taken in front of the colorful "Happy Birthday, Ron" banner, while on that same day thousands of

Anonymous protesters showed up at Scientology organizations around the globe.

Despite the vast amount of information the Church amassed on Anonymous, and despite all the work we'd done to help counter their attacks and paint them as an anti-religious terrorist branch of the Internet Hate Machine, I remained convinced that the attacks had begun simply as a prank by online troublemakers who had accidentally kicked a hornet's nest of disparate Scientology haters.

Miscavige and OSA had a vested interest in pumping up Anonymous as a formidable foe rather than a small group of pranksters who caused existing anti-Scientology movements to coalesce into one massive effort—remember, cults need a devil to flourish. It made it easier to play the victim if Anonymous was a Goliath rather than a handful of geeks living in their mothers' basements.

In an attempt to tease out what I believed was the real origin story of the Anonymous anti-Scientology movement, I secretly, without any authorization and in my spare time at night, set up an anti-Anonymous YouTube channel designed to look as though it was created by one of the original protesters who'd triggered the movement in the first place and was now using YouTube to ridicule the protesters for having taken the prank so seriously that they were willing to take to streets. I suspected that the original Anonymous hackers who attacked Scientology online, were in reality a small group that had stayed true to their manifesto to do battle exclusively on the Internet, and above all to remain anonymous. While creating anti-Anonymous videos for Scientology, I'd spent considerable time on 4chan, 711chan and other imageboards, reading the chatter and cross talk regarding project Chanology while absorbing its language and culture. I noticed a considerable number of negative posts commenting on the protesters, referring to them as losers with no real power of their own. They were apparently despised by the original Anonymous "hacktivists" because, lacking any hacking skills, they had turned to demonstrating in the real world where they hoped to meet up with their fellows and party on for the LULz. The Anons were happy to see Scientology being attacked, while at the same time deploring the Guy Fawkes mask-wearing "pawns" demonstrating in the streets.

So, I created the YouTube channel, AnonPawnBeGone and posted several videos, executed in the unmistakable style of the original *Message to Scientology* video, except that this video was meant to call out the protesters for having strayed from the original Anonymous manifesto to wage war on the Internet, not in the real world. Before long I began receiving private messages from an individual identifying themselves as one of the original Anons, claiming the videos were exactly on point and supporting my belief that the individuals who triggered the whole thing had never participated in the demonstrations, as they never operate in the real world. I had no reason to doubt their authenticity. None of this made the protests any less valid

SCIENTOLOGY - THE BIG LIE

or deserved. In fact, in my mind, the fact that a prank could explode into a global protest movement meant Scientology's reputation was far worse than anyone imagined.

Regularly scheduled strategy meetings to deal with the ongoing Anonymous protests continued to be held at the International Base. Linda Hamil, the Commanding Officer of OSA, and OSA spokesperson Karin Pouw, and a few other OSA staff, had taken up residence in an office located near the Gold editing bays. No one noticed when I entered the office for the day's meeting, they were all huddled around a computer monitor and fixated on the screen. Linda turned to me and asked, "Have you seen this?" On the screen was my YouTube channel playing my original message to the pawns (protesters). I hesitated for a moment, then unable to resist, replied, "Yeah. I created it." They all froze, literally speechless. After a long and uncomfortable silence, the meeting came to order. Even though I'd committed the grievous sin of acting on my own without authorization—something for which I could have been severely reprimanded—no one from OSA ever mentioned the YouTube channel. I am certain it was out of fear that they'd be blamed for not knowing I created it outside their purview.

As much as I wanted to explain that, as far as I was concerned, the entire Anonymous fiasco was triggered by a small group, I could never find the right moment. They needed their gargantuan foe; any other explanation would not be believed. Plus, it didn't really matter if the entire Anonymous anti-Scientology movement was triggered by a small group of hackers playing a joke on Scientology, who then stood by and watched as an angry mob burned down the city or were themselves among the huge mob of torch and pitchfork carrying participants. It was all the same: the intensity and frequency of the protests had shown that Scientology was reviled around the World.

Following the Anonymous protests, the Church of Scientology spent millions and expended tens of thousands of man-hours attempting to improve its online reputation. They hired high-priced experts in reputation management and search engine optimization (paying one firm $100k a month), as well as spending millions on online advertising. Thousands of hours of new media were created, and existing media reorganized specifically for the web, covering all aspects of Scientology and the organization. At the same time, reports of alleged abuses against its members and staff only increased, adding fodder to the anti-Scientology movement. When considering the need to counter Scientology's rapidly deteriorating reputation, led in no small measure by the Internet Hate Machine, Miscavige would often repeat Hubbard's battle cry to "fill the vacuum." He strongly believed there was a vacuum of truthful information regarding Scientology, and that vacuum was being filled by hatemongers. The solution to rescuing Scientology's reputation was to fill that vacuum with thousands of web pages hosting hour after hour of glossy self-promotion. But no matter how hard Scientology tries to "fill the vacuum," as long as it continues to cover up its abuses and as more and more Scientologists defect and become whistleblowers, publish books, speak out to the press, and launch social media channels dedicated to exposing the truth about Scientology, Miscavige has been unable to stem the tide of a growing public bent on seeing the organization and its leader held accountable. He would, however, spend $100 million to establish Scientology Media Productions, referred to as S-M-P, a broadcast facility whose sole purpose was to fill that vacuum once and for all and, as Miscavige put it, "to fuck them up," referring to the media he claimed had treated him unfairly.

As for the Anonymous movement, like so many individuals and organizations who interacted with Scientology over the years only to find themselves dispersed and deflated, Anonymous's battle with Scientology would be their last hurrah, with the exception of a few skirmishes trolling Trump, calling out ISIS, and supporting women's rights they've pretty much disappeared from the landscape, cyberspace or otherwise.

TWENTY-TWO

SUPER POWER:
INSIDE THE REALITY DISTORTION FIELD

A super fantastic, but confidential series of
Rundowns that can be done on anyone whether
Dianetic Clear or not that puts the person into
fantastic shape unleashing the Super Power of
a thetan... It consists of 12 separate high-power
rundowns which are brand new and enter realms
of the tech never before approached.

—LRH

BUD TRIBBLE WAS ON
the team that designed the original Apple Macintosh
operating system. But apart from his work on the Mac OS
interface, Tribble is perhaps best known for his use of the
term "Reality Distortion Field" to describe Steve Jobs' ability
to—as fellow Apple alum Andy Hertzfield put it—"convince
himself, and others around him, to believe almost anything
by using a mix of charm, charisma, bravado, hyperbole,
marketing, appeasement, and persistence." Tribble attributed
the phrase to an episode of *Star Trek* titled "The Menagerie,"—

considered by many to be the greatest *Star Trek* episode of all-time—where it was used to describe how an advanced alien society created its own virtual reality through mental force. L. Ron Hubbard could also be said to be a master of the Reality Distortion Field, as is David Miscavige after him—though Miscavige's technique calls for applying physical force as well as mental force. There is perhaps no better example of Scientology's Reality Distortion Field than the series of auditing actions and physical drills known as Super Power.

The history of Super Power begins with the development of the original Hubbard-directed technical training films. Back in 1978, Hubbard directed his staff to begin studying filmmaking. At that time, he was in Sparks, Nevada, where he had fled seeking refuge after the FBI simultaneously raided the Scientology complex in Los Angeles and its headquarters in Washington, D.C. The raid resulted from an investigation into the Church's infamous Operation Snow White, under which Church operatives infiltrated and wire-tapped government agencies for the purpose of purging documents critical of the Church. In all, eleven top Church executives, including Hubbard's wife Mary Sue, were sent to prison for their part in the program, which was later deemed to be one of the largest infiltrations of the United States government in history. Hubbard was named as an unindicted co-conspirator, but otherwise successfully evaded any blowback from the Snow White fiasco. Returning to his La Quinta base of operations, he began working in earnest on his technical training films.

It should have surprised no one that Hubbard had great difficulty accomplishing film production. After all, Hubbard was the only one working on the films who knew anything at all about filmmaking, but he had no practical experience in film production. He ordered textbooks for his staff to study and learn what they could. Needless to say, the tech films got off to an abysmal start. Instead of attributing the production difficulties to a lack of experience or talent, Hubbard concluded the crew's failures were the result of spiritual deficits. To address this, Hubbard developed twelve individual "rundowns"—a "rundown" being a scientific-sounding term used to designate an auditing process that addresses a specific subject or area of a person's life. The first eleven rundowns fit the conventional model of Scientology auditing, taking place in an auditing room with an auditor, a preclear, an E-meter, and instructions from a case supervisor. The twelfth rundown—the "Perception Rundown"— was unlike anything Hubbard had previously concocted. Hubbard surmised that humans have a total of 57 sense channels or perceptions, and that past trauma results in mental "charge" (negative mental energy) that inhibits a person's ability to perceive. Once the charge on a specific sense channel is resolved with auditing, the person performs drills focused on each perception, thus increasing their ability

SCIENTOLOGY - THE BIG LIE

to perceive and to communicate. Unlike the first eleven audited Super Power Rundowns, which were compiled from existing technical information as instructed by Hubbard, he left no specific instructions for the perception drills, only a list of the 57 perceptions and an order to produce drills for each one. By the mid-2000s, none of the perception drills had been completed—no small problem as Super Power was the main marketing driver being used to capture donations for the new Flag building, which was currently under construction. The Perception Rundowns were slated to take up the entire fourth floor of the new five-story, 127,000-square-foot Flag Building; to keep public interest high, and donations rolling in, Miscavige would need to tease the public about the upcoming Super Power release. While the audited Super Power rundowns had been completed, the Perception Rundowns had barely gotten off the ground. To make matters worse, the Perception Rundowns were being produced under the auspices of the Church of Spiritual Technology (CST) which was woefully unequipped for the task. Before L. Ron Hubbard departed this Earth, he established three separate corporate entities, each with separate but equal authority, to carry on after his death. They were: the Church of Scientology International, which would be in charge of running Scientology organizationally; the Religious Technology Center (RTC), which controls and oversees the use of all of the trademarks, service marks, symbols, and texts of Dianetics and Scientology; and the Church of Spiritual Technology (CST), which owns all of the copyrights, trademarks, services marks, and texts of Dianetics and Scientology. He set it up this way so that no one entity or individual could gain control of the Church. Unfortunately, he hadn't anticipated the cunning of David Miscavige who had gained control of all three corporate entities.

I received an urgent communication from Miscavige briefing me on the status of the Perception Rundowns. He stressed that the Perception Rundowns were being produced by CST and that Gold was strictly forbidden from having anything to do with the project. All resources—including personnel and finances—had to be kept entirely separate. He hinted that this was a requirement of the Church's tax-exempt status. How my participation figured into that equation, I never found out, and honestly didn't care to know.

He revealed that they'd set up a confidential skunk works in a warehouse in the middle of Hollywood, where they had designed and built a couple of the key machines needed for the Rundowns. The machines were impressive space-age-looking devices, sculpted out of anodized aluminum and stainless steel, that looked like they belonged in a lab at NASA, perfect for being filmed to produce a teaser that could be used at fundraising events. They'd also assembled a small team of computer artists and technicians, all Sea Org members and including the art director I'd apprenticed on the tech films, but they were making slow progress. In addition to the Super Power project in Hollywood, CST had hired a company in Florida that specialized in designing and building attractions for theme parks—kind of a bush-league version of Disney Imagineering. Despite having worked on the project for a couple of years and billing the Church $2 million dollars, they had hardly made any progress and Miscavige was growing impatient. It was time to begin showing donors the fruits of their donations, yet there was nothing tangible to show.

I was standing not far from where I had witnessed Miscavige terrorizing those three executives over the lack of a Dianetics marketing campaign when Marc Yager rushed up, the way people do when they've been looking for you. "COB wants you to get the Super Power Perception Rundowns done. You can use any resources at Gold." Strange, I thought. I can use any resources at Gold. I wondered what happened to the admonition that Gold was absolutely forbidden from being considered a resource for producing Super Power. I knew better than to ask, for that kind of benign curiosity would only cause suspicion.

The first thing I did was fire the Florida company. The only thing they actually managed to do was to acquire the rights to some stock footage that was intended to be used in one of the drills. In this drill, you strapped yourself into a kind of gimbal seat, not unlike that of a machine gunner in a WWII bomber, or even more apropos, a seat in one of the gunner bays on the *Millennium Falcon*, like the one Luke Skywalker famously mounted in order defend against the Empire's TIE fighters. You'd strap into the gimbal seat and then a highly realistic movie would play on a small video monitor in front of you. The monitor was attached to the gimbal chair, simulating the view out the front window of a vehicle. There were various films you could choose from: a death-defying roller coaster ride; a high-speed drive on a twisty mountain road which eventually misses a corner and flies off into space; a wild ride in a runaway mining cart; or the view from a train as it careened down the narrow ledge of a snowy granite mountain, hugging the tracks for dear life. The motion of the gimbal chair provided a physical sensation, while the on-screen visuals—which played in sync with the chair's motion—provided the visual cue that tricked your brain into thinking the motion you were seeing was actually the motion you were experiencing. You were also hooked up to an oximeter that read your heart rate and displayed the beats per minute on the screen in front of you. The purpose of the drill was to enable you to use your mind to lower your heart rate. As you began to "zoom through space," your heart rate would climb. If you concentrated on the fact that what you were experiencing was an illusion, your heart rate would lower. The goal was to get it to return to normal. The participant believed they were actually controlling their heart rate. In reality, they were merely taking notice that there was no danger. The images that played on the screen were the only part of the project that the Florida company made good on. However, when it came time for them to deliver the goods, they were only able to provide prints from the original negatives. Two million dollars well spent.

There was a mountain of research to get through and very little time to do so. In going through all the documentation that had been compiled thus far, I noted that there were no instructions from Hubbard on how to design or operate the drills. All the material had been compiled by CST staff and was, in my estimation, their best guess on how to design drills for each of the 57 perceptions. In addition to the audio-video material needed as part of the drills, "orientation videos" were needed that comprised two or three minutes of material instructing the participant how to do the drill. One particular drill was intended to teach participants "relative size," meaning the relative size of their physical body versus everything else in the universe. For the orientation video of this particular drill, CST had purchased the rights to Charles Eames' classic documentary short film "The Powers of Ten," a film dealing with the relative size of the universe and the effect of adding another zero to the number 10 over and over. The film opens on a straight down angle at a couple having a picnic by a lake. The frame captures an area of one meter square. The camera jumps back, adding one zero to cover an area of 10 meters square. In a matter of 23 such jumps, we reach the edge of the universe, 100 million light years out. And then the action reverses until, in not that many jumps, we arrive at the nucleus of an atom. I have great admiration for Charles Eames. I hated the idea of trivializing an Eames film, utilizing it as an add-on for one of the Super Power drills. Any number of filmmakers had already made their own version of "Powers of Ten," the most notable version was produced for IMAX and narrated by Morgan Freeman. So, I thought hell, I'll just make a new version appropriate for Super Power.

Many of the drills were actually fun. In fact, if you had encountered some of them at an amusement park or science expo, you would not be disappointed. But inside the Reality Distortion Field—at a cost of thousands of dollars—those drills led participants to believe they were gaining super powers. When all the drills were complete, I flew to Clearwater to supervise the final installation. Up until this point I'd been working remotely with the staff at the Flag Building to get the drills installed.

The fourth floor of the Flag Building looks like something out of a science fiction film, lots of translucent or transparent glass etched with geometric patterns. The surfaces were all a gleaming atmospheric light blue, white, and stainless steel. The lighting was soft and shadowless. I spent four days, 12 hours a day, on the fourth floor getting everything ready for Miscavige's inspection. By the fourth day, I began feeling very disoriented. I'd already been having mental issues, experiencing extreme anxiety, a fear of flying and claustrophobia, none of which I could explain. After all, I was an OT and had done a considerable amount of Scientology auditing and training. I felt I was on the verge of having a complete mental breakdown. Something, SOMETHING, was amplifying whatever was troubling me mentally. Then it struck me. I was suffering from extreme color deprivation. I'd spent most of four days in an environment devoid of all color except silver, white, and light blue tones. I don't even know if color deprivation is a thing, but at that moment I quickly exited the building and just started staring at anything with color, and sure enough, I calmed down. No one was expected to stay in that environment for as long as I had. Participants would spend a couple of hours a day in there. The staff who work on the floor would be in and out of their offices, not stuck on the floor. Standing on the sidewalk in the late afternoon, drinking up the colors of everything I could get my eyes on, my mind settled and my wits returned. I should have spotted it then, but I didn't. Something was happening to me. I was starting to deteriorate mentally.

By the fifth day, everything was ready. All the drills were in place and functioning as intended. Miscavige arrived with his usual entourage and the tour began. He approved the entire thing with only a few modest changes.

But for me, there was no sense of relief or accomplishment.

The years and years of pressure, of seeing staff abused, of never knowing when I'd get home, or when I was home, when I'd get that call to drop everything and get my ass up to the Base, had taken a toll. I was divorced, I had two kids I rarely saw, and I was so rattled I did not think I could set foot on an airplane.

Tom Vorm was an executive with CST. An inordinately tall fellow with a strange, gangly gait. And an awfully nice guy. I'd been working with Tom since I started on the Super Power project. Miscavige caught wind of the fact that I was in no shape to fly and ordered Tom to rent an SUV and drive me back to LA. The Church's in-house travel agency arranged for luxury hotels along the way, mostly at high end resorts. The drive was a welcome distraction, except for the West Texas Plains with their never-ending vanishing points, rolling past like an endless film loop. The drive seemed to unspool the pressure I was under and by the time we reached the Arizona border, I'd pretty much decompressed.

The new Flag Building opened later that year. Super Power was a bona fide success. As I toured the fourth floor with a group of 30 or so Scientology public members—scores of such groups would tour that day—I couldn't help but think that all these people thought Hubbard had envisioned the Super Power Perception drills and had left detailed instructions concerning how to design and operate each drill. In fact, nothing could be further from the truth. The drills involving audio-visual elements were a product of my art school education coupled with a hefty imagination. The rest of it was just a creative group of young Sea Org members making shit up that seemed to fit the bill.

It was just one giant Reality Distortion Field.

TWENTY-THREE

NARCONON REDUX

I DON'T REMEMBER
the exact year David Miscavige left the International Base,
setting up shop at Author Services, Inc. in Hollywood, never
to return to the Base again, but in a one-on-one conversation
he made it clear that he was fed up with all the people at the
Base who had, as he put it "fucked me over," and who he never
wanted to see again. I assumed he was mainly referring to
the hundred or so executives he'd held captive in the Hole—
the ones that hadn't escaped. Personally, I thought he feared
the day one or more of the detainees might get violent and
take him out. But it was certainly before 2014 that he vacated
the International Base, leaving behind the $50 million office
building he'd supervised as the plush headquarters for his
relatively small staff. I recall he hadn't been at the Base in
some time when I received an urgent request to meet him at
Author Services to go over plans for reinventing the Narconon

drug rehabilitation program. That request came via my friend and writing partner Timothy Jones. (I'm using a fictitious name for privacy reasons. Timothy is deeply embedded within Scientology's Reality Distortion Field, and I have no reason to call him out.) I was just finishing up lunch when Timothy appeared, breathless and energized, saying "We're going to LA, the boss wants to meet." Any excuse to leave Gold was welcome, especially when it meant being closer to home at the end of a workweek, and an invitation to meet with Miscavige was particularly welcome. Keep in mind that despite a few rough conversations we'd had over the years, things between Miscavige and me were generally pretty chill. I always thought he made sure to keep it that way because it meant a higher likelihood I'd defend him if called upon to do so, and of course if something having to do with film or media blew up, he could always count on me to solve it.

All film production at the International Base must be part of a plan that has been approved by David Miscavige—from this arises the often-heard phrase, "approved planning." For the prior six months or so, Gold had been producing a series of films to be included in an update of the Narconon program. What followed is pretty much the anatomy of a major production fuck-up in the Cine Division of Golden Era Productions. To be specific, we were producing films that were assumed to have been approved at some planning stage, but were later discovered not to be what was wanted. How big the disaster was when the fuck-up was discovered depended entirely on Miscavige's mood.

Narconon is run under the auspices of The Association for Better Living and Education, otherwise known as ABLE. It comprises four Scientology-sponsored social betterment programs: Applied Scholastics (Scientology's secular outreach that aims to export its educational tools to schools); Criminon (the Church-sponsored rehabilitation program for prison inmates); the Narconon Drug rehabilitation program; and, the Way to Happiness Foundation (dedicated to disseminating Hubbard's non-religious moral code of conduct). These organizations were originally established and run by the old Guardian's Office—which Miscavige disbanded after Operation Snow White. These "social betterment" programs were specifically run so that the Church could point to its good acts—they are essentially puff-PR-piece-generating, do-gooder machines.

ABLE International, the governing body over the four programs, was once a strictly secular organization staffed by public Scientologists under the auspices of the Church of Scientology International. Miscavige restructured ABLE International so that it is staffed solely by Sea Org-only members, while the individual programs remain staffed by non-Sea Org Scientologists. ABLE International, located on Hollywood Boulevard in a building that was once the headquarters of the Screen Actors Guild, happens to be

SCIENTOLOGY - THE BIG LIE

conveniently located next door to ASI. After leaving the
International Base, Miscavige took up residence at the El
Cadiz apartments on Sycamore Avenue located directly behind
ASI. The Church had purchased the building for his use and
had constructed a secret tunnel so he could travel undetected
between the El Cadiz and ASI.

Security at ASI was tight. There was the usual complement
of a couple of Sea Org security guards in uniforms that
resembled rent-a-cops, as well as two or three private security
guards who could pass for ex special forces—the type who'd
retired, returned to Iraq as independent contractors, and then
took work with a private security firm that contracted with the
Church. They favored tactical cargo pants and military-style
desert boots. They were friendly enough, but no small talk—
ever. When you arrived at the ASI parking structure, if there
was a desert-boot-wearing-Glock-carrying private security
guard on-duty at the gate, then you knew Miscavige was in
the house. When Timothy and I pulled up, the private security
guard pushed the intercom button to let the receptionist know
to open the gate. We were instructed to park and head over to
the ABLE conference room next door.

The first leg of the meeting was just Miscavige, Timothy,
and me. He was in a pretty good mood. The agenda was a
briefing on the recent Narconon fiasco.

Narconon had been under intense fire in the media. On
July 24, 2012 *The Oklahoman*, an online news service reported

on deaths at Narconon Arrowhead, Narconon's flagship training and rehab facility in Oklahoma. The story said:

> After the death of 20-year old Stacy Dawn Murphy at a Church of Scientology-backed drug rehab program in Pittsburgh County, the state enacted a new law to provide more oversight of drug and alcohol rehabilitation centers.
>
> However, Narconon Arrowhead, where Murphy and three other clients died, continues to operate legally because the law allows only limited supervision from the Oklahoma Department of Mental Health and Substance Abuse Services.
>
> "I am very surprised they are still open, I sure am," said Gary Richardson, a Tulsa attorney who represents former Narconon Arrowhead clients and their parents, including Murphy's parents, in nearly a dozen lawsuits against Narconon.

Murphy had just returned to the center after a brief home visit. According to Sheriff Joel Kerns, "It appears she brought back with her prescription drugs that she did not have a prescription for." Staying true to his vulgar way of framing a conversation, Miscavige's version of the story had Murphy returning from a weekend pass with a condom containing heroin "stuffed up her cooch." He did not mention that she'd been left unattended for two hours in the withdrawal section of the facility when, tragically, she died of an overdose. The Church was being sued because Narconon never explicitly stated anywhere in its policies that smuggling drugs into the facility was forbidden. In other words, Murphy hadn't broken any rules and Narconon was being sued for having failed to look after her well-being. According to Miscavige's always-blame-the-victim point of view, in Murphy's case, the lawsuit was due to her greedy parents looking for a payday."

These lawsuits brought the entire Narconon program under Miscavige's intense scrutiny. He was intent on exposing any vulnerability in the Narconon program, its policies and procedures—anything that might have contributed to their being held liable for the deaths of clients in Narconon's care, and to revise the program so that they could never be sued due to a client's death. According to Miscavige, the Narconon program, had been kludged together over the previous decades, and it was time for a full revamp. The program originally began in a California prison when heroin addict and convicted felon William Benitez read Hubbard's *The Fundamentals of Thought* and was inspired to create a drug rehab program based on Hubbard's description of core human abilities. Benitez wrote to Hubbard from prison, Hubbard gave his blessing, and Narconon was born. As time went on, various components were added to the program: the *Purification program*—the sauna, nutrition-based detox; "objective processes" that supposedly returned a person's attention to present time after drug use had knocked them about; *The Way to Happiness* book—a study of Hubbard's moral code; and some study of the principles contained in Scientology ethics, intended to help the person disentangle themselves from their drug culture connections and behaviors. While Scientology-based elements formed the bulk of the Narconon curriculum, it wasn't branded as Scientology. Miscavige wanted to throw the entire program out and create it newly from scratch.

The first step was to expunge William Benitez as the original founder of Narconon. Miscavige wanted Narconon re-credited as being "based on the discoveries of philosopher and humanitarian L. Ron Hubbard," and that was that, no more Willie Benitez. The other big change was to expunge *The Way to Happiness* from the Narconon program. As Miscavige explained it, one of the precepts in *The Way to Happiness* calls for individuals to be "temperate." Apparently Narconon clients, upon reading that precept, thought it meant they could take drugs and drink alcohol in moderation.

Following our briefing, Gary Smith, the Executive Director of Narconon International, joined us. Gary was a rough looking ex-addict who'd been a Narconon executive for a couple of decades, most notably running the Narconon Arrowhead flagship facility where Stacy Murphy had died. If Gary had been in the Sea Org, he most certainly would have been sent to the RPF. But as a public Narconon staff member he would be spared the RPF and only subjected to months of brutal interrogations. Miscavige briefed us as though Gary would be participating in the revamp, but I never saw him again in the year or so that I worked on getting the program redone. He was, as they say, disappeared.

The Narconon revamp, was a huge deal in Scientology. New buildings for Narconon facilities on all major continents had been purchased, including actor Larry Hagman's hilltop mansion in Ojai, California, with the intention of turning it into a five-star, celebrity-worthy luxury rehab. Massive renovations of all Narconon facilities were taking place. Every aspect of the program, from new policies to ensure Narconon was complying with the law, to uniforms to give the staff a polished, professional look, to new study materials and films, were being developed, documented, and put in place. The films were being produced to guide the Narconon clientele as they progressed through the program, and of course furloughs were banned. If a client left the facility before they had completed the program, they were not allowed to return. To further insure against a repeat of the Stacy Murphy episode, a drug-sniffing dog was acquired for each facility. But for me, the good news was, I'd be relocating to LA for the duration of the Narconon project and working out of ASI.

The large office on the fourth floor of ASI was set up to accommodate about ten people. It had a million-dollar view of Hollywood Boulevard, looking out at the El Capitan Theater across the street, and was only a few doors down from the famed Chinese Theater and the home of the Academy Awards ceremony, the Dolby Theatre, formerly named the Kodak

Theatre. Between tapings of *Jimmy Kimmel Live!* show at the El Cap, and premieres and awards shows at the Dolby, traffic could sometimes be a nightmare, but parking was never an issue as ASI had parking for about 200 cars and only needed space for about 30.

The office would do nicely for Timothy and me, a place to settle in and get to work on reconfiguring the Narconon Program. The only drawback was that the space was sometimes a thoroughfare for anyone needing to get to the other side of the floor or to the large office next to us that was currently being occupied by Danny Sherman, the official L. Ron Hubbard biographer and Miscavige speech writer, lap dog, and apologist. Working with Danny was the ever-present biographer's assistant, Fleur, sister of Lou Stuckenbrock, Miscavige's assistant-paramour-bulldog.

It seemed like a daily occurrence, Miscavige popping his head into the office to say, "Danny's on his way up," at which point Timothy would quickly gather up his laptop and phone and scram. Danny hated Timothy and had no qualms about letting him know it right to his face, and in the most vulgar, toxic, venom-spewing manner you can imagine. It wasn't just that Danny hated Timothy. He hated the scripts Timothy wrote for event videos, most specifically the "Winners Videos"—the video presentations that preceded the announcement of IAS Freedom Medal winners—and he thought Timothy's work was amateurish. He also hated Amber O'Sullivan Mellor, the

Cine Sec at Gold, my former titular boss. In a fierce tirade, he once famously brandished a .38 Special in her face. I think he hated her because she was a duplicitous sycophant who specialized in getting things done while pissing people off. She'd been busted out of RTC, where apparently she'd become expert in the Miscavige style of management, which dictated that if your staff didn't fear you then you're a lousy manager. Amber was a petite (if I wasn't adverse to body shaming, I refer to her as scrawny) Irish redhead who, while lacking in physical weight, threw the weight of her position around as though it had the girth of a Sumo wrestler. Danny also hated Taron Lexton, a young director who I'd brought on to direct the *Youth for Human Rights* videos, as well as a feature length film adaption of Hubbard's book *The Way to Happiness*, and other projects. He hated Taron because he thought his work was superficial eye-candy that cheapened Scientology—all artifice and no art. That was the short list. In the previous few years Danny had risen to new levels of toxicity, and he seemed to have reached his zenith. This wasn't helped by, and was probably a byproduct of, his crippling arthritis, which he treated with any opioid he could get his hands on to the point of becoming severely addicted. This became one of Miscavige's most guarded secrets—the man he'd appointed to the exalted position of official L. Ron Hubbard Biographer was an opioid addict. In the midst of the national opioid crisis, while himself addicted to opioids, Danny Sherman was writing speeches extolling Scientology's role in helping to counter the drug problem and heal its victims. Scientology is, unequivocally, a bottomless pit of hypocrisy.

Mostly, Danny hated all these people because they weren't what he considered "cool." I wasn't on the list of those Danny hated. I was on the list of those people Danny considered cool. To Danny, I was one of the inventors of cool because I grew up in Laurel Canyon and was an ex-surfer, ex-drug addict, and a filmmaker with a seemingly endless supply of film trivia and film history factoids at my fingertips. I had lots of off-beat friends, I was always introducing him to quirky, thought-provoking books, like David Reese's must-read, *How to Sharpen Pencils*—which for awhile became Danny's raison d'être. And I was one of Miscavige's go-to guys. Danny was fond of saying, "COB considers you and me to be tent poles of Scientology." Danny wrote all of Miscavige's speeches, including the LRH bio speeches featured at the annual March 13 event commemorating Hubbard's birthday. Miscavige would have Danny read the speeches to him out loud before he rehearsed them. After hearing Danny read one particular speech, he said, "Danny, you should get up on stage and give that speech." From then on, Danny became a presenter at every Birthday Event and an internationally known celebrity within the Scientology bubble—the L. Ron Hubbard Biographer. Little did the public know that when Danny was spinning his tales of L. Ron Hubbard's daring do, his heroism in battle, or

SCIENTOLOGY - THE BIG LIE

his spectacular achievements in social reform and the arts, he was loaded on OxyContin and propped up with steroids.

Danny had been one of my oldest friends, at least within a professional work context. I first met him shortly after arriving at Gold. We were the same age and had both grown up in LA, me in West Hollywood, he in the wealthy West LA beach-adjacent neighborhood of Pacific Palisades. The term "purple prose" could have been invented to describe Danny's speechwriting style—it meets the definition according to Wikipedia: "Purple prose is a flowery and ornate writing style that makes a piece of text impenetrable. It is characterized by long sentences, multi-syllabic words, excessive emotion, and a plethora of clichés. It's typically melodramatic and often too poetic." There has never been a more accurate definition of Danny's speechwriting style. He once told me he wrote that way to make Miscavige appear smarter than he was. He was also a master at never letting the truth stand in the way of a good story. In one of his bio speeches he referred to Hubbard as "having been exiled from Rhodesia." After the event I pointed out the inaccuracy: "Danny, he couldn't have been exiled. You can only be exiled from your native country. He was deported." To which he smugly replied, "Exiled sounds better." What he really meant was—"exiled" sounds cooler.

So, there we all were, me, Timothy, and Danny, on the fourth floor of ASI, Timothy and I working to revamp the Narconon Program, and Danny writing speeches for

Miscavige to give at international Scientology events. It was a vastly better scene than working at the Gold base 90 miles from home. ASI was a short, seven-minute drive from where I lived and I wasn't expected at the office until lunchtime. It was the first real sense of independence I'd felt in a long time. I'd been sprung from the cog-in-the-machine, grind-you-down routine of working at Gold and was now working in Miscavige's rarefied bubble—inside the belly of the beast. I would exercise in the morning, do whatever research was needed to prepare for the day's work, then head to the office.

Meanwhile, a few miles east of ASI, at 4401 Sunset Boulevard, renovations on the Church's new broadcast facility were approaching their final phase. The Church had acquired the old KCET Studios in 2011, a cultural landmark in Hollywood dating back to 1912. The property, spanning 4.5 acres, was home to a 300,000-square-foot facility comprised of two sound stages, post-production facilities, offices, and a satellite uplink. In 1978 it was designated a Los Angeles Historic Cultural Monument—the perfect kind of trophy real estate Miscavige was so fond of purchasing, which he referred to as "statement buildings." The Church of Scientology paid $45 million for the studio and then spent an additional $50 million on renovations and upgrades.

I'd known Miscavige had been looking to purchase a broadcast facility for some time. Ever since a meeting a few years prior when randomly changing the subject he said, "Hey

Mitch, I don't mean to push your buttons, but how'd you like to have a bunch of young people working under you?" Silently, I thought to myself how much I'd love to be working anywhere but at Gold. And "young people working under me?" Why not? He'd been looking at a facility north of LA in the Santa Clarita area, but that deal had fallen through, and he'd been grooming a bunch of young recruits currently training at Flag to staff a new production facility.

As long as I'd known him, Miscavige spoke of wanting to produce international events somewhere, anywhere, other than Gold, which was originally established by Hubbard to be a film production facility not a live event production facility. Miscavige wanted to keep film production running without interruption, yet producing live events at the same time as film production routinely threw the studio into chaos resulting in film production being shut down. Put another way, Hubbard established Golden Era Productions to produce the films he deemed were vital to the survival and expansion of Scientology. David Miscavige turned Golden Era Productions into his personal vanity production studio, producing live events that would solidify him as the singularly unchallengeable leader of Scientology and as a fundraising powerhouse. These two things did not play well together. As a result, when international events went into production, Gold would experience an extreme form of whiplash caused by film production being suddenly halted while everybody went onto producing all the graphic elements, music, documentaries, performance pieces, and speeches that went into putting on a three-plus hours long event. As I was not involved in event production, when an event hit the fan, I'd fade into the background, drift back to LA and wait it out until film production started back up, and I'd enjoy the time off. After a time, I began to organize my entire life around the times when Gold was absorbed in the chaos of event production.

In his search for a facility to house event production, Miscavige finally settled on the old KCET studios—home of LA's public television station. Per the Church's press release, the new facility would be a, "centralized global communications hub for the Church's media activities, which include public service announcements, television programming, advertisements, magazines, brochures, Internet, and every other conceivable type of content." The new facility would be christened "Scientology Media Productions."

You would think that having event production relocate from the International Base to a new facility would be a cause for celebration at Gold—an end to the chaos and the whiplash effect. After all, the Gold staff would no longer be forced to put on the brakes and do a 180-degree turn four or five times a year, switching from film production to event production—which was like a weeks-long Bataan Death March—and then back again to film production. But, in reality moving event production to a new facility represented an existential threat to Gold as it made them appear less relevant. Much of their identity and self-esteem had been derived from being the organization that produced the international events, and now that activity was being moved to a new studio.

The word on the streets was that Gold was being left for dead. To make matters worse for Gold, Miscavige used Scientology Media Productions as another poison-tipped arrow in his quiver of emotional insults he loved to hurl at the Gold crew. He had been telling me for years that he wanted to move event production away from Gold so that Gold could focus on what it did best and on what L. Ron Hubbard had originally intended for Gold—namely, film production. Yet, when the KCET facility was purchased and Scientology Media Productions was in the planning stages, he told Gold staff that, as a result of their monumental failure to produce live events without crashing film production, they had forced him to buy another studio. Miscavige pointed at the new broadcast facility as a symbol of their failure to perform, and he guilted them with the $100 million-dollar price tag for good measure.

On Miscavige's invitation, Timothy and I took a tour of the new studio facility, which at the time was far from complete. The property had passed through many hands on its way to becoming the home of Scientology's broadcast facility. Its original, industrial age brick structures dating back to 1912, combined with its 1970s administration buildings that had been inspired by a post-war obsession with the modernist grid, was like touring an archaeological site dedicated to an epoch of Hollywood studio history.

With the Church's vast financial resources, a pennies-on-the-hour work force of skilled Sea Org labor, and a partnership with internationally renowned Gensler architects, the property could not have found a more attentive landlord than the Church of Scientology. The renovations were nothing short of spectacular. Even *The Hollywood Reporter*, which had never been kind to Scientology, described the new facility as "plush." To give you an idea of the attention to detail, the surfaces of all original bricks were returned to factory-new freshness, given new mortar, and damaged bricks replaced with exact matches, found by exhaustive searches of old demolished buildings. Missing doorknobs were replaced with vintage originals. The original factory window mullions were stripped down to bare metal, and the brass hinge hardware polished to a gleaming shine.

Restoring old buildings is something the Church of Scientology is expert at, and for good reason, considering Hubbard's adage—"They will know us by our MEST." Miscavige is obsessed with purchasing old buildings and renovating them to such a degree that the renovations, in and of themselves, generate good press. In his mind, the renovations alone command respect, and prove to the world that Scientology is not a cult or a scam. "What kind of people would go to that length to preserve a Hollywood landmark?" He literally asked me this.

Even though the interior spaces and much of the hardscape had yet to be completed, I looked around and marveled that this was potentially my new home. It had not been decided if I'd be relocated to SMP or remain at Gold as the Senior Director over film production. Fingers were crossed I'd be moving to SMP where, not only would I have authority over a brand-new creative venture, I'd have more autonomy than at Gold. But most importantly to me, I'd be working 15 minutes from home, and maybe for the first time in many years, I could have a personal life outside of work.

There was another advantage to working close to home, my concern that the hepatitis I'd contracted at 17 might cause complications and need immediate medical attention. Being stuck out at Gold presented a very real problem. I was far from my doctor, and the medical resources in the nearby town of Hemet were, in my experience, substandard. Even though I'd been asymptomatic since recovering from the virus decades prior, and I didn't drink or use drugs that tended to weaken one's liver, my doctor cautioned me that end-stage liver disease came with little warning: "You'll feel fine with no symptoms. Two weeks later you'll be dead." No matter how asymptomatic I had been, just having the virus meant I had a 20% chance of developing liver failure.

Gerald Duncan was the Director of Inspections and

Reports, or Dir I&R. One of only three Black Sea Org members on the Base, at about 6'1" and 300+ pounds, he's a formidable figure, though his voice is only slightly higher than Michael Jackson's. The Dir I&R is an enforcer within the Ethics department. Gerald exhibited what I consider to be a bizarre behavior pattern that is trained into all ethics staff specifically, and into Scientologists in general, namely, an artificial way of regarding people differently if they are in trouble or doing well. For example, if you get a reject on something you submitted to Miscavige and happened to pass by Gerald on your way somewhere, assuming he hadn't already gathered you up to go over your reject, he would glower at you, clench his jaw, shoot bullets out of his eyes and muster up every item of body language he could in order to make you feel as ashamed as possible. Then, once you've handled the reject, and gotten a "Thank You" or "Well Done," etc. he'd be all smiles and thumbs up.

Gerald grabbed me for an interview one day, wanting to know that I was doing everything possible to handle my health situation, adding that if I wasn't taking care of it then I was being "out-ethics." I assumed the MLO had sent him a report regarding my health issues. I explained my situation with hepatitis C and that my doctor was strongly urging me to start Interferon treatment, a chemo-like drug that involves giving yourself a weekly injection for about 12 weeks, usually on Friday night, then spending the weekend bedridden with flu-like symptoms. Most patients took a leave from work during treatment. Gerald was adamant that I start the treatment. When I told him it would mean taking 12 weeks off work, without skipping a beat, he replied, "Let's find an alternative solution." He might as well have said, "I'll take my chances that you'll drop dead before I'll okay you missing 12 weeks of production." I never did start the Interferon treatment— not because of Gerald's reaction, but because I preferred to hold out for a better, less troublesome treatment. As I sat there looking at Gerald across the interview table, I felt pity for him, pity for the conditioning that led him to think that way. If he was that disconnected from the humanity of others, how disconnected must he be from his own humanity?

My doctor mentioned there were new hepatitis treatments on the horizon that were 90% effective and had little to no side effects. I was working at ASI when I heard about the release of the new miracle drug Sovaldi. I called my doctor. "Let's get you started," he said eagerly over the phone. Picking up my first prescription of Sovaldi, from across the counter the pharmacist said, "That'll be $1,300.00," and that was for one week of a 12-week regimen. The blood left my face. "Don't worry" she reassured me, "you've just hit your co-pay. The next 11 weeks will only be $6 a week." The nurse provided me with a phone number I could call 24/7 if any complications came up. "There's a small chance your blood cell count will drop and you'd need an emergency transfusion. It's rare but it happens." There was more: "It's not likely but there's a chance you might have severe fits of anger and depression so let your family and co-workers know to stay calm if that happens. We can give you medication if you'd like."

When I arrived at work the next day, I informed Laurisse, Miscavige's assistant, that there might be days when I would not be able to come into work. She was completely understanding. Two weeks after starting treatment the virus had gone undetectable, and my blood count had dropped slightly, causing a bit of fatigue. Other than that, I experienced no side effects. Unless you consider wanting to beat someone to death with your bare hands to be a side effect.

The afternoon weekday traffic heading through Laurel Canyon feels like it moves at the speed of a mouse passing through the digestive tract of a boa constrictor—a lot of pressure, not much movement. I was headed over the hill to ASI when Timothy called. Our conversation distracted me from the traffic light at Lookout Mountain Drive, a stone's throw from the house Graham Nash shared with Joni Mitchell when he wrote "Our House." Missing the red light, I almost gridlocked. Fortunately, the alert driver behind me left room for me to back up. To my right, a gentleman and his wife, in a late-model Mercedes, began to turn left onto the Canyon passing in front of me. Apparently I had caused the guy a nanosecond or so delay while he waited for me to back up, and he had much to say about it. He rolled down his window and started screaming obscenities—something about being inconvenienced by outsiders who used his neighborhood as a shortcut over the Hollywood Hills. HIS NEIGHBORHOOD! I'd grown up down the street and currently lived less than a mile from that intersection. Not to mention, two of my best friends had died of heroin overdoses back in the day within a few blocks, and this guy is screaming at me like I'm some punk kid from Queens who's clogging up the Midtown Tunnel to get to a disco on a Friday night. The Mercedes came to a stop. My window was down and I'm screaming back at the guy. He's opening his door to get out of the car. My hand is pulling the door latch. His wife is pulling him back into the car. Just then the light turns green, and cars start honking at the guy to move. I hear Timothy's voice over my car's sound system. I'd forgotten all about the call. I literally wanted to beat that guy to death and would have done so, given the chance. But that was about the extent of the side effects I experienced from Sovaldi.

Timothy and I were having a good laugh recalling the phone call when Miscavige walked in and asked. "What's that all about?" I explained what happened. He took a long beat, then looked at me and said, "Did he deserve it?" He smiled and walked off.

A few weeks later a group of us flew with Miscavige on Tom Cruise's jet to attend the IAS event held yearly on the grounds of Saint Hill in the UK. I was in the middle of hepatitis treatment and so had to request extra medication in case the trip was extended. I spent the next week working on the scripts for the Narconon program out of a comfortable office at Saint Hill Manor with a beautiful view of the lush green English countryside. I was being waited on hand and foot and felt eerily like I was being groomed, but I was enjoying the experience too much to question it, so I tamped down those feelings and carried on.

The yearly IAS event consists of the main event, followed by a couple of days of fundraising seminars. That is the main purpose for holding such events—to raise money. There is also the Patrons' Ball, an exclusive event where Miscavige hands out gaudy trophies to top donors who earn status levels such as the "Patron of Legend," awarded to the Duggan family for having cumulatively donated $300 million. The patriarch of the family, biotech billionaire Bob Duggan, is Scientology's wealthiest member, and ex-husband of Scientologist Trish Duggan. But the most exclusive event of the week is the Patrons Dinner, held in the opulent dining room at Hubbard's former residence, St. Hill Manor. I was invited to attend the dinner and sit at Miscavige's table, along with his assistant Lou, Tom Cruise, Australian pop-star Kate Ceberano and her husband Lee, Karin Alpers, head of the IAS, and Dianna Hubbard. I'd forgotten that Kate and Lisa Schrorer, my former assistant and disgraced Commanding Officer of Gold currently being held captive in the Hole, were close childhood friends, and that they had grown up together in the tight-knit Scientology community of Melbourne, Australia. Though I was unaware of Lisa's current whereabouts, I was aware she'd gotten into serious trouble and had vanished. Out of the blue, Kate asked me how Lisa was doing. I could literally hear Miscavige and Lou tense up in anticipation of how I might answer. They both knew exactly how she was doing and that, while being held captive in the Hole, she'd taken a leadership position as head bondage mistress in Miscavige's torture circus, cheering on such gruesome punishments as Debbie Cook being made to stand in a trash can wearing a sign that read "lesbo" while ice-cold water was poured over her. If you've heard of or read about that gruesome episode, it was Lisa who placed the sign on Debbie Cook. There we were, in this opulent setting that was once the home of L. Ron Hubbard—feasting on a meal prepared by caterers to the Royal Family, we were in the company of the biggest movie star in the world, surrounded by the most generous of all Scientology donors, and I'm being asked by a celebrity Scientologist about her friend who David Miscavige, sitting two chairs to my left, was holding captive in hellish conditions and had personally traumatized. "She's doing fine," I said. And, in the standard vernacular all Scientologists use, especially Sea Org members, when asked about a person's situation that they can't be truthful about, I added, "I haven't actually seen her in a while as she's been off on a special project." Miscavige and Lou started breathing again. Kate, satisfied with the answer, simply said, "Well, tell her I said hello if you do see her," and the conversation continued from there. And that was that. Bullet dodged. If I had given the slightest indication of Lisa's actual predicament, I would have been toast. I willingly lived in a rarefied bubble, isolated from the worst aspects of Miscavige's bloody reign. And as such, I was obligated to support the lie that everything was fine. Hubbard coined a phrase to describe the answer I'd given. I had not lied; I had told "an acceptable truth." I had not seen Lisa in a while, and she *was* on a *special* project.

The day before I left, Lou paid me a visit at my temporary office at Saint Hill Manor. They were flying on to Dublin, then Denmark, and had come to say goodbye. Her message was simple: "We'd like you to take on a broader role in the organization." All I could think of was the people I'd known, who, having been drawn closer and closer into Miscavige's orbit, found themselves broken and defeated. I didn't want to end up in that pile. I didn't even want to think that such a pile existed, but I'd seen it happen to the Sea Org members I'd worked with who were busted to the galley, or to the grounds crew trimming trees, or jumped the fence in the middle of the night with little or no money to their name and nowhere to go. Or worse, were confined to the Hole. Surely, I thought, it would be different for me, that I could continue to live my life at the top of Scientology unscathed—satisfied in the thought that if bad things were happening to people, they probably deserved it—or at least I was clever enough to avoid the same outcome.

Nothing ever came of the conversation with Lou. I did end up being posted as the Senior Director at Scientology Media Productions, but I don't think that's what Lou was hinting at. Whatever it was, it got lost in the confusion of launching the new broadcast facility and ultimately forgotten.

On the flight back to LA, I couldn't help but reflect on the relationship between Tom Cruise and David Miscavige. The dinner I attended with them that night at St. Hill Manner was the first time I'd actually seen them together in many years, though I'd often hear Miscavige refer to Tom, relating anecdotes about Tom's latest high-flying hijinks, or ordering a bunch of us into a conference room to be force-fed Tom's latest "sizzle reel," movie speak for hastily thrown together sequences from the latest Tom Cruise blockbuster that studios often put together to tease the press in order to generate advance buzz—a kind of insider sneak peek on a thumb drive.

But it wasn't until the years had passed and I gained the advantage of distance that I realized Tom and Dave are not friends. Tom is Dave's highest profile victim. Here is a man who came to Scientology in a vulnerable state, a budding star with a reading disorder that made it painful for him to read scripts. Somehow, his interaction with Scientology had afforded him the means to lick that problem—not that unbelievable to me as it had afforded me the means to kick a drug habit. But Cruise's interaction with Scientology, and his friendship with Miscavige, would also see the destruction of Tom's three marriages. The first to Scientologist Mimi Rogers, was literally engineered out of existence by David Miscavige's personal operatives to make way for his second wife Nicole Kidman, with whom he adopted two children. When Nicole's lack of enthusiasm for Scientology met Miscavige's paranoia that she might be a potential threat to Tom making Scientology the most important thing in his life, Miscavige had that marriage killed off as well. They say, "Three is a charm," and when Tom jumped on Oprah Winfrey's couch, as silly and manic as that may have seemed, no one questioned he was in love with Katie Holmes.

Their dream wedding in an Italian castle was called the wedding of the century, but it was also a portent of the disaster to come. Ex-captain of the Apollo, Norman Starkey, made a stir when he drunkenly hit on Brooke Shields, earning himself a stint in Miscavige's makeshift prison, the notorious Hole, but the big news was Leah Remini noticing Miscavige's assistant Laurisse playing grab-ass with her boss and then asking foot-in-mouth spokesperson Tommy Davis why Dave's wife, Shelly, wasn't at the wedding. Tommy's answer, "You don't have the fucking rank to ask that," was the trigger point that led to Leah exiting Scientology and becoming its most outspoken and effective critic.

Nearly six years later Katie Holmes discovered she was

as married to Miscavige as she was to Cruise, and made her dramatic escape. When I hear statements that Tom Cruise is David Miscavige's co-conspirator, or his best friend and that they have some special bromance, I wince. When you survey the wreckage of Tom's personal life, when you consider that all three of his ex-wives have been declared enemies of the Church, that he's estranged from his only natural child, that his two adopted children are estranged from their adopted mother and are deeply committed to a cult, and when you calculate the tens of millions he's donated to Scientology, there is only one conclusion to be made. Tom Cruise is David Miscavige's number one victim. But that does not mean he isn't accountable for his participation in allegedly mistreating his staff and accepting free labor from Sea Org members. Or, his role in girlfriend-gate, wherein Church resources were used to audition a girlfriend for Tom after his pre-Katie Holmes romantic partner Penelope Cruz, abruptly ended their relationship, and Tom complained he couldn't get a girlfriend. That role was awarded to actress Nazanin Boniadi who, not understanding the arcane rules and rituals of Tom and Dave's relationship, was kicked to the curb and made to do penance by scrubbing a bathroom floor with a toothbrush. She too left Scientology and is now considered an enemy of the Church.

Back at ASI, the work of revising the Narconon program continued. It seemed the revisions would never end. No matter how much we completed, Miscavige kept expanding the list—one more film, and what about uniforms for the clients? Narconon should have their own branded film for the Purification Rundown (the sauna based detox program), and they'll need a Narconon branded playback system for all the new films. By the time we were done, the project had ballooned to include 25 instructional and indoctrination films, a slew of new operating policies that filled two 4 inch binders, uniforms for both the staff and the clients, there were also course materials, and even a cute drug sniffing beagle. Each Narconon facility would be receiving one to ensure the type of situation that lead to the death of Stacy Dawn Murphy—who had died of an overdose from the drugs she smuggled into the Arrowhead facility—would never recur.

With the newly revised Narconon program now complete, it was time to release it to the world. As it was a huge departure from the previous program, Miscavige felt it was vital to get the Executive Directors of all Narconons from around the world on board with the new program. Narconon centers operate much the same as franchises; private owners are granted a license to run a Narconon facility and are obligated to send a portion of the fees they collect to ABLE International. Miscavige was concerned there might be some blowback from some of the Narconon old-timers seeing their precious program undergo such radical change. He wanted to bring them all to LA so that the new program could be presented to them in person. That way, any potential negative reaction could be handled right there on the spot, and not given a chance to fester in some remote part of the world. There was a lot for the Narconon Executive Directors to digest—and a lot for them to be concerned about—and Miscavige wanted to brief them as close to home as possible. His solution was to hold a three-day conference in the small ABLE Auditorium, next door to ASI. Generally speaking, the public would expect Miscavige, and no one else, to present a release of this magnitude. Miscavige explained that he could not do the briefing himself because Narconon was a secular organization, and he is Sea Org, and therefore can't be seen as being in charge of Narconon. He was adamant that he could not possibly be involved in the presentation, yet he had micromanaged every step of it along the way. This made absolutely no sense as ABLE International is run exclusively by Sea Org members, so how could he, being the top Sea Org official, deny his association with ABLE and therefore Narconon. The only logical reason for him avoiding the briefing would be to keep him at a distance from any potential liability arising from future lawsuits. To keep himself out of it he chose Timothy and I to headline the presentation along with CMO International executive Jason Hoertling, and an attorney they'd hired to author Narconon's new legal policies—an attorney who happened to be the top lawyer in the country practicing in the field of drug rehabilitation, and who had helped a number of major drug rehabilitation facilities navigate the tricky path leading to claiming outcome based success. In other words, this attorney laid out what would have to happen for Narconon to be able to go from claiming an unsubstantiated 80% success rate to legitimately claiming that statistic based on actual outcomes—which the attorney thought they could achieve. What he didn't know was that they were lying to him about their success rate.

Over the course of three days, about 25 Narconon Executive Directors from around the world sat in attendance as the new Narconon program was presented to them in detail. From the new legal protections, to the uniforms for staff and clients, to their own terribly cute, drug-sniffing beagle. As Miscavige had anticipated, there were grumblings amongst a few of the Narconon Executive Directors. They were concerned with how much the upgrades were going to cost them. The form fitting, athleisure uniforms were a big problem for many of the body conscious executives who were struggling with weight issues. Throughout the conference executives who'd expressed their concerns would go absent for hours as, presumably, they were being given "extra attention" by Miscavige operatives. By the end of the conference all the Narconon owners were on board, with the exception of one who either bailed or was kicked out after which his franchise contract was picked up by another, more loyal, Narconon operator.

Shortly after the Narconon briefing, with renovations still ongoing, we moved operations to SMP. There was plenty of space to work out of; we just had to dance around the plumbers, painters, and carpet installers doing their finishing touches. More and more, Miscavige's comments were focused on his primary reason for wanting to open the new broadcast facility. It was the reason he'd alluded to earlier when he told me he was going to use the studio to "Fuck them up," meaning, flip the script on the negative press. He intended to do this by creating a broadcast version of the Scientology published magazine *Freedom*. Initially, the entire focus of Scientology Media Productions was to take *Freedom* magazine to the airwaves, transforming it into *Freedom TV*.

Published since 1968, *Freedom* describes its focus as "Investigative Reporting in the Public Interest." Psychiatry, Scientology's favorite enemy and devil trope, was a common target of *Freedom* articles. As was the IRS, and any entity that had reported negatively on Scientology. It was essentially the mouthpiece of Scientology when it came to pushing back against negative press. It was Miscavige's personal beer bottle that he could hurl at anyone he chose.

Miscavige was convinced that once he had control of his own media outlet branded as *Freedom TV*, he could level the playing field on the negative press, as though it was as simple as throwing the switch on your own broadcast media production facility. But for that to be successful, they would need a great deal more than just the capability to broadcast news and publish magazines. They'd need to have an audience that was interested in consuming their content. In that respect, Scientology Media Productions was, and remains to this day, a monumental failure. Its audience has never grown beyond members of the Church who are mandated to consume its content. In fact, much of the programming on Scientology TV is intended to keep devotees indoctrinated into believing that Scientology is expanding and having a positive impact on the world. *Freedom TV* never saw the light of day. In fact, as of this writing, there hasn't been a issue of *Freedom* magazine since 2019. The Scientology Media Productions broadcast facility—with its 24/7 stream of eye candy infomercials and faux documentaries, simply devolved into another element of Scientology's Reality Distortion Field, intended to keep loyal adherents fixated on donating their time and money.

Our first order of business at the new, yet-to-be-opened studio was to create more of those websites intended to impugn the character of Scientology's critics—commonly referred to as "hate sites." Slandering critics, or per Hubbard's dictates on the matter, attacking the attackers, was a favorite tactic of David Miscavige. In the case of ex-members who were speaking out, the information was culled from their Auditing sessions, given in a confidential setting supposedly governed by priest-penitent privilege, then used out of context to assassinate the person's character. But mostly the information was composed of outright lies. For example, critics were accused of having been sex workers, sex tourists, wife beaters, thieves, embezzlers, or just plain lazy and incompetent—disgruntled apostates who had been kicked out and were retaliating. Even as I was assisting with those sites, it never ceased to amaze me how, while characterizing ex-members this way, the Church was admitting to having allowed such people to be members in the first place, some for decades, and some even ascending to top management positions. Ultimately, it was an admission that Hubbard's technology was utterly incapable of detecting such people, let alone "curing them of their 'aberrations.'"

To assist with the creation of the hate sites, a veteran journalist—let's call him "R"—was hired who had formerly written for *The Hollywood Reporter*, whose digital and print editions were known for their decidedly negative bias against Scientology. Having come from *The Hollywood Reporter*— considered a salacious tabloid compared to the more respected industry journal *Variety*—he was no stranger to spilling poisoned ink when the job called for it. One day, in an almost unbelievable twist of fate, "R" was standing in line with a friend at a popular fast-food restaurant, telling his associate that he was working for the Church of Scientology and that, as far as he was concerned, they deserved every inch of their bad reputation. He was apparently taking a paycheck from the Church, writing hate sites on its enemies, while ridiculing the Church to his journalist friends. To his misfortune, the wife of one of the other hate-site writers—who happened to be a dedicated Scientologist—was standing in line directly behind him and overheard the entire conversation. As a dutiful Scientologist, she wrote a Knowledge Report. The guy was subsequently investigated by the ethics department where it was revealed he had a cocaine problem and had gotten fired from the *Hollywood Reporter* due to his drug use. The story only gets worse from there.

"R" was originally brought on board to write for *Freedom*, which at the time, was located not far from SMP in the Hollywood Boulevard headquarters of the Office of Special Affairs. Some months prior to first meeting "R," I was asked to give a soon-to-be onboarded journalist a tour of Gold. I'll call her "J." She had been working out of the *Freedom* office at OSA, and, as the *Freedom* journalists—a handful of professional writers none of whom were Scientologists— would be relocating to the SMP facility and taking on an expanded role on *Freedom TV*, Miscavige wanted the *Freedom* writers to tour all of Scientology's major production facilities: Gold; SMP; Bridge Publications; The Dissemination and Distribution Center; and the ginormous warehouse where all Hubbard writings and recorded lectures have been arranged, in date sequence, in an effort to make sense out of all the random material that comprises the so-called technology of Scientology. It's a bit like expecting a thousand monkeys to type Shakespeare. That facility is known as Compilations.

Over the next few months I got to know "J" a bit. She was a single mom who had survived a bitter divorce with a successful

Silicon Valley entrepreneur, and had the most delicious way of stringing words together into meaningful and digestible prose. As I read "J's" work, I became aware of how gifted she was. In my estimation, the most skilled writer the Church had ever hired to work on *Freedom*. As a result of having been introduced to Scientology at the highest echelon, given VIP tours, love bombed and offered choice writing jobs, "J" only knew Miscavige as he wanted her to know him—an intensely dedicated, hard working leader. She admired Miscavige to the point of loyalty. She and "R" had both been working out of the *Freedom* OSA offices when she became aware of "R's" cocaine use and that he'd been using coke in the men's room at OSA and felt obligated to rat him out to Miscavige. There was, however, one huge problem. When the Church of Scientology hires someone, especially anyone working in close proximity to Miscavige, OSA is required to perform a thorough background check, and I mean thorough. Scientology maintains, at great expense, scores of private investigators armed with weapons-grade investigatory tools dedicated to vetting individuals before they are allowed anywhere near Miscavige's "lines"—shorthand for *communication lines* but also includes any activity that might involve access to inside information. That "R" slipped through OSA's vetting machine represented a colossal security failure that would most likely result in the entire 10th floor of OSA being assigned to the RPF, or at least severely reprimanded. When it was discovered that "J" was about to rat out "R," panic set in. An immediate investigation was launched. "J" had been 100% transparent in her vetting process, to the point of disclosing a two decade-old incident of little consequence where she'd used a company credit card without authorization and wound up in some minor legal trouble, which resulted in her being given probation. Unfortunately she violated her probation when she moved to a different county for work, resulting in a black mark on her arrest record. This was known about and no-one seemed to care when she was hired. Suddenly, in the wake of her wanting to rat out "R," she was a criminal and had to go. She was summarily frog marched off the studio premises (by this time she and "R" had moved from OSA to SMP). She was made to sign an NDA and paid off to keep quiet. Miscavige was subsequently told "J" had a criminal past and had to be let go. He was unhappy about losing a talented writer and utterly furious they'd allowed her onto his lines to begin with.

As for "R," his undoing was the aforementioned incident at the fast food restaurant wherein he tragically ratted himself out to a card-carrying, knowledge-report writing Scientologist in good standing. When Miscavige found out about it, wanting to avoid a wrongful termination suit, he had his people make the guy an offer—SMP would pay him $100K in monthly installments, and in exchange, he would write a book on the perils of cocaine use. The Church would own the rights to the book, and he was banned from ever setting foot on the property, or ever discussing anything regarding the Church or from bringing any litigation against them. He took the deal. I never saw him again, though I did hear he overcame his drug problem and is doing well.

By any measure, "J" deserved to be treated with compassion and understanding, especially from an organization that claimed tax-exempt religious status—even more so considering her potential contribution to Scientology's image. She had produced effective articles for the Church—writing that, in my opinion was a cut above anything they'd previously published. As for "R," who had genuinely expressed his desire to get off of drugs, and was employed by an organization that claimed to be better equipped than any organization in the world to help people with addiction, they could have easily sent him to their VIP Narconon and likely made him into a friend for life, if not a loyal Scientologist.

In the intervening time since I first arrived at Gold back in 1990, something in the way the organization dealt with pros had changed. And not for the better. Despite the fact I had been an intravenous drug user who'd had a couple of youthful scrapes with the law, I was hired to direct Scientology's most sacred films. As a measure of how far things had gone awry, consider this. A few years after my arrival, Gold hired a professional audio mixer, a young man in his thirties, who was on probation for involuntary manslaughter after his best friend died while he was driving drunk. Rather than disqualifying him, Gold sought to counsel him to put his life back together again. While this was most certainly part of their cultish method of bringing a person under their control, it was also the right thing to do, the kind of thing you'd expect from a legit religious group. Their response was to help the guy. He did become a Scientologist and he did straighten out his life and find some degree of happiness. Unfortunately, he died of cancer a few years later.

In another example, in the early 2,000s Gold hired another pro-mixer who, among many other credits, had been the head of music mixing at Paramount Studios for over twenty years. They hired him because the audio department at Gold could never figure out how to properly mix surround sound, and this guy was one of the top surround sound mixers in Hollywood. Like me, he too had been an intravenous drug user, and additionally had been an alcoholic. When Gold first approached him about working for them, he was severely depressed, had begun drinking again, and was on psychiatric medication following a failed attempt to cure his Hepatitis C. Gold helped the guy to sort out his life, stop drinking, and no longer need antidepressants. He became a dedicated Scientologist and led the Gold audio department to a new realm of quality. Unfortunately he died of liver cancer on December 22, 2019.

So why did Miscavige react so negatively to the single-parent mom with the minor infraction on her arrest record, overlooking her spectacular work, classifying her as a criminal to be gotten rid of rather than someone worthy of help as he had once done with the two pro-mixers at Gold? Her "crimes" were far less troublesome than the two mixers were, and her talents and willingness to put them to work for the Church were already proven. Something had changed. Whatever sense of humanity and desire to help people, I had experienced when I first arrived at Celebrity Centre, and then briefly witnessed at Gold years later, was gone. Put aside that such assistance was partially motivated to draw people into a cult—it had been expunged by a ruthless leader. David Miscavige had become so paranoid that something might dent his image, that he would sacrifice people with the ability to play an instrumental role in shaping the Church's image just because of the potential that someone would find out the person had made a mistake in their past and had a prior, minor legal problem. But the worst wasn't the change in attitude that had ostensibly gone from "Let's help these deserving people" to, "Get them the fuck out of here and make sure they can't sue us." The worst was about to arrive at Scientology Media Productions in the guise of Miscavige's "Establishment Team," and with that, things were about to get a whole lot darker.

TWENTY-FOUR

Scientology Media Productions

I N   A   S C I E N T O L O G Y
organization, whether it's a Church that services the public,
or a Sea Org production facility such as Gold or SMP, Division
One holds the responsibility of establishing the organization.
The term "Establishment" in this context, includes the hiring
of new staff and ensures that they know how to do their jobs,
setting up the lines of internal and external communication,
collecting and reporting the organization's statistics, making
sure executives are informed of anything stopping the
organization, and most importantly, ensuring that the staff
maintains the highest level of ethical behavior. Division One,
also known as the Hubbard Communications Office, or
HCO, are the Scientology organization's thought police, its
gestapo, and its Big Brother, with some telecommunication
and IT skills thrown in for good measure. If you get hauled
in and subjected to a "Committee of Evidence," Scientology's

kangaroo court version of a military court martial, it's HCO that does the hauling-in and runs the show. Shortly before the opening day of the Scientology Media Productions, Miscavige's hand-picked HCO establishment team showed up from Flag, some of them were repurposed from HCO Flag and some new trainees were specially hand-picked for SMP. Their favorite pastime seemed to be interrogating staff in one of the tiny interview rooms located in the basement of the main administration building. Generally speaking, problems in an organization trace back to leadership style. When considering Miscavige's leadership, I am reminded of a quote from author Tom Robbins:

> Since when has leadership been a criterion for sanity? Or vice versa. Hitler was a gifted leader, even Nixon. Exhibit leadership qualities as an adolescent, they pack you off to law school for an anus transplant. If it takes, you go into government.
> —Tom Robbins, Still Life with Woodpecker

The same could be said for joining the Sea Org—if the anus transplant takes, you go into HCO.

An organization can suffer from too little establishment, resulting in no, or faulty communication lines, untrained staff, computers that don't work, etc. But SMP had the opposite problem—too much establishment. When you find yourself struggling to balance your time between spending

SCIENTOLOGY MEDIA PRODUCTIONS

it conforming to the rigors of compliance and reporting, as mandated by HCO, and the work you need to get done that you actually get paid for—that is too much establishment. When you are constantly scrutinized, and when, just like I'd witnessed at Gold, the cost of failure is so high it sucks all the oxygen out of the room, that is too much establishment. That high cost the Sea Org places on failure? HCO exists to ensure that cost stays high and that staff members pay up when they screw up.

In addition to the ex-coke-snorting-ex-Hollywood Reporter writer, and the highly-talented-single-mom writer who ratted him out for snorting coke in the men's room at Scientology's Office of Special Affairs, a slew of other non-Scientologist staff were hired to fill positions as marketing and magazine copywriters, graphic designers, a couple of broadcast professionals, a documentary director or two, and a couple of video editors. Generally, Miscavige doesn't like dealing with people he doesn't know personally—especially people who will be working around him on projects he will need to approve or reject and who he may run into on a daily basis. What do these people know about him? What have they heard? What have they read? For that matter, what did SMP staff know about the accusations and rumors that had been leveled at Miscavige for decades? Scientology was gearing up to embark on its greatest public relations and information venture ever: a venture intended to "fill the vacuum," displacing the torrent of negative information that had been swirling around Scientology for decades. Miscavige understood that the staff at SMP, and the professionals he'd hired, would be tasked with piloting that new venture straight into the headwinds of an aggressively negative press. In his speech at SMP's grand opening, Miscavige paraphrased author Frank X Walker's often repeated quote. "If you don't write your story, somebody else will," adding his own personal touch, "So, yes, we're now going to be writing our story like no other religion in history." Miscavige, like Hubbard before him, is obsessed with information control. That "story," the one he alluded to, would need to be based on facts, and he knew well that whoever controls the facts, controls the story. Not long after the grand opening, I was invited to attend a mandatory briefing, along with 50 or so pros and staff, that was intended to ensure we all had our "facts" straight.

As we filed into the softly lit auditorium, the first thing I noticed was the eight-foot folding table on which sat a half dozen or so thick three-ring binders. At the table, arranging the binders was Lynn Farny, OSA Legal Liaison. Lynn is not a lawyer, but he has been involved in every major Scientology legal action for decades, and has a working knowledge of Scientology's and Hubbard's legal history going back as far as pre-Dianetics days. I thought it was bizarre when it was happening. Looking back from my current position, it is even more so. Farny covered everything from accusations that

Miscavige murdered Hubbard, to his having been responsible for the death of his mother-in-law—some of it was based on persistent rumors and some of it, like the Lisa McPherson wrongful death suit, were based on legal action brought against him personally. I can only attribute the briefing to Miscavige's narcissistic need to play the persecuted victim. One thing that wasn't mentioned, despite it being a lightning rod for bad press, was the mystery surrounding his wife Shelly's disappearance from public view.

I first met Shelly Miscavige shortly after arriving at Gold. I thought she was even tempered and friendly. My interactions with her were mostly confined to social things— arranging for birthday and Christmas gifts for Miscavige and such, or at post-event formal dinners. For the years running up to her disappearance she had been a constant fixture in Miscavige's entourage. A few years after she was relocated to an undisclosed location in 2007, I ran into her while stopping for lunch in Redlands, California on my way to the international Base.

Redlands is a sleepy little town just off the San Bernardino freeway about two thirds of the way from LA to Gold. If you're into Victorian, Carpenter Gothic, or Mission Revival architecture, Redlands is worth a tour. Continuing east past Redlands, you'll discover it's the last outpost of civilization until you hit the golf course-riddled, star-studded playground of Palm Springs. Nonetheless, Redlands is a great place to stop for lunch before driving off into the wasteland of Moreno Valley and then on to the International Base. If Gold were Dante's Inferno, then leaving Redlands traveling eastward towards Gold, you'd find the inscription, "Abandon all hope, ye who enter here."

Redlands was my usual lunch stop on my Monday drive to the Base, and it was a straight shot down a winding mountain road from Big Bear and the CST compound where Shelly was rumored to be living. Leaving Starbucks on the way back to my car, I spotted Shelly in the company of two other RTC staff members and an executive from CST. I knew all four of them, one of them had been my auditor, the one who first told me about Jason Beghe's car accident. Sitting there chatting under a cafe umbrella on a warm late spring day, they appeared no different than any four girlfriends out for a friendly lunch. Until that moment I hadn't thought about the fact that I had not seen Shelly for some years. After all, people disappeared from the International Base all the time, often for no other reason than having been sent on an extended mission to some other part of the world. Not to mention, I'd been well indoctrinated into the mindset that I was at Gold to make films, not to poke around in Sea Org business, or ask too many questions. That she'd been moved to a secretive location during a time when I wouldn't have noticed her absence, meant running into her was inconsequential.

Somehow, I'd caught their attention and they all looked

SCIENTOLOGY MEDIA PRODUCTIONS

over at me. What followed was a brief, awkwardly polite conversation. Thinking back on this, all evidence pointed to Shelly having been relocated to the CST facility near Big Bear, and she was having lunch in Redlands in the company of her handlers. As one of the women in her group was wearing a CST uniform, I assumed she was on a special project for CST.

One thing was for certain, no sooner did Shelly disappear from public view than Miscavige's personal assistant became a ubiquitous presence at his side. Unlike Shelly, who was not always with Miscavige and sometimes not even on the same schedule, Lou was never absent from his side and always seemed to be on the same schedule. That time I flew with them to the UK on Tom Cruise's jet, Lou and Dave spent the night together in the master bedroom, although there was plenty of room for her to sleep in the very comfortable forward passenger cabin. I never thought they were anything but a secret couple. In my opinion, Laurisse Stuckenbrock is the mystery woman behind Shelly's disappearance. Insiders have speculated that the flashpoint for Shelly's disappearance was her suspicion that her husband was in a relationship with his assistant.

When I was living in one of the 'G' units at Gold, Miscavige and Lou lived in an adjacent unit. On Friday mornings, I'd often see them returning to their cottage after pulling an all-nighter spent analyzing the statistics that poured in from Scientology organizations around the world following the 2 PM Thursday deadline. Lou wasn't even-tempered and friendly like Shelly. She could mimic Miscavige's angry outbursts and is the only Scientology senior executive who ever screamed at me.

With the renovations complete, and the Establishment Team having put everything in place, on May 29, 2016 Scientology Media Productions held its grand opening in the main courtyard just off its Sunset Boulevard entrance. The entire staff, the pros in business attire, and the Sea Org crew in their newly issued SMP uniforms, sat in the bleachers as Miscavige introduced us all to a densely packed crowd of Scientologists, beaming with pride at what their Church had accomplished, many of whom had donated to the project.

If I were keeping a ledger of the things that, over the years, pried me away from Scientology and inspired a return to rational thinking, high on the list would be that day at Gold when I witnessed Miscavige traumatizing those three executives he'd made to sit on the blistering hot concrete while he verbally assaulted them, humiliating them in front of their fellow Sea Org members. Also high on that list was a particular phrase Miscavige uttered during his grand opening speech when he referred to Scientology as "The coolest religion on Earth." I played those words back in my head a few times. I was at once embarrassed and disgusted. Even back when I was a true believer, I never thought of

Scientology, or any other religion, as cool. The words "cool" and "religion" didn't belong in the same sentence, let alone next to one another. It's not that religion is uncool, though it certainly can be, it's that pop-culture adjectives are not capable of capturing the essence of religion. The phrase "Hey dude! Check out my cool religion." Doesn't really work, does it? Miscavige often invited local religious leaders to attend the grand opening ceremonies of Ideal Orgs. I imagined one of them, say a Rabbi, hearing Miscavige's description of Scientology being the coolest religion (implying that the Rabbi's religion was less cool).

Like all Scientology facilities, SMP has an office for Hubbard. The LRH office at SMP is located in one of the brick buildings that once housed the original Monogram Studios. Not long before the grand opening, a letter from a producer at Monogram Studios, addressed to L. Ron Hubbard and inviting him to come write for the studio, was miraculously discovered amongst Hubbard's papers. The framed letter was included as part of a display in the small conference room located in the LRH office. Conveniently, the office had an exterior door that opened onto Sunset Drive, a side street located at the back of the studio, and the street to which the letter to Hubbard was addressed. Just for show, metal address numbers were added to the interior entrance of the building. I'm not claiming the letter was a forgery, but its provenance is highly suspect. Despite an exhaustive search,

SCIENTOLOGY - THE BIG LIE

I was unable locate any historical connection between Hubbard and Monogram Studios. No credits in film archives, and no posters or advertisements of any kind, such as the ones advertising the Columbia Pictures serials that featured a Hubbard writing credit. That letter is the only thing connecting Hubbard and Monogram. A letter to Hubbard inviting him to work at the studio which Scientology now owns—a letter from the '30s no less—suddenly surfaces just in time to be included as an anecdote in Miscavige's grand opening speech, and then to be permanently memorialized in an office dedicated to Hubbard's screenwriting career. It takes an enormous stretch of the imagination to accept such a coincidence with nothing to back it up. Miscavige likes to paint a picture in which L. Ron Hubbard—living or dead—is somehow involved in every aspect of Scientology history. The Church purchases a broadcast facility and lo and behold, a letter from the 1930s suddenly surfaces, addressed to Hubbard from that very same address, offering him work as a screenwriter.

With the new broadcast facility now open, the first order of business was to complete the programming for the Scientology Network. Miscavige wanted to announce to the world that Scientology had its own television station, and that meant leasing a channel from a service provider. In today's world, television comes in two flavors: Over the Air, known as OTA, the signals beamed across the airways and picked up at home via an antenna just like the early days but digital rather than analog; and Over the Top or OTT, which is broadband Internet delivered by cable, satellite, or IPTV (Internet Protocol TV) enabling subscribers to reliably receive programs from alternate providers like Netflix, Amazon, Hulu, etc. While you wouldn't think of subscribing to a service provider that didn't carry your favorite streaming services, the Scientology Network could only afford to be on one service. The service they chose was DirectTV, who for a multi-year contract worth $10 million dollars, provided Scientology with a channel in a mostly unoccupied section designated for religious programming. You can find ScientologyTV at DirectTV's channel 320, alongside Christian stations, televangelists, and the 700 Club. For a mere $10 million in taxpayer underwritten dollars, Miscavige could boast to parishioners that Scientology had its own television station. If you weren't a DirectTV subscriber (which most people aren't) you could access Scientology TV via the web at scientology.tv or a streaming app available on most popular devices. But the big question was, what to put on the network?

I bumped into Miscavige one day in the hallway of the administration building—the building that housed, among other things, his plush top-floor executive suite, Internet and social media operations, marketing (which mostly consisted of designing and writing magazines and brochures), international event planning, and HCO. Every Thursday, just after 2 PM

(Scientology's end-of-week, immutable deadline for turning in your weekly statistics), the entire Sea Org Staff at SMP would head to the basement of the admin building for their weekly Meter checks, consisting of a moment spent in silence holding the E-meter cans while an HCO staff member stared at the Meter's needle to make sure your needle was "clean." They were looking for erratic needle movement, a "dirty" needle, which supposedly meant the person was up to no good or had unclean thoughts about the organization or its managers. Anyone found with a "dirty needle" was held for further interrogation. It's the strangest thing watching a bunch of Sea Org members waiting in line for a meter check. On the surface they seem cheerful, full of team spirit and camaraderie. But beneath the surface, they are straining to keep their spirits high so as not to accidentally trigger a movement of the E-meter needle that might cause undue scrutiny.

Miscavige pulled me aside and informed me he'd bumped onto Kirstie Alley at Flag and that she wanted to meet about her ideas for a Scientology television show. He said I should give her a call. I said, "Okay great," and that was that.

I first met Kirstie Alley at AOLA, back around 1986, at the Advanced Organization of Los Angeles. We'd both enrolled on the confidential course, Operating Thetan I, or OT 1, and like much of the study in Scientology we were required to team up with a study partner, or twin, and Kirstie and I were "twinned up." We weren't hang-out-together friends, but we were friendly. We bonded over the similar paths that had led us into Scientology—our history with drugs. Over the years, I interviewed her in her capacity as the spokesperson for Narconon, we'd see one another at Scientology functions or at a party she was throwing or a launch event for one of the products she endorsed. My point in mentioning all that is simply to say that when Miscavige suggested I give her a call, I don't think he was actually aware of how well I knew her, that her cell number was in my contacts, and that shooting her a text and then calling was not a problem. What happened next is a perfect example of how Miscavige has to control everything, and has to be the one pulling the strings.

Since the request to call Kirstie was SMP business, and it came form Miscavige, rather than contacting her directly I thought it appropriate to reach out to her via the President's Office at Flag—the office responsible for looking after VIPs. The following day, Kirstie called, and we arranged to meet at SMP the next week when she returned from Florida. Later that day I ran into Miscavige again and mentioned I'd spoken with Kirstie. I thought he'd be pleased that I complied with his request so quickly. But instead, he flipped out, "You what?!" Apparently when he asked me to contact her, he did not mean literally go off and contact her. He meant, send him a proposal in the form of a CSW (Completed Staff Work—a cumbersome request for approval, the form of which Hubbard lifted verbatim from an Air Force Manual). The CSW would lay out the nature of the call and the reason why it should be approved. Submitting a CSW would allow Miscavige to micromanage the phone call, and apparently, I had denied him that. He didn't specifically tell me I should have submitted a CSW, but I could tell from the veins bulging out of his neck that's what he wanted, or at the very least, a dispatch stating, "Dear Sir, thank you for asking me to contact Kirstie to discuss her ideas for a TV show. Before I contact her, I wanted to let you know exactly what I intend to discuss with her, and to assure you that I won't make any kind of commitment to her. I'll listen to her ideas and then we'll consider what she had to say." I could tell he was about to rip me apart, then realizing we were in a busy hallway, he backed off. I continued saying "She'll be back in town next week and will call to set up a meeting." Realizing I hadn't caused any actual damage, he responded, "Oh, okay. Thanks for letting me know." I'm pretty sure everyone within earshot began to breathe again. That wasn't the first time I'd acted on my own volition without authorization from Miscavige.

If you're going to announce the launch of a new television network, and you want to get noticed by the broadcast industry, you're going to need some kind of presence at the National Association of Broadcasters (NAB) convention, the world's largest event covering filmed entertainment along with the development, management and delivery of content across all mediums. With the planned launch of the studio barely two months away, Scientology Media Production's "broadcast consultant" insisted they needed to announce the upcoming launch of Scientology TV at the NAB convention. The plan was to create a two-minute video, a "sizzle reel," that established the network's mission statement and teased the yet-to-be-produced programming. The plan called for the "broadcast consultant" and the CMO Project Ops who was over SMP, to load the sizzle reel onto an iPad, fly to Vegas, and network with industry bigwigs, operatives, and thought leaders, creating as many opportunities as possible to generate buzz. The broadcast consultant had overseen the launch of DirectTV's digital streaming service, so they weren't going in entirely unknown. They needed to leave for Vegas in two days to make the convention, which meant there was no time to submit the video to Miscavige for approval, who was also out of town.

Two days later, they were out the door, sizzle reel in hand. That two-minute video would give the industry, and the world at large, its first look at Scientology's new television network. They cornered broadcast executives in elevators, showing the video on an iPad. They set up a hospitality suite where the sizzle reel played nonstop on video monitors. They booked time in the digital theaters that had been set up for exhibitors' use. Most importantly, they collared as many HBO representatives as they could get their hands on. With HBO's "Going Clear" documentary still fresh on everyone's mind, they thought that making HBO aware of the upcoming Scientology TV network would be tantamount to thumbing their nose at them, "Ha, ha, ha, you hit us with that documentary and look at us now! Bigger and stronger than ever, and with our own television network. Boy, are we gonna fuck you up, HBO!" Is this what Miscavige meant when he told me he was launching a broadcast facility so that he could, "Fuck them up?" I doubt HBO gave it a second thought, likely they had a good laugh over it, like when Miscavige sent ABC's 20/20 producers a basket of baked goods prepared by Gold's Italian pastry chef. But my concern at that moment was that Miscavige had spent $100 million on the studio, was about to spend another $10 million on a multi-year deal to lease a channel from DirectTV, and I had just sent off a two-minute video giving the world its first glimpse of Scientology TV—and I'd done so without any authorization.

I made sure a copy of the video, attached to a proposal, was on Miscavige's desk before he returned to LA. Though he never officially approved the video, or asked for any changes, he did authorize it for broad use, saying that he would have done it slightly differently—such high praise. Having pulled that off, contacting Kirstie Alley without first jumping through the expected gauntlet of bureaucratic hoops, didn't seem that big a deal.

When the day of my meeting with Kirstie arrived, she thought she was showing up at the studio for a casual brainstorming session. But the Sea Org executives running SMP, thought differently. They rolled out the red carpet and began her visit with a VIP tour of the new facility. It's not that she didn't want a tour, but it was clear from her body language, it was not what she was expecting.

Following the tour, we all converged on the main conference room, the one in the admin building, not one of the other dozen or so other conference rooms located around the facility. One thing about Scientology organizations, they love their conference rooms.

Kirstie kept looking over at me sitting at the opposite end of the conference table, throwing me this look of "What the fuck are all these people doing in our meeting?" At one point Kirstie stepped outside for a smoke and motioned for me to follow her. Wanting an explanation, I told her that I had nothing to do with it and did not know it was going to go down like this. Even though I hadn't anticipated that the SMP Studio Manager and the young woman in charge of public relations internationally, who also acted as an executive at the studio, would commandeer the meeting, I understood why they had done it—out of sheer paranoia that the meeting would go badly. Just as shit flows downhill, apparently so does the compulsion to micromanage. There was also their unstated, but very palpable, distrust for having an NSO (non-Sea Org member) take the lead on the meeting. I'd known the two of them for years. Before becoming the studio manager at SMP, Chandra Lorentzen had run Mad Hatter Studios—the recording studio once owned by jazz legend Chick Corea and later sold to the Church and then absorbed into SMP. The other executive, Erin Banks, joined the Sea org with her husband Nick, son of a wealthy Australian businessman, and quickly rose through the ranks to become the emcee at Ideal Org openings. I'd known Erin as a struggling actor. Before joining the Sea Org she'd won a couple of small parts in Gold films. Regardless of our previous experience with each other, the two of them were openly antagonistic towards working with a non-Sea Org person, which I assumed was mitigated by the cachet I'd earned for my years of valuable work for Gold—we had a kind of one-sided, interoffice rivalry. I left Kirstie to finish her smoke and went back in the conference room to explain to Chandra and Erin that Kristie just wanted to meet with me. They were not pleased. I used to joke at Gold that I directed films for free and got paid for putting up with the politics. This was a perfect example.

When we resumed, Kirstie made it clear the meeting was over and let Chandra and Erin know I'd be continuing the meeting at her home about 10 minutes away.

I met with her the next day. She laid out her ideas for a talk show that featured comedy sketches which poked fun at religion in a non-derogatory way—all religions, including Scientology. It was the don't-take-yourself-too-seriously brand of comedy. One sketch segment featured a spinning wheel inspired by Wheel of Fortune. Her ideas were creative, funny, and irreverent, kind of like Kirstie herself. It was also vastly more entertaining, informative, and watchable than anything Miscavige would authorize for airing on the channel. Unfortunately, her ideas went nowhere. That was the last time I ever saw Kirstie. Shortly after our meeting, she sold her house in LA and moved to Clearwater, Florida. On December 5, 2022, she passed away.

Meanwhile, Dan Sherman's opioid addiction continued to rage on, and with it, his angry outbursts aimed at the "uncool." Apparently Miscavige had had enough. It was time for Danny to get off drugs. The plan was to rent a secluded house and to bring in a doctor who specialized in medical detox, after which Danny would be put through a Purification Program— Scientology's sauna-nutrition based regimen for clearing the body of toxins, especially drugs. I never understood why they just didn't clear out the new VIP Narconon in Ojai, the facility located in Larry Hagman's old hilltop mansion, and use it for Danny's detox and rehab. I assumed it was because knowledge of the LRH Biographer's drug problem had to be kept so confidential that only a handful of Sea Org members and myself could know about it. Fleur, Danny's assistant, went over the details. She said he'd requested I be with him every step of the way. "He wants you there, Mitch. You're part of the process." I had no problem helping Danny, but I had no idea the obligation would simply be piled on top of my already heavy workload.

A mere 40 miles northwest of downtown Los Angeles there are about 50 vineyards in what is referred to as "The Malibu Wine Country." A few of the wineries offer secluded rentals for visitors seeking more than a day's excursion. One particular rental was a perfect detox house for Danny—located on a vast estate known as Malibu Wine Tours. Each day for about two weeks I'd leave the studio around noon, and head out to Malibu, finally returning home between midnight and 2 AM. Or I'd simply not go into the studio at all. The detox doctor would usually arrive in the early evening—a Porsche-driving physician who specialized in providing concierge medical services to addicted celebrities. He'd check Danny's vitals, then give him whatever medication he needed to help him through opioid withdrawals. I'd arrive early on days when it was my turn to prepare dinner, something I did not mind doing.

After a couple of weeks of medical detox, Danny was scheduled for the Purification Program. Considering that Danny's predicament needed to be held in strictest confidence, there was a question as to where he should do the Purif. Celebrity Centre in Hollywood had a VIP Purification facility, but regardless of having its own private parking entrance and private entrance into the Purif Center, and that it was entirely isolated from the rest of the Org, it was not considered confidential enough to host Danny's Purif. The solution was to rent another house—a lovely multi-story Mediterranean villa with a jetliner view of West Los Angeles and the Pacific Ocean beyond, located near the top of the celebrity-strewn neighborhood of Sunset Plaza. A small, portable sauna was installed and each day a two-person Purif delivery team would come down from Gold to supervise Danny's Purif. I had, of course, been assigned to do the Purif with him as the procedure forbids being in the sauna alone.

The Purif house had a small, private patio behind a street-level wall. The other two stories wound their way down the hillside. Each day on the Purif begins with 20 minutes or so of jogging "to get the blood moving." As the narrow hillside roads lacked sidewalks, and there were no parks nearby, two treadmills were set up in the garage. We would jog with the garage door open, facing the street, watching the Bentleys, Lamborghini's, Ferraris, and every other imaginable breed of exotic car drive by, mostly piloted by a range of chubby producer types, Kardashian wannabes, or escaped Russian oligarchs. Though I could not care less, I wondered what they must have thought about the two dudes on the treadmills being supervised by an athletic looking Black girl who was taking notes on a clipboard.

The Purification Rundown has gained a lot of controversy in the press, driven by reports claiming the mega-vitamin doses and lengthy time spent in the sauna can be hazardous to one's health. Personally, I think the Purif is an expensive and godawful waste of time—but the fact remains, it might be far worse than that. The Purif requires you to get a medical exam to ensure you don't have a heart condition, high blood pressure, or an infectious disease. Unless there's a medical emergency—such as suffering a stroke, or a heart attack, or needing emergency medical attention due to dehydration or heat stroke—that exam is the only medical supervision you'll receive while on the Purif.

On the surface, the Purif appears to be comprised of healthy lifestyle choices. You are required to be well rested, and to eat fresh, healthy foods daily. You exercise everyday, and you take ever increasing doses of vitamins, some of which you may actually be deficient in, and all of which are mostly going to turn into expensive pee when urinated out of the body. In particular, the supplement niacin may be dangerous in the amount one is required to take on the Purif. The worst part about the Purif is the mind-numbing boredom of spending about 4.5 hours a day in the sauna, taking short breaks to shower off when you feel too hot, or a few minutes to eat a salad.

The entire premise of the Purif is based on the idea that toxic substances can remain trapped in fatty cells for years. While this is true of some insecticides, the amount of stored toxins is negligible. In particular, Hubbard claimed drugs such as LSD can later be released into the system and cause a person to re-experience the effect of the drug as thought they'd taken it newly. He further stated that this is the cause of LSD flashbacks, and why it is so hard for addicts to withdraw from drugs like heroin, the reason being, the drug keeps being re-released into the system keeping the addict in a continuous state of withdrawal. The entire premise of the Purification Rundown relies on the never proven and unscientific notion that drugs—especially LSD—remain lodged in fatty tissues. However, a 2013 article in Popular Science titled "Are Acid Flashbacks a Myth?" traces the idea that LSD molecules can indeed hide in fat cells, and can later be re-released, to an urban legend pushed by anti-drug campaigns. A recent study published in PLOS ONE done by the Norwegian University of Science and Technology's neuroscientist Teri Krebs, found "no association between using psychedelics, including using LSD in the past year, and seeing things other people don't." The study went on to conclude that "Contrary to what some anti-drug campaigns will have you believe, dropping acid probably isn't going to make you depressed or psychotic. In fact, psychedelics might actually be associated with better mental health."

But the "LSD Flashback," regardless of its origin as urban legend, remains crucial to Hubbard's narrative validating the Purification Rundown, and it is at the core of its sales pitch. That sales pitch would have you think that even if you've never taken a drug more powerful than aspirin or Advil, your body is riddled with toxins absorbed from the environment, radiation from the sun, pesticides in our foods, and pollutants in the air we breathe and the water we drink, all preventing you from thinking clearly and making spiritual progress in Scientology. The Purification Rundown is the gatekeeper to Scientology's Bridge. In other words, the Purif is the big lie at the foot of Scientology's Bridge of lies. I did the Purif a total of three times. I also helped to market the hell out of it.

About two years into my stint at Gold, I was given the assignment to produce a TV spot for the "Clear Body, Clear Mind" campaign—a mainstream marketing campaign designed to sell the Purif. The ad called for a shot of a pristine waterfall. A location was found near Mt. Shasta in the northernmost region of California. I'd been shown photographs of the waterfall. It was perfect. About 30 feet tall and 100 feet wide, sheets of clear water cascading down a craggy rock face set in a dense emerald forest.

The nearby Hemet-Ryan airport, located a short 20-minute drive from the International Base, is noted for two things: it's one of 19 strategically located attack bases used by the US Forest Service to stage its airborne firefighting tankers; and being a backwater airport, it's a good place to earn a pilot's license without breaking the bank. The cameraman, script supervisor and I waited with our gear next to the twin engine Cherokee we'd chartered to fly us to Mt Shasta. Our pilot, described to us as the local flight school's top instructor, was late—very late. Finally, a young man in a brown double-breasted pinstripe Armani suit, wearing only a white undershirt under his jacket and Gucci loafers with no socks, approached and introduced himself as our pilot. He couldn't have been older than 25. He had a thick Dutch accent, a shock of blonde hair falling to his aviator sunglasses, and a Marlboro dangling from his lips. He looked startlingly like Rutger Hauer's cuter younger brother who had never made it home from wherever he had been shacked up the night before. He helped us stow our gear and we were airborne.

When we finally arrived at the location, we all stood in shock staring at the waterfall. Following one of the driest winters in years, it had been reduced to barely a trickle. In my early days at Gold, I assumed whoever was responsible for scouting and securing locations would have a least contacted the local ranger station, or Bureau of Land Management office to inquirer about the current status of the waterfall. We wasted a bit of time searching on foot for an alternative location then, defeated, headed back to the airport.

By the time we arrived the sun had already sunk beneath the horizon and the runway was quickly being swallowed up by the darkness. Our pilot, who had been waiting patiently, hustled us into the plane. Being a small VFR airport, meaning it was governed by Visual Flight Rules which dictate that if you can't see the runway, you are not allowed to take off or land. According to those rules, we'd be spending the night at a cheap motel and leaving in the morning. According to our pilot's rules, we'd be airborne momentarily, dark or no dark. Poised for takeoff, it was now pitch black, a moonless night with only the dim blue lights outlining the runway to guide our departure. The voice from the tower was stern, demanding the pilot turn the plane around and return to the apron. The pilot keyed his radio, click, click, click, click and in his Dutch accent told the traffic controller "You're breaking up." Then he gunned the engines and off we went into the wild black yonder. I thought that sort of thing only happened in movies.

We made it back safely to Hemet-Ryan. I made a mental note to always hire the same pilot. I flew with him a few more times and he never disappointed. We did find another location, and at some point the Purif ad was completed. Beyond that, I directed the instructional film that is used by Scientology Orgs to administer the Purif, and then later another "secular" version for Narconon.

But none of the Purification Rundowns I'd done in the past, nor any of the harrowing experiences I'd had shooting ads promoting it, could match the experience of doing the Purif sitting next to Dan Sherman. That truly stands out as the most bizarre Purif experience of them all. About six weeks later we were complete with the Purif and it was time to get back to work.

I assumed the time I'd put in helping Danny to kick opioids

would buy me some air cover for having been mostly absent from post for a couple of months. And I assumed that my spectacular production record, earned over many years, would hold me harmless against any problems that might have arisen because of my absence. But this was the Sea Org, and this was SMP being run by Miscavige's hand-picked Department 3 whose primary statistics was "number of situations found and handled." If they couldn't find any situations, then their stats were down and they'd be in trouble. It was not long before I got the dreaded call. "Hello," I answered. Without the slightest hesitation and without announcing who it was, the female voice on the other end of the line simply barked "Come to HCO."

The "interview rooms" that HCO maintains at SMP for interrogation purposes when giving Meter checks, metered interviews, and Sec Checks, are no bigger than a small closet and always triggered my claustrophobia. The worst were the interview rooms at Gold, where you literally had to turn sideways and suck in your gut to squeeze past the tiny desk to take a seat, and the person administering the interview, who always sat in the chair closest to the door, would have to stand up and step aside to open or close the door. That arrangement, with the interviewer sitting in the chair closest to the door, was mandated by a Hubbard Technical Bulletin titled "How to Set Up a Session and the E-meter." Such an arrangement makes it nearly impossible for the person on the other side of the table to decide to walk out without the interviewer's, or in the case of an auditing session, the auditor's consent. Scientology auditors, and interrogators, are taught that they must do everything within their power to prevent a person from leaving the room without their consent—and that includes the use of physical force.

I'd known the HCO Sec Checker sitting across from me in the tiny interview room located in the basement of SMP since she was a baby. I was once friends with her parents. I recognized her voice when she ordered me down to HCO. And now here I was sitting across from her in a tiny interview room and she's questioning me about the most intimate, personal aspects of my private life. Were there things I'd done that I didn't want them to find out about—things I'd done in my private life that I wanted to keep private, and that had absolutely zero to do with my work or job performance? Absolutely! Among other things, she wanted to know who I'd had sex with, what kind of sex had I engaged in, and so on. In Scientology, there is no such thing as privacy.

Every day for the next few weeks I had to report to HCO in the basement of SMP where I was routinely screamed at by the HCO staff—one of whom accused me of being "worse than a wog"—"Wog" being Scientology slang for someone who's not a Scientologist, the term used in Britain as a racist slur for a non-white person. I was given the task of sculpting every Precept in Hubbard's book, "The Way to Happiness" in modeling clay—a sort of three-dimensional illustration intended to test your understanding of a Scientology concept or principle. Making "clay demos" is a part of Scientology "study technology." When complete, the clay demo is scrutinized by a Scientology instructor and if they can recognize the concept being illustrated, the student is given a pass. I was required to spend scores of hours creating demos of concepts illustrating moral conduct, as well as reading Hubbard references and listening to lectures. When Miscavige was on the lot, I had to leave as I was not allowed to be anywhere in his vicinity.

So why didn't I just leave, walk to my car and drive away? After all, I was not contractually bound. I wasn't in the Sea Org. Why was I allowing myself to be taken off work, and put through that hell? Of course it was nothing compared to being sent to the RPF or being locked up in the Hole, but for me it was a nightmare. For the first time in all my years working for Scientology, I had lost whatever power and authority I had. I was no longer respected, and my income was canceled. But I was still a Scientologist. I was still hopelessly trapped in the Reality Distortion Field that dictated Scientology was the only hope you had to achieve spiritual freedom, and was long past having any professional connections outside of Scientology. So, I kept showing up. I kept agreeing to be traumatized, humiliated, and accepted that I was a bad person who needed to reform.

In the lexicon of Scientology, there are two words that hold special significance: "Overt" and "Withhold." An overt is a contra-survival (against survival) act, something you've done that could discredit you. A withhold, is simply the act of withholding the overt act. A man robs a bank. He has committed an overt. Weeks later he's driving in traffic and a cop pulls up next to him at a stop light and looks over at him. He wonders if the cop knows about the robbery. This is called a "Missed Withhold," wondering if someone knows about your overt, or nearly found out about it.

In an auditing session, any overt you are unwilling to disclose is considered a withhold. You are told that if you do not tell your auditor every detail of every aspect of your life, every secret, every private thought, every overt you've ever committed, then you are damning yourself to an eternal hell in which you will have destroyed any chance of achieving spiritual freedom. If it's discovered that your auditor failed to "find" your withhold, whatever ethics or justice action could be levied at you for having committed the overt, will be levied against the auditor and worse. If the person had done something deemed particularly egregious that the auditor failed to find, that auditor would most certainly be banished to the RPF.

L. Ron Hubbard was obsessed with loyalty. He thought the surest way to maintain loyalty was to keep track of his follower's deepest held, most intimate secrets, because those

SCIENTOLOGY MEDIA PRODUCTIONS

secrets might contain a plan or a plot to do him in. In 1960, he developed an interrogation technique known as the Security Check, which I've talked about extensively in this book. The technique was incorporated into the Scientology auditing process known as "Confessional Procedure." On the lower levels of Scientology's "Bridge to Total Freedom," there is an entire level devoted to confessional procedure, sold to parishioners for its "therapeutic value," allowing a person to unburden themselves of the turmoil resulting from their transgressions. Receiving a confessional is a requirement of attaining "the State of Clear." In a Scientology confessional, the preclear "gets off" their withholds and is told they are forgiven for anything they have honestly and fully disclosed. The "Security Check" is the weaponized version of Scientology confessional technology. The person receiving the Security Check is told, "I am not auditing you," and everything they disclose is written up as a "knowledge report" and sent to the Ethics Section who will follow up with whatever corrective actions are deemed warranted.

Scientology parishioners are routinely sec checked. In order to progress past Clear, Scientologists must be granted "eligibility" to continue with the confidential OT levels. Eligibility also requires high-dollar donations as well as time spent volunteering for Scientology-sponsored programs. In other words, before you are allowed to participate in your own spiritual advancement, you are required to prove yourself

SCIENTOLOGY - THE BIG LIE

worthy. Those eligibility Sec Checks will continue, at least twice yearly, for as long as the person remains in Scientology. The content of those security checks is a main reason most people who leave Scientology don't speak out—fear of having their secrets spilled all over the Internet.

Based on my metered interview, a Committee of Evidence or "Comm Ev" was convened to adjudicate my "crimes." A Comm Ev is the Scientology equivalent of a court martial. In reality, it is a kangaroo court that rarely, if ever, finds in favor of the accused. I'd been in Scientology for over 40 years and during all that time, I'd never come anywhere near receiving a Comm Ev.

Based on the findings from my Comm Ev, I was ordered to undergo a sec check and do 50 hours of amends. Exactly what the 50 hours of amends was comprised of, no one would say. It was left up to, "You figure it out and we'll get back to you." I had seen this happen to so many people in. They'd get in trouble for some infraction: their statistics were down, they'd done something inappropriate with a member of the opposite sex, or they'd failed to meet a deadline. The list was long. Suddenly, the division, or in some cases the entire organization, had a reason for it's recent troubles—a scapegoat had been found. Such was the situation I'd found myself in—I was the cause of why content for the network wasn't being completed, and for why the programming lineup was so far behind schedule.

From that point on, I became a designated scapegoat for all the problems the studio was having with the upcoming Scientology Network launch. I was essentially banned from the studio lot and told to report to the "HGB," the middle management building on Hollywood Boulevard, where a Sec Checker would take me in for my daily dose of interrogation. I thought if I could just get through this I could land on my feet and get back to work. I was determined to be 100% honest, to tell them everything they asked. I literally threw myself at their mercy. I didn't want to be thrown out of Scientology.

My Sec Checker at the HGB seemed friendly and warm. She seemed to genuinely want to help me get "cleaned up" and back on post. After all, I had that reputation for being the person who directed all the technical training films and had spearheaded the look of Scientology, jumpstarting the global propaganda machine, and steering it away from looking like a two-bit cheesy offbeat religion, to being high quality. Miscavige used to say I was responsible for creating visual work that commanded respect for Scientology. None of that seemed to matter now. It wasn't enough to get me off the hook. But the woman who was sec checking me seemed to think it did, and wanted to see things get back to normal.

About three weeks into the sec check, I started to see light at the end of the tunnel—meaning, the trauma they'd inflicted on me they were now easing. It's no different than an abusive marriage where the abused partner cooperates with their abuser hoping to get those good feelings back and those good feelings were coming back. My daily sec check appointment wasn't until 1 PM so I'd taken myself to lunch. I was taking a leisurely stroll down Ventura Blvd in Studio City when I got the call. It was the same HCO staff member that had screamed at me accusing me of being "worse than a wog." "Please come to HCO now." "But I have a session scheduled for 1 PM," I replied. The response was simply, "Come to HCO now." I called the HGB and spoke to my auditor. She said she'd heard someone at SMP had canceled our session and that I'd been ordered to SMP. It was highly irregular to cancel someone's Sec Check before it was complete, especially when it was going well and almost done.

Arriving at HCO, I headed straight for the basement where I was asked to wait in one of the small interview rooms. Eventually the person in charge of the Ethics division showed up to let me know there was someone I needed to meet with. It was a total mystery. Right on cue, the mystery person swung open the door. It was my old "senior" from Gold, Amber O'Sullivan Mellor. Somehow Amber had managed to intervene and convince HCO at SMP that I should be sent back to Gold. This was an entirely political power move on her part. With me now being the Senior Director at SMP, Gold had lost its most valuable creative individual and Amber had figured out a way to haul me back up there. The MAA (Ethics

Officer) who'd been working with me on my Ethics program informed me I had two weeks to prove myself and get back to SMP. Amber had other plans for me.

TWENTY-FIVE

HURTLING TOWARDS DESPAIR

GOLD WAS THE LAST PLACE on Earth I wanted to be. I was no longer the valued director who could wriggle out of Ethics trouble on reputation alone. Nothing I'd done in my personal life or on my job had created any actual damage to the Church's production or reputation, yet here I was being driven to Gold—in my own car no less because I hadn't slept in days; extreme anxiety had left me too fatigued to drive. For the first time in all my years of being in Scientology, I was experiencing the full brunt of the Scientology Justice system—not to mention the unbridled shaming of its puritanical culture. When I look back on that time, I can't believe that I simply didn't just leave, can't believe I was so brainwashed—so trauma-bonded—that I was unable to sever the connection even though it was becoming more and more difficult to deny the methods the Church of Scientology uses to strike fear and obedience into the hearts of its members.

387

I recalled seeing a BBC documentary entitled *How Art Made the World* which featured a segment explaining how cultures down through the ages had used images of death to control their populations. At the great Aztec pyramid of Tenochtitlan, executioners would regularly sacrifice prisoners made to stand in lines four deep, each line stretching two miles long. Before they were ritualistically killed, the victims were forced to climb up the pyramid's 237 steps. At the top were two killing rooms, and priests wielding sacrificial knives. It was through the imagery of this wholesale slaughter, that the Aztec leaders instilled loyalty and obedience throughout the population.

While in today's modern society, blood sacrifices have become socially unacceptable, that mechanism of threat has remained a mainstay of high control groups such as Scientology. In Scientology, the deathful imagery has been swapped out for deathful language and other means of striking fear into the hearts of its members—not unlike the kind of fear I imagine a typical Aztec citizen probably felt when seeing rivers of blood cascading down the stone steps of the pyramid.

To provide a glimpse into how Hubbard wove images of death and destruction into his Scientology justice system, consider this: On page 229 of the book, *Introduction to Scientology Ethics*, Hubbard wrote: "Labeling as a suppressive is our 'hanging.'"

A suppressive is Scientology's designation for an enemy of the Church, requiring the person so labeled to sever all contact with anyone in Scientology, whether social, familial, or professional. A suppressive is essentially excommunicated from Scientology. The list of acts that can get one labeled, or "declared" a suppressive, is long and complicated.

On the same page of that book, Hubbard stated: "Too many bad indicators and too goofed up a situation and we must put a head on a pike."

Meaning, someone has to pay. The "head on a pike" being the example of what will happen to you if you step out of line. On page 228 Hubbard wrote this: "We start to 'hang' people and keep right on 'tying the noose' in a workmanlike fashion right up to the instant we can get tech in—which of course makes the 'noose' unnecessary."

By "get tech in" Hubbard meant that the person had become compliant and in lockstep with the program.

On page 166, Hubbard provides a lesson on the correct way to serve a person in power. As the lesson goes, the person in power notices the legs of a dead woman poking out from under a desk. The underling explains to his boss: "*She* over there, those pink legs sticking out, didn't like me." To which the person in power replies: "Why are you bothering me with it if it's done and you did it. Where's my blue ink?"

Beyond the use of deathful imagery, Scientology employs a variety of techniques to create a threatening atmosphere for its members. Adherents are cautioned that in order to be safe, they must remain inside the bubble—donating their time and money,

SCIENTOLOGY - THE BIG LIE

and progressing up the Bridge, while ignoring and avoiding any information that disagrees with their beliefs. On page 225 of *Introduction to Scientology Ethics*, Hubbard writes:

> "The dangerous environment of the world, of injustice, sudden dismissals, war, atomic bombs, will only persist and trouble us if we fail to spread our safe environment across the world."

In other words, the world is a dangerous place and you will only be safe if Scientology prevails.

While keeping its members in line with metaphorical threats of hanging, proclamations that the environment is dangerous, and lessons teaching you that your boss needn't be bothered if, in the course of performing your job, you commit a murder, there is the threat of what will happen to you for failing to make your participation in Scientology your number-one priority.

At the beginning of every major Scientology course, the student must study the Hubbard-authored policy letter titled, *Keeping Scientology Working*, or *KSW* for short. No other document in Scientology contains more threat per sentence than KSW:

> "When somebody enrolls, consider he or she has joined up for the duration of the universe—never permit an 'open-minded' approach. If they're going to quit let them quit fast. If they enrolled, they're aboard, and if they're aboard, they're here on the same terms as the rest of us—win or die in the attempt."

And then there's this:

The proper instruction attitude is, "You're here so you're a Scientologist. Now we're going to make you into an expert Auditor no matter what happens. We'd rather have you dead than incapable."

In a policy letter Hubbard issued on 5 January, 1968, "Overfilled In-Basket, Bad News," he writes, in all caps:

MAKE THE PENALTIES FOR NONCOMPLIANCE AND FALSE REPORTS TOO GRUESOME TO BE FACED AND ENFORCE THEM.

"Too gruesome," became an often-heard noun as in, "Give him a too gruesome." The degree of "gruesomeness" is entirely subjective. It can mean different things to different people. To Hubbard it meant throwing crew members overboard, locking them in a chain locker, or making them clean the bilges—practices first initiated on the Flagship *Apollo* soon after the *Too Gruesome* policy letter was issued. Miscavige took the *too gruesome* concept to new heights. A short list of his penalties includes: physical assaults and verbal abuse; forcing subordinates to jump into a sewage lagoon; holding executives captive in the Hole; and making staff sit on scalding hot cement while verbally abusing them in front of their co-workers; and much more.

A group will take on the characteristics of its leader—mean dog-owners beget mean dogs. Miscavige owns a pack of snarling beagles that would rip you to shreds if they got the chance—as I discovered firsthand at the cost a ruined pair of expensive jeans. Like his dogs, many of the staff at the International Base took on his violent persona.

Most of staff at the International Base, at least the ones in high-pressure positions, possess two emotional states: a default, artificial politeness that they used to keep their seething rage in check, and the seething rage that would leap forward whenever they needed to put someone who worked under them in check. I believe this is partly due to the mentality that if anyone screwed up, they and their immediate cohort got punished. Those who worked the closest with Miscavige tended to be the most adept at fashioning themselves in his persona.

Amber O'Sullivan Mellor, my titular boss at the time, had worked in RTC as a transcriber—a mind-numbing job requiring one to spend the day in front of a computer, wearing headphones, starting and stopping an audio playback system via a foot pedal, and typing Miscavige's words into a text editor. The text was then formatted into a "dispatch" and then "routed" to the relevant "terminals." Any meeting you had with Miscavige, formal or casual, anything that needed to be followed up on, would be recorded, transcribed and routed as "traffic." Whenever you received traffic, you went straight to a "word clearer." Then, while holding the E-meter cans you were required to read the dispatch aloud. Any hesitation or stumble, any physical manifestation other than smoothly reading aloud, and the word clearer would stop you and ask if there is something in the text you did not understand. A large number of RTC staff were engaged in transcribing, formatting, filing, and routing anything Miscavige uttered that required some action to be taken. I never had much occasion to visit the RTC offices, but sometime in the '90s, prior to the construction of the lavish new RTC headquarters building, I was walking through the office with Miscavige. As we passed through the filing room on one side of which there sat four or so transcribers, their feet tapping away on the foot pedals, fingers tapping away on their keyboards. Across from the transcribers there was a bank of rolling filing cabinets containing all the traffic going back and forth between him and whoever he was dealing with. He threw a gesture at the filing cabinets and said, "There's more traffic in there between me and you than between me and anyone else on the entire planet." I was unsure what to think of that comment. Did that fact come with some obligation I'd not yet become aware of? I had no idea. Was it even true?

I'm not sure how someone screws up enough as a transcriber to get themselves booted out of RTC, but Amber had managed to screw up big enough to get punitively transferred to the Cine Division where she worked as a set painter, eventually climbing the ladder to Cine Sec—the divisional secretary of the Cine Division.

It was well into the evening by the time I arrived at Gold. I was driven straight to my old room at the Gs. Eve Stumbke, the Commanding Officer, stopped by to assure me they would get me through my ethics program and back to SMP as quickly as possible.

The following morning Amber was waiting for me in my office. Arms folded, glowering, jaws clenched, eyes narrowed into slits. Her take on the matter of how long I would stay at Gold was different than Eve's, "You need to kick your kids out of the house, get rid of the house, sell your car, and be prepared to be up here for the next year." Her words trailed off as the sound coming from her mouth was drowned out by the noise in my head. She continued on saying something about how the main unit crew—the one I'd spent years developing—was no longer mine, but was now under the young man I apprenticed as a director, who also happened to be her husband. The next few days were a blur. Everyday Amber would come into the office I was working out of, put her hands on her hips, and berate me in ever-increasing volume until she was screaming.

This went on for about two weeks—Amber storming into the office, screaming threats at me: "I should lock you in the dish room," (which I took to mean, lock you in the galley to wash dishes). Or (though not at the time) my favorite: "You're creating fodder for [noted anti-Scientology journalist] Tony Ortega."

A few days later, on Easter Sunday, I ripped those tiny blades out of a Gillette safety razor and slashed my wrists.

. . .

Two weeks later, I was walking along Zuma Beach in Malibu, one of the most popular beaches in Los Angeles.

It was a warm spring day. The crisp, clean air smelled of brine. Swells gently rolled across the blue Pacific on their journey to crash on the shore, sending children running madly with joy. The water was a dazzle of sparkling sunshine, undulating like the tiara on a drunken prom queen. I was not so much walking along the shore as I was trying to run away from having cut myself with a razor—and from all the reasons that precipitated my having done something that was so against my values. I didn't do it because I wanted to die, but because I wanted a different life. The life I had been living up to that point was essentially over, or at least that's how it seemed, and I didn't see a pathway to any other life. I'd been doing that same walk on the beach, or along the trails of the section of the Santa Monica Mountains that overlooks the Pacific, for about a month; ever since the cutting incident when the Gs housekeeper barged in the back door of my unit to find me standing in the kitchen, surrounded by a significant puddle of blood.

Soon, every security guard on the Base arrived—must've been a slow day. Eve, the CO, showed up soon after. She surveyed the room, then in her polite British accent and "be-calm-and-carry-on manner," she picked up the phone and called Amber. "Mitch won't be coming to post today." That was the extent of the phone call. Anyone who'd done such a thing would be automatically classified as a security risk and forbidden from ever being allowed on Base property—at least I'd accomplished that, or so I thought.

An EMT-trained security guard bandaged my wrist, and before I knew it, I was in a car with the MLO being driven to Orange County. Knowing a standard emergency room would have a legal obligation to report self-harm, likely resulting in a 72-hour psychiatric hold, the MLO opted to drive me to a clinic owned by a physician who was a Scientologist and ran a busy private practice that did a huge business in vanity-branded nutritional supplements and quack intravenous infusions known as drips. The MLO knew full well that "Dr. Drip" would disregard his legal obligation to report my self harm, for in Scientology doing so would be considered a suppressive act.

In spite of it being Easter Sunday, the doctor was waiting when we arrived. Very thoughtful of him to break away from his family dinner to stitch me up. I left 45 minutes later with 11 stitches that looked like they were done in Dr. Frankenstein's lab. Since he was a nephrologist, I don't think he'd executed a suture since sewing up a medical dummy back in med school. By the time we'd arrived back at my room at the Gs, the housekeeper was packing my suitcase. The CO informed me she had arranged a rental on the beach, and, in the company of an Auditor, a security guard and the MLO, I was going to "destimulate," the word Scientologists use when they mean decompress. But more importantly, I was a suicide risk and therefore not eligible to be allowed back on the property. Even more important, if Miscavige learned of the incident, that HCO SMP had sent me to Gold on an Ethics program, he would have personally held Gold responsible for my having wound up like that while in their care. And how exactly had I wound up like that? After two weeks of daily verbal abuse from my "senior," I was ready to pack it in. That I hadn't slept in all that time did not help the situation. It wasn't just Amber, but at least half the population of the Base now saw me as a degraded being who had discredited them.

The first few nights after driving away from Gold, we wound up in a luxury timeshare in Laguna Beach and then Malibu where we spent a lovely week in a cozy house a block from the shore. We finally ended up in spectacular, contemporary mini-estate on a bluff overlooking Zuma Beach, owned by a tech billionaire who ran it as a non-profit with all of the rental fees being donated to Doctors Without Borders—likely the only money Scientology ever gave to a legitimate cause.

Every morning after breakfast, I'd walk the three or so blocks to the beach, my entourage in tow a safe distance behind. And on every walk, I'd see the same young woman, maybe late twenties, rummaging through the trash barrels collecting plastic bottles and aluminum cans. One day I stopped to speak with her. I don't recall our exact words, but it went something like this:

"Excuse me. I see you here every day. I'm curious to know how you got into this situation? How do you survive? I don't mean to pry or to be disrespectful, but sometimes I think I may end up in the same situation."

She put down her collection bag of bottles and cans, looked at me unfazed, then softened, seeming to believe my question was sincere.

"No. I don't mind," she began to explain. "I grew up in Malibu. I graduated from Malibu High. My parents had always been employed by a wealthy family. My mom's a housekeeper and cook. My dad does landscaping and maintenance. We always lived with the families we worked for. Over time, things changed. Houses got sold. New owners weren't interested in having us around, so we ended up homeless."

"Where do you sleep?" I asked.

"We sleep in our car on Westward Beach Road. We all collect bottles and cans. My mom finds coupons in discarded papers. The local grocer helps us with day-old stuff and dented cans. The gas station lets us use their microwave so sometimes we have hot food. There's plenty of showers here at the beach."

We chatted for a bit about nothing in particular. As I turned to walk away, she suddenly said, "Hey, I really want to thank you for not thinking we're bums. We're homeless and we're struggling to get back into the system." I just smiled at her and wished her good luck.

A few days later I was in a car with my handlers driving down Westward Beach Road, headed to the south end of Zuma Beach, when I saw the young woman with her parents, parked by the side of the road, rearranging the contents of their Honda SUV. My first impulse was to pull over and say hello, but I then realized the other passengers in the car with me were incapable of seeing these people as anything other than "degraded beings" who had done something to land themselves in their current situation. In Scientology, the less fortunate such as the unhoused or the mentally ill, are seen as the flotsam and jetsam that have washed ashore after having crashed upon the rocks known as the mental health industry. Their mindset is, "Why should we clean up psychiatry's messes? Our job is to help the able be more able."

I never got her name, the young homeless woman I met at Zuma Beach during my desperate walks. I think of her and hope she's doing well.

A few weeks later I was back home—still mentally shaken but no longer in danger. Amber was unrelenting in her attempts to lure me back to work—apparently what I had done had not disqualified me from working at the International Base. They posted a staff member to stay with me, which they considered was for my well being, but it felt more like damage control. Soon, I began receiving writing assignments for Gold. Shortly after that, I agreed to come back to work at the Base with the proviso that I did not have to live on the property, and that they would provide transportation to and from Los Angeles. Each morning, a Cine staff member would make the 90 minute drive from the Base to my home, picking me up at 9 AM, then drive me to the Base, arriving at about 10:30 AM, and drive me back home at 8 PM, arriving home around 9:30 PM— that's nine and a half hours of work, not counting short breaks, and three hours a day commuting.

For the next year and a half or so I commuted to the Base five days a week. The crew I'd trained was now under the direction of my former protégé. Amber insisted that, as part of my amends, I was going to train a second crew, most of whom were inexperienced, having spent little or no time on a film crew. Nonetheless, I had them trained to the point that our work was indistinguishable from that of the main crew. Most of our projects consisted of producing filmed versions of a series of articles Hubbard had written in the 1950s and '60s, that were originally published in the Church's *Freedom* magazine, focusing on Hubbard's staunch anti-government government, and anti-mental health industry views, as well as societal ills targeted by Hubbard to be viewed through his distorted lens. And that pretty much covers the grind at Gold for the next couple of years.

In mid-December 2018, I wrote David Miscavige a letter. I wanted to reconnect after being booted out of SMP. In all honesty, he seemed to take little notice of my absence from his sphere, which struck me as very odd considering our relationship over the previous twenty-plus years. I thought his lack of notice might have had something to do with HCO SMP (the Ethics division of Scientology Media Productions) not wanting to be perceived as letting me "get away with something" as that is considered a serious crime in Scientology, and had subsequently overreacted and were now covering it up. That, and Gold's self-centered need to have me working back at their facility. After all, I had been instrumental in fulfilling their mission to operate successfully as Hubbard's film studio. His reply took me by surprise, especially one particular section where he referred to me having been sent back to Gold:

> Truth be told, I do not know what happened. I was informed that HCO SMP returned you to Gold. I asked what had occurred and they, bluntly, didn't want to tell me. I asked why and they told me that, quite in addition to our working relationship all these years, they knew we were close friends. They felt it better not to tell me because they did not want me to, I assume, think badly of you. So I left it at that.
>
> —David Miscavige, letter dated January 10, 2018

Wait a minute. Did I read that right? Close friends? I thought close friends would run interference for each other. Sure, I had failed to live up to Scientology's standard of ethical behavior, but what about our mutual "close" friend Danny Sherman, who'd gotten himself severely addicted to opioids and had—not uncommonly—brandished a firearm at Gold staff members, and who had HCO SMP so terrified of him that they wouldn't dare call him out on his "out-ethics" behavior. And what about Miscavige himself? His wife Shelly hadn't been seen since 2007 while he's been ostensibly carrying on an intimate relationship with his assistant. I'm not saying their behavior excuses mine, I'm just asking, what's with the double standard?

There are specific Hubbard policies governing the sexual activities of Scientologists—also known as 2D activities, the 2D or Second Dynamic being that zone of life covering sex and the rearing of children. The policy that governs the sex lives of non-Sea Org, Scientologists is called Second Dynamic Rules and is dated August 11, 1967. It contains the following text:

> "No Ethics Order shall be issued by reason of Second Dynamic activities. All Ethics Orders now in force relating to the Second Dynamic are cancelled.
>
> No staff member may be punished, transferred or dismissed because of Second Dynamic activities.
>
> No student or preclear may be suspended or dismissed because of Second Dynamic activities."

Nothing Hubbard ever wrote superseded Second Dynamic Rules. Yet, for my 2D behavior, I was removed from post, called before a committee of evidence, subjected to months of interrogation, humiliated in front of my coworkers, had my income cancelled, and was "returned" to Gold.

While the 2D rules pertaining to public Scientologists

may seem somewhat lenient, the 2D Rules governing Sea Org members are anything but. According to Sea Organization Flag Order 3739 of 21 December 1978, 2D Rules:

> 1. 2D couples may not live or sleep together under any circumstances unless legally wed. Legal marriages are required.

> 2. Women have their own quarters. Men may not enter these and visa versa [sic].

> 3. S.O. members may not engage in any sort of 2-D activities with public students or PC's.

> 4. No new 2-D relationships may be created while one or both members are LEGALLY married to another person. It is the ethical responsibility for one to terminatedly end cycle on a 2-D before starting up new 2-D. Adultery is against the law.

> 5. No heavy petting is acceptable among un-wed S.O. members.

My point is not to say that Miscavige is a naughty boy or that his behavior with regard to sex was better or worse than mine, but to call him out for the hypocrisy of likely having banished his wife to a mountain compound while engaging in an intimate relationship with his assistant, while at the same time leading a system that has ruined the lives of countless Sea Org members and public Scientologists simply because he was "offended" by their private sexual lives. And, while there is only anecdotal evidence that his relationship with his assistant Laurisse Stuckenbrock is of a sexual nature, just the fact that he spent the night with her in the same master bedroom cabin of a movie stars private jet during a transatlantic flight to England, is enough to land him in serious trouble in the Sea Org—the kind of trouble that gets one sent to the RPF. That's not a second hand rumor. I was on that flight.

The story of Lou and Dave, like so many stories I encountered at the International Base, has a tragic beginning. Before taking up with Miscavige, Laurisse was married to a handsome Sea Org officer from Germany by the name of Uwe Stuckenbrock. When I originally met Uwe, he was a member of the Gold security force, the picture of good health, and had done a small part in one of my films. Tragically, Uwe died at 46 from Multiple Sclerosis following an 11-year decline. Laurisse left Uwe shortly after he was diagnosed, and Miscavige ordered the couple to divorce.

I read Miscavige's letter a few times, trying to decipher any hidden message. There was none. He was basically saying, "Dude, you fucked up and I'm going to pretend I don't know what happened, and I'm perfectly happy with you slaving away at Gold as the second unit director, making documentaries for the Scientology Network." It was at that moment I realized even his declarations of friendship were part of his manipulative psychopathy. His response made it perfectly clear that this person whom I'd considered a friend for almost three decades, and whom I had once admired, was entirely unaware that I had needs; that being isolated on a Sea Org base had been the most difficult circumstance I'd ever experienced; and that after having accomplished so much for Scientology over so many years— having completed projects that generated countless millions of dollars for the Church, reshaped the aesthetics of both its internal design and its outward face, played a crucial role in redefining its messaging as the chief architect of Scientology's global propaganda machine—I would have thought that perhaps he might want to ask, "Mitch, what would you like to do now?" Though being so easily discarded doesn't rise to the level of being thrown in the Hole, beaten and humiliated daily. It was enough for me. And with that, I was done.

TWENTY-SIX

LEAVING SCIENTOLOGY

The simple truth is, we all make mistakes, and we all need forgiveness. There is no magic wand we can wave to go back in time and change what has happened or undo the harm that has been done, but we can do everything in our power to set right what has been made wrong. We can endeavor to make sure the harm never happens again.

—Desmond Tutu

I ASSUMED THAT ONCE I had made the final decision to leave Scientology, all that would be left would be to wait for the adrenaline to wear off and then move forward. In the early stages of leaving, I had no idea how broken I was. I soon discovered that the decision to leave, and then leaving was not enough to propel me forward into a brighter future. I soon discovered that thinking the decision was all it would take is really the same kind of magical thinking that was keeping me trapped—the narcissistic belief that I was perfect enough to pull up my stakes and walk off. I often hear people who've left Scientology—and other cults—refer to their recovery process as "peeling an onion." I would agree, if the onion were composed of layer upon layer of sedimentary rock that one had to excavate with explosives.

What attracted me to Scientology to begin with? I was a 23-year old film school dropout who was addicted to heroin and the closest person to me in life had just died of an overdose while I was asleep in the next room. Subsequently, I was introduced to a group of people who seemed to genuinely want to help me free myself from the grip of addiction; they offered community, structure, and an opportunity to interrupt the cycle of drug use. Perhaps most importantly, they expressed an idealism, a desire to build a better world that aligned with my values. More than anything else, it was that sense of idealism that attracted me to Scientology and captivated my interest. What I got was a far cry from how it first appeared—something which became grotesquely different as the power struggles within the Church, waged within the walled garden of Scientology's international management structure, raged on until finally a diminutive tyrant took the reins.

I thought I had failed Scientology—failed to live up to its impossibly high standards of ethical conduct. Then one day it began to dawn on me that the shame I felt for having failed it, had in fact been engineered by an organization that then turned around and offered to sell me a solution to the very the shame it had instilled in me in the first place without my awareness or consent.

For its ability to pull that off, Scientology may go down in history for being the most successful confidence game of our era; both in the way it gets people to willingly donate their money with no expectation of receiving anything tangible in return other than feeling connected, and for the way it creates need in its members—often by manipulating them into feeling guilt and shame and then convincing them those feelings are proof they need further help.

It's difficult to imagine an organization that charges people to give up their core identity, but that's exactly what Scientology "technology" is designed to do. The fact is, the further one ascends up Scientology's Bridge to Total Freedom, the more of one's true identity—what is authentic about them—becomes replaced with a false mythology, until finally, and unbeknown to the person, they are utterly lost in a belief that they are something that in reality doesn't exist.

Orson Wells famously said, "If you want a happy ending, that depends, of course, on where you stop your story." More concisely: if you want a happy ending, you end the story before shit gets bad again. I don't know where my story will end. No one does. But I am fairly certain the blue sky I see before me is actually just that and not a mirage seen through a distorted lens.

Writing this book has been analogous to taking a 20-pound

sledgehammer to what I refer to as my cult mind. I'm still picking out the little shards that lodge in the shadows.

I suspect I will be doing so for some time to come.

ACKNOWLEDGMENTS

Sincere thanks to my friend and former colleague Mike Rinder for his encouragement and for connecting me with talented and generous individuals who selflessly gave their time and talent to assist me in editing this book:

Heather K. Gaynor

Rebecca E. Rumbo

Amanda Johnson

A special thanks to my dear friend Caroline Mustard, who originally approached me to work for Scientology. Without Caroline's support, this book would likely never have been realized in its final published form.

Thank you to Jeff Hawkins for his friendship and support.

To the incredible artist known as Mermaid Cafe who designed this book as a work of passion.

To Iris DeMent for granting me permission to excerpt a lyric from her epic song, "Let the Mystery Be."

And lastly, I'd like to thank someone whom I've never met, author Cheryl Strayed, who's fearless voice inspired me to tell my story.

ABOUT THE AUTHOR

Scientology today promotes itself with slickly produced films and TV programs, but it wasn't always so. In fact, in the 1970s, their films were embarrassingly amateur.

That all changed when they hired film director and Scientologist, Mitch Brisker, to come to their international headquarters and work to upgrade the quality of their films.

Mitch became one of the few "outsiders" to ever work at their secretive international Sea Org headquarters, and the abuses he saw behind the scenes caused him to finally quit his job as Scientology's film director and ultimately to leave Scientology altogether. Mitch's journey into and out of Scientology began back in 1973 when, as a heroin addicted, film school drop out, he awoke the Sunday morning before Christmas to find his partner dead from an overdose. A film director with whom he'd recently worked introduced him to Scientology. After becoming drug free, Mitch returned to college earning a degree in cinema from California Institute of the Arts and embarked on a career as a commercial director. In 1990 he was invited to Scientology's secretive International Base to direct a film for the training of

Scientology practitioners, ultimately ascending to the highest levels of the organization and becoming the chief architect of its global propaganda machine, until, in the wake of the Covid lockdown, he left Scientology and began to speak out.

Made in the USA
Las Vegas, NV
26 December 2023